$5.00

To Nor̄ ⟩

Whose Rock is God!

With My Love,

Carol Nordman

GOD,
MY ROCK

Faith Adventures
of a
Missionary Mom

CAROL NORDMAN

WESTBOW
P R E S S®
A DIVISION OF THOMAS NELSON
& ZONDERVAN

WestBow Press books may be ordered through booksellers or by contacting:

WestBow Press
A Division of Thomas Nelson & Zondervan
1663 Liberty Drive
Bloomington, IN 47403
www.westbowpress.com
1 (866) 928-1240

Scripture taken from the NEW AMERICAN STANDARD BIBLE®, Copyright © 1960,1962,1963,1968,1971,1972,1973,1975,1977,1995 by The Lockman Foundation. Used by permission. www.Lockman.org

ISBN: 978-1-9736-9188-4 (sc)
ISBN: 978-1-9736-9186-0 (hc)
ISBN: 978-1-9736-9187-7 (e)

Library of Congress Control Number: 2020908824

Print information available on the last page.

WestBow Press rev. date: 7/13/2020

For Vance, the love of my life and partner in the adventure.

My soul, wait in silence for God only,
For my hope is from Him.
He only is my rock and my salvation,
My stronghold; I shall not be shaken.
On God my salvation and my glory rest;
The rock of my strength, my refuge is in God.
Trust in Him at all times, O people;
Pour out your heart before Him;
God is a refuge for us. Selah. (Psalm 62:5–8)

ON MONDAY, AUGUST 19, 1991, WE AWOKE TO THE NEWS ON BBC RADIO that the Kremlin had announced that Mikhail Gorbachev was unable to perform his presidential duties due to illness.

Our concerns rose as we reached the bridge crossing the Moscow River near Moscow State University. On both sides of the street, at the entrance to the bridge, was a tank. Driving over the long bridge, we saw tanks on the opposite end, also guarding the bridge.

We watched the hourly news summary filled with information about the coup in Moscow. After watching CNN for about fifteen minutes, we prayed. At the top of each hour, we watched the news summary then went back to our prayer meeting. We planned to pray until three o'clock and then go to the storage facility, which contained thousands of Bibles, and pass them out in the street so the Bibles wouldn't be confiscated if the coup succeeded.

CONTENTS

Appendix

PREFACE

≈

"YOU SHOULD WRITE THAT STORY," EXCLAIMED MY DENTIST AS I TOLD him of the unusual root canal he discovered in my mouth. I intended to write the stories someday. Then I read in the Bible:

> They will still yield fruit in old age;
> They shall be full of sap and very green,
> To declare that the LORD is upright;
> He is my rock, and there is no unrighteousness in Him.
> (Psalm 92:14–15)

I sensed God telling me to write the stories now, proclaiming the goodness of God and that he has been my Rock. He has always been there for me.

When we lived overseas for fourteen years, I wrote home once a week to my parents and to my mother-in-law. My parents kept the letters, as did my mother-in-law. I also had our ministry prayer letters and my journals. My husband, Vance, and I sorted and filed the letters by date. I searched my writing for stories proclaiming the goodness of God and how he has always taken care of me and our family.

Some names have been changed to protect people's privacy.

EARLY LIFE

≈

MY PARENTS MARRIED AT TWENTY, AND THE DOCTOR TOLD THEM they could not have children. They tried to adopt but couldn't. Then, at thirty-two, I was born, to their great joy. My mother dedicated me to God. As a young child, I believed in God. When I was five or six, I remember writing letters to Jesus and the angels, and walking to a neighborhood church. My parents were lying in bed one Sunday morning when I came into their bedroom, dressed up; I told them I was leaving for church and walked to a church in the neighborhood. I enjoyed listening to hymns on our record player. But I knew I was guilty. Desperate to make things right, one day, I washed my mouth out with soap. It was awful, and I never put soap in my mouth again.

In my fourteenth year, my grandmother died. I worried about dying. I'd heard of heaven and hell from church but didn't understand the way to heaven. Frightened of the dark, I had a Bible from my great-grandmother, and I listened to a Christian radio station at night in my bedroom. Pacific Garden Mission's stories of men on the street becoming Christians and the soothing voice of the host on Haven of Rest spoke to my soul. I read Romans 10:9, which says, "that if you confess with your mouth Jesus as Lord, and believe in your heart that God raised him from the dead, you will be saved." I understood this must mean saved from going to hell.

God can do everything, so I had no trouble believing he raised Jesus from the dead. I walked to a church down the street and responded to the altar call. To fulfill the rest of the verse in Romans 10:9, I told the pastor I wanted to say, "Jesus is Lord." The pastor desired to baptize me at once. I didn't understand it, but I wanted to do whatever it took to go to heaven, and I trusted the pastor knew more than I did. So he baptized me.

I tried going to the youth group for people my age at the church but found it hard to relate to the kids. They didn't seem very interested in God. I got involved with a different group of friends. I had a girlfriend, Ann, who was a Mormon. I knew her from school, and we had fun, wholesome parties with friends from her former home near downtown Los Angeles. We made a movie together and had pool parties at Ann's home. The Mormons I met were such nice people, I considered becoming a Mormon. But I read in the Book of Mormon that marriage continues in heaven, and I read in the Bible that Jesus said there is no marriage in heaven. This discrepancy prevented me from becoming Mormon, though I still enjoyed spending time with Ann and her friends.

When I entered the University of California, Los Angeles, I was a confused freshman. Different philosophies and religions surrounded me. I chose to rely on myself, not people or God. My roommate was a Communist and held drug parties in our room.

While eating lunch one day, a woman from Campus Crusade for Christ approached me. She talked about totally trusting my life to Jesus. I wasn't ready to do that, and she stopped our discussion. Meanwhile, life with my roommate was becoming intolerable, as I spent nights in the lobby to avoid the drug activity in our room. After I met a nice girl named Linda in the cafeteria, we moved in together.

Linda took me to a Bible study at the home of the Campus Crusade director, Wes Brenneman. His wife, Suzie, led the Bible study. Linda planned to attend a summer project sponsored by Campus Crusade in Lake Tahoe, California. I determined the solution to my confusion required a change of scene, so I decided to go too. I applied and was accepted.

About thirty college students stayed in cabins in the mountain resort, and we got jobs in town. We spent evenings in group Bible studies and talking to people about Jesus, standing in front of the resort's casinos. But a change in my location didn't solve my confusion. In desperation, I fled to a staff woman and poured out my heart. She read 1 John 4:18 from the Bible, which says, "There is no fear in love; but perfect love casts out fear, because fear involves punishment, and the one who fears is not perfected in love." She pointed out that God loves me perfectly, so why was I so afraid to trust him with my life?

A light bulb flipped on, and I gave God three problems I couldn't solve: where to live the next year on campus, what to major in, and my relationship with my boyfriend. I read in the Psalms over and over that God is our refuge. Instead of trying to run from problems, I ran to him for help. Back on campus, I found a Christian sorority (Alpha Delta Chi), joined it, and moved into the apartments they lived in. The women surrounded me with love and support, taking me to a good church every Sunday, where I learned from the Bible. As for my studies, I discovered kinesiology—the perfect combination of my love of science and sports. I enjoyed the classes and planned to pursue physical therapy as a profession. I broke up with my boyfriend, who didn't share my faith, and was much happier. God took such good care of the three areas I had entrusted to him. I gave him everything else in life too. That was the start of learning to trust God, and it transformed me. My fear and confusion disappeared, and life became an adventure. Light and free as if a weight had fallen from me, I grew closer to God.

Involved with Campus Crusade for Christ, I learned how to talk to other students about my faith. A friend, Carolyn, invited me to join her. Carolyn said we didn't have to force students to trust in Christ. We just asked them what they thought and then told them what we believed. We had many good discussions. We thought it might help if we prayed first and asked God to lead us to interested people. God knows everyone and could guide us to the right person. One day, we met Lynette, sitting on the grass. She had questions about Jesus. After meeting several times, Lynette gave her life to Jesus. As we studied the Bible with her, we watched Lynette become a happier person.

She changed before my eyes. I started a Bible study with Lynette and another new Christian, Betsy. They asked so many questions. Then Betsy talked to her boyfriend, and he became a Christian. I learned a lot by finding answers to their questions and saw that God could use me. I wanted to give my life to helping people know Jesus, who transforms lives—as he did with mine and Lynette's and Betsy's lives.

As a senior in college, I applied to work with the staff of Campus Crusade for Christ. I had five options after college, including pursuing physical therapy, public health, and seminary. But the wish to join Campus Crusade just kept growing. I worried about money, as staff raise their own salary. Without a home church except for the one I had just attended in college, the only Christians I knew were college students. One day, two verses jumped out at me from the Bible, and I sensed God saying, "These verses are for you."

> I will go before you and make the rough places smooth;
> I will shatter the doors of bronze and cut through their iron bars.
> I will give you the treasures of darkness and hidden wealth of secret places,
> So that you may know that it is I, the Lord, the God of Israel,
> who calls you by your name. (Isaiah 45:2–3)

The money I needed to join the staff of Campus Crusade for Christ was hidden in a secret place because I didn't know where it was. They accepted me on the staff, and I prepared to attend the summer training in Colorado. My father was out of a job, and I worked as a cashier at the school cafeteria while taking classes. Friends and acquaintances came up and gave me money to go. When I arrived in Colorado, there was just enough plus twenty dollars extra for spending money. God was faithful to his promise. This was just the start of watching him provide, often in unexpected ways.

There were many things I didn't understand when I arrived in Colorado; several thousand other staff members attended the same

CAROL NORDMAN

training. I received my textbooks for classes. Textbooks? I had just finished school. Over the years, I received a seminary education from many excellent professors. My knowledge of God and the Bible deepened. We received ministry training and instruction on how to raise our own finances. Then we scattered to all corners of the United States to find the people God had called to support us with prayer and finances.

I stayed with my parents in their one-bedroom apartment, sleeping on the couch. They didn't yet share my personal faith, but my father drew a large thermometer on paper and taped it on the closet door, filling it in as the money arrived.

God often provided through ways I didn't expect. The church I attended in college told me they only wanted to sponsor people who grew up in their church. That was a blow. Next, I talked to my friends from college. They gave what they were able. I called churches through the phonebook. Most had their own missionaries. One elderly pastor couldn't give money but made me prayer cards to pass out. Another pastor agreed to meet me. As I told him how Christ changed my life, he didn't appear to have a personal faith himself. He was too busy teaching a class on automobiles at the university to attend a ministry training I told him about. But he suggested I talk with the high school class in his large church. Matthew 6:33 promises, "But seek first his kingdom and his righteousness, and all these things will be added to you." A college friend and I spoke to the high school group. We shared the Gospel, and three students indicated they asked Christ into their lives. Afterward, one student told me how good it was to hear about God in Sunday school. They usually talked about other things, like mountain climbing.

After another invitation to speak to an adult Sunday school class in the same church, I arrived at a small group, sitting in a circle discussing how to get to heaven. They each said they needed to live a good life. One lady exclaimed she felt she would never be good enough. Someone introduced me as the speaker. From my training with Campus Crusade, I picked up with the fact we can't be good enough but need to accept the payment Jesus made for our sin. When we personally turn from our sin to God and accept his forgiveness, asking him to come into our lives and take control, we have assurance of heaven according to the promise in 1 John 5:11–13: "And the testimony is this, that God has given us eternal life, and this life is in His Son. He who has the Son has the life; he who does not have the Son of God does not have the life." Afterward, one lady said it was interesting how my talk fit into their discussion.

Then I spoke to an adult home group. As it appeared most people in the church didn't understand how to have a personal faith, I passed out the tract I used on campus: "The Four Spiritual Laws." I explained that I planned to use it with college students and read the tract out loud to them. At the prayer asking Jesus to come into their lives, I invited them to pray after me. A loud chorus of voices repeated the prayer after me. I met a few people in the church with a personal faith. They were praying for their church, and a couple agreed to help fund my ministry. One man who owned a car dealership put new tires on my car.

In the hills above Los Angeles, I looked at the vast metropolis below, thinking, *Somewhere out there are the people who will support me.* Later, I lay facedown on the floor, telling God this was how helpless I was to tackle the job before me. But I held on to promises from the Bible. First Thessalonians 5:24 says, "Faithful is He who calls you, and He also will bring it to pass."

God continued to surprise me. Someone suggested calling morticians, as they work with churches. So I looked up morticians in the phonebook and made some calls. I met with one mortician, a large, jovial man, who gave me a thousand dollars. I attended a church Bible study near my parents' apartment and wanted a guitar to sing praise songs in my devotions. Without knowing this, a young man at the Bible study came up and gave me his guitar. He said God told him to do it and explained that he only used the guitar to sing praises to God. My mother wrote a letter to my aunt saying that anyone who watched what was happening would believe in God.

One day, I attended an alumni event for the Christian sorority I was in at UCLA. Alpha Delta Chi began around 1920 and had many alumni. They gave me a book with the names, addresses, and phone numbers of the alumni. This was it. Here were the people to call. I sent a letter to the ladies, called, and visited them. It wasn't long before I had the money I needed and a team of people to support and pray for me. I packed everything I owned into my little car and took off for Houston, Texas—my first assignment.

FAITH LESSONS
IN TEXAS

≈

Aʟⱼₜₑᵣ SEVERAL DAYS OF DRIVING, I ARRIVED IN HOUSTON AND MET MY team. Dale and Jewell Erickson were newly married, and Dale was the new director. Debbie, Ron, and I rounded out the team. Debbie and I rented a house right across the street from the University of Houston, where we worked four days a week. One day a week, we all went to Rice University—a small, prestigious private university.

I loved my team and our work. Each morning, Debbie and I jogged on the grassy banks along a bayou. Then we had our personal devotions, and the team met at our house for Bible study, prayer, and planning the day. Most days; we talked with students, taking a religious survey and talking with those who wanted to know more about God. We formed Bible studies for interested students and trained student leaders to work alongside us. In the evenings, we often had meetings and events for the students to help them grow as Christians.

I loved it all but soon found that I was working in a different dimension than I was used to. The University of Houston was a commuter campus, and students were busy with school, work, and commuting. It was a difficult campus to minister on, and we had only a handful of students from the previous year. I had never worked in a job that had no end. There were always more people with more needs. And sometimes—no matter how hard I tried—nothing seemed to happen. I started three Bible studies the first year, and every girl dropped out. I worked, not stopping for rest, and soon got sick. I couldn't seem to get well. One doctor told me I needed to rest. I learned that God was wise to give us a day off each week—and I should take one.

On campus, I felt like I was walking through mud. Students weren't responding. It was just so hard. I took an hour during the day to stop and just pray. After I prayed, things happened. I felt like I was running rather than wading through mud. Students responded. In fact, the other campus ministries also were having troubles. The leaders of the different ministries met together to pray. I was learning the truth of Ephesians 6. Our battle is in the spiritual realm, and we need spiritual weapons to see things happen.

Something big was also happening across the country. The "I Found it!" campaign was launched in America by Campus Crusade. Billboards and television ads proclaiming, "I Found it!" appeared—making people curious. Gradually, "it" was disclosed as "a new life in Jesus Christ." But first, a citywide prayer movement began. We all got involved, and I helped with prayer workshops. Prayer groups multiplied throughout the city.

Finally, it all broke open. Throughout the city, people became Christians. At the university, students responded. It was thrilling, like riding an ocean wave. In fact, I wrote a song after attending a retreat in the little city of Galveston, on the shores of the Gulf of Mexico. As I walked on the beach and gazed at the pounding waves of a stormy sea, I felt like one of those little drops of foam riding on God's power. Borrowing from Campus Crusade's materials, I wrote:

> Every day can be an exciting adventure for the Christian who is filled with God's Spirit and who lives under his control. As a drop of foam rides a mighty wave—so my soul is thrilled as I ride on God's power.

I wanted to do it again. I wanted to go somewhere where things were difficult and watch God work. It was so exciting. I would see God work in more amazing ways in Houston. Faith is like a muscle. The more you step out and trust God, the stronger your faith grows—and you can trust him with more. Speaking in a classroom and witnessing a miracle at the dentist would strengthen my faith muscle.

Rice University

≈

My director, Dale, decided to send me full time to Rice University. I was to work with a lay couple close to my age—Wally and Ann Ford. Wally had graduated from Rice, and both he and Ann worked in ministry during college. Wally was busy as an architect in Houston. Ann went with me on campus, and together, we talked with girls and started Bible studies.

I loved Rice's old brick buildings and tree-lined streets. It was small, and students lived on campus. People said hello, and students and professors ate meals together. Even though it was near downtown Houston, there was a quaint village nearby with interesting restaurants. The girls I worked with fascinated me. I taught them Bible, and they taught me geology, art, music, and much more. I had gone to a good school, but my scores weren't high enough to get into a college like Rice. It often amazed me that I could teach Rice students anything. I discovered that just because a person is smart and knows a lot, they may not know much about God. Sylvia, a girl in my Bible study, was a PhD student from Germany about my age; she was also an opera singer. We had fun together doing many things. I remember going to an art museum, and she translated the foreign titles of paintings and explained the meanings.

One day, Dale announced that this semester, all the staff would speak in classrooms. A ministry of Campus Crusade had developed talks on various subjects we could use in classrooms. I thought, *Maybe you will speak in a classroom, but I work at RICE and I will not speak in a classroom there.* However, the whole staff team was working together, with each of us picking a topic and working on a talk. Okay, I could do that. I chose a Christian answer to the book *Beyond Freedom and Dignity* by B. F. Skinner and prepared a talk. That wasn't so hard since the Crusade ministry had already done a lot of the work.

Then, one day, I was visiting a girl from my Bible study in her dorm room at Rice. I saw the book *Beyond Freedom and Dignity* on her desk. *Oh-oh,* I thought. "Um, are you studying that in class?" I asked, hoping that she wasn't. She told me she was. "Um, do you think, um, your professor might let me speak in your class?" I hated to ask it but felt I had to. Anyway, why would he let an unknown person like me speak to his students?

My friend took me to visit her professor in his office. Stacks of books about five feet high covered the floor, with a narrow, winding path leading through them to the professor's desk. A disheveled man with shoelaces untied looked up from his papers. I made my request, and to my surprise, he invited me to speak—not to the lecture but to a study session. *Oh, no,* I thought. *This will really happen.*

Somehow, I went to that study session and faced the professor and about thirty students and gave that talk. I even answered questions afterward, and I remember people clapping. Well, after that, I knew God could do anything. I was never a public speaker; no one could hear my quiet voice, but if God could use me to speak at Rice, everything else was insignificant in comparison. My faith muscle was growing.

My Weakness, God's Power

≈

In Houston, it seemed God was continually teaching me not to rely on myself but on him. Here's something I wrote in December 1975:

> Burned out it's
> Apathy. Hearts are so cold! People don't want You.
> Christians don't care … the spiritual battle …
> Burned out it's …
> Trying, working, obeying, continuing. It's just too
> hard, Lord—too much—too big! I just want to pack
> boxes, something mechanical that I can do. But this
> Lord, it's beyond me!
> Burned out it's …
> Worn out. My body is tired—my being says, Stop!
> Rest, it's of You. You chart my path. You supply. Your
> burden is light … if only I'd just … listen … to Your
> plan.
> I can't continue—Lord, I really can't. I'm helpless! I
> would control—I would be independent. Thank you,
> Lord, for drawing me ever more intimately to Yourself.
> Such a wise lover You are, so strategic in Your wooing

of my heart, till I yearn and long for my Lord who alone can give rest, power, strength, adequacy, hope.

Burned out ... the answer? How will I respond? Yield, lean on God, run to Him, cry to Him? Or rebel, harden, give up?

Burned out ... the answer? It's You, Lord! (See 2 Corinthians 1:8–11.)

Another time, I realized how sinful I was and focused on that, thinking it was a spiritual thing to do. I became increasingly discouraged. Then, I realized that this thinking was a trap. I was focusing on myself instead of on God. I realized that sin is best dealt with by confessing it, asking God to cleanse and restore me (1 John 1:9), and then focusing on the Lord, not myself.

One morning in October 1976, I felt impressed to ask God to do something supernatural—so I did. I wrote about what happened:

That day I went to the dentist (a Christian dentist). I walked into the office at the same time a man walked in. The dentist and his wife took their time as we shared about the Lord and what He had done in our lives (we had such a good time I almost didn't need any Novocain). When he finished, my dentist felt impressed not to charge me. As I walked to the waiting room, his wife had just talked with another patient—a Christian—who had sent in more money than her bill called for. The patient had said she was impressed by God to send that much. Her extra money covered my bill! That's not the end of the story. The man who walked in with me heard the entire conversation from the time I first sat down in the chair until the dentist, his wife and I rejoiced at the way the Lord had paid my bill. After I left, the man sat in the dental chair while the dentist talked. This dentist witnesses to his patients by asking them, "When did you receive

CAROL NORDMAN

Christ?" He asked this man also, and the man said he never had. My dentist read him the Four Spiritual Laws, and the man prayed—inviting Christ into his life—right there in the dental chair! My dentist was so excited he called me that evening. He also laughed and asked me not to pray for the supernatural before coming to his office because it took him several days to recover from the excitement!

Well, there is still more to the story. Later, I needed more finances and found a copy of a Christian business phone directory. I started at the beginning and called Dorothy Armstrong. Dorothy said she had been supporting a Campus Crusade staff member who left our staff, and she was wondering what to do with the money. When I visited her, I discovered she was the patient who had felt impressed to send in extra money for her dental bill. She was a faithful friend and supporter for many years until she went to be with her Lord.

I wrote the following song:

Wait Before the Throne

I am weak; you are strong
I am finite; You are infinite.
I come and wait before Your throne.
For those who hopefully wait for You will not be put to shame, Lord.
I need healing; You're the healer.
I am needy; You are wealthy.
I come and wait before Your throne.
For those who hopefully wait for You will not be put to shame, Lord.

DATING LIFE

≈

SINCE I WAS AN ONLY CHILD AND NEVER AROUND BOYS GROWING UP, MEN seemed like another species—a mystery. As a college student, I went to Crusade conferences and learned that it isn't good to date someone who doesn't share my faith. Second Corinthians 6:14–15 says, "Do not be bound together with unbelievers; for what partnership have righteousness and lawlessness, or what fellowship has light with darkness? Or what harmony has Christ with Belial, or what has a believer in common with an unbeliever?" I also learned from a speaker, Josh McDowell, that it is good to limit physical contact. He spoke on 1 Corinthians 7:1, which says, "It is good for a man not to touch a woman." This was referring to unmarried people. He said this meant to arouse or light a fire under a woman. So I decided I would not even hold hands with guys I dated. I told them this was my standard—and since the men I dated walked with God, they respected it. I found I could have mutually beneficial relationships with men under these conditions. Another important thing was to be honest with how we were feeling and to stop pursuing the relationship on a romantic level if one person knew their feelings weren't there. Most of the time, this worked well. After I joined Campus Crusade and before I met my husband, I dated several godly men, and we had fun and encouraged each other.

Sometimes, there were no men in my life. I remember talking to the Lord about it once during staff training in Colorado. Philippians 4:19

says, "And my God will supply all your needs according to His riches in glory in Christ Jesus." In the context, this refers to monetary needs. But throughout scripture, God meets all the needs of his children in his way and time. Praying about this and sitting on the grass, a girlfriend came by, and we had a heart-to-heart talk. I found the emotional need I had been feeling was satisfied after that talk. I hadn't needed a man at all; I needed some good conversation. I realized that God is ready to meet my needs if I allow him to do it in his own way and not insist on the method I think best.

Norma was an elderly single woman who supported me. Norma was so happy and involved in the lives of people all around her. I was in my early twenties and amazed that she could be so happy. I asked her how she could be so happy when she was single. I will never forget her answer: We never live for ourselves. She was so busy helping and giving to people that she forgot about herself. I hope to remember her example and follow it.

After I was on staff with Campus Crusade for four years in Houston, I worked on a staff recruiting team for a short time in Austin, Texas. I felt drawn to something international, applied to five different international ministry opportunities, but got none. Instead, my assignment was a beach project in San Diego for the summer and the leader of the women's ministry at San Diego State the following year. These were the last things I wanted to do. But as I prayed about it, God helped me see that this was his will. He provided a coworker to drive behind me from Houston to San Diego as I pulled a U-Haul behind my little Datsun. I downshifted to first gear over the mountains as the clutch kept slipping. I think the car was too little to pull a U-Haul. God kept confirming this move was his will, though it made no logical sense. So I went.

After moving to San Diego, I dated a man from my church, but when I read Proverbs 4:23, "Watch over your heart with all diligence, for from it flow the springs of life," God impressed on me the importance of guarding my emotions and only getting involved with someone who had the same calling of going international with Campus Crusade for Christ. That calling was clear. I told the man at church I couldn't keep dating him because I felt called to go international with Campus Crusade, and he didn't.

He responded by saying he felt sorry for me, as I would probably never marry. I thought perhaps he was right, as I was twenty-five, and there wasn't anyone I knew around me who had the same calling I did. I had asked God for someone to share life with—even a roommate who didn't move away. I claimed the promise in Philippians 4:19, "And my God will supply all your needs according to His riches in glory in Christ Jesus."

MEETING VANCE

≈

I ENJOYED WORKING AT SAN DIEGO STATE WITH THE CAMPUS MINISTRY. The students were full of faith, and we met regularly for prayer. I lived in a rented house with three other women; one, Simone, was from Switzerland. They helped with the ministry.

The Campus Crusade single staff in Southern California would occasionally plan outings together to get to know one another. Through these events and Campus Crusade conferences, I got to know my future husband, Vance Nordman. I had met Vance earlier when my Texas roommate introduced us. She and Vance met on a summer project in Santa Cruz, California. My former roommate was the best judge of character of anyone I knew and said she felt Vance wasn't for her—but she respected him. I hadn't heard her speak that way about anyone, so I felt curious to meet him. Vance planned to go overseas with Crusade but was seriously dating an acquaintance of mine on our staff. I saw Vance at a conference during the fall and noticed he seemed sad. Later, I found out he didn't receive an overseas assignment, and the relationship he was in had ended.

Our first date was by accident. A Campus Crusade singles group planned a trip to Tijuana, Mexico, for the day. My coworker and I had to go later, as we had a commitment, and Vance offered to drive us. Somehow, my coworker found the rest of the group, but Vance and I didn't. We still can't figure out how this happened. So we ended up in Tijuana together and went out to dinner in a restaurant that was a remodeled prison. I'll never forget eating a delicious dinner behind the bars of our cell—serenaded by a Spanish music group.

At Christmastime, staff and students from many campuses traveled to the Campus Christmas Conference near San Francisco—held in a massive hotel with many hallways. I have a terrible sense of direction, and as I wandered lost in the halls, Vance ran into me and helped me find the meeting room. He has been pointing the way in our lives ever since. (I help him wander off to smell the flowers.) As I drove back to Los Angeles with other staff women, we stopped along the rugged California coast at a hilltop motel. I walked out in the evening to the cliffs and watched the pounding waves below. I had the distinct sense that just as the ocean was powerful, so a powerful God was up to something that affected my life.

The next conference for the campus staff was in Dana Point, California. During the conference, Vance asked to talk—and we sat on a low wall outside. He wanted to pursue a relationship and laid down some ground rules. The main one I remember is that we would be honest and communicate what we were feeling. By this time, I had a crush on him and readily responded to his suggestion. We opened our notebooks with our ministry schedules and tried to find a time to see each other. The campus ministry is very busy—even in the evenings and on weekends. I had an opening on a weekend or two—but everything else was booked solid. An amazing thing happened, however. Every weekend, something was canceled or worked out so we could see each other. Vance would often spend the weekend in San Diego staying with the staff men so he could see me. My parents lived in Garden Grove, near where Vance was serving with Campus Crusade, so I sometimes spent the weekend with them so we could see each other. We had a great time dating and getting to know one another.

I didn't trust my judgment and had asked God to make it very clear when the right guy came along. In the early spring, my grandmother was in the hospital. I had come home to my parents' apartment and wanted the comfort of talking to Vance. But I didn't feel comfortable yet calling him. One day, my mother took a walk during her break at her work and prayed. Her mother was sick, and her daughter would never get married because she wouldn't call her boyfriend. Mother put it all into God's hands, about ten o'clock. At the same time, I sat at home with my father. I had a nagging thought I should call Vance. Finally, I silently prayed, *If this is from you, God, have my father leave the room.* No sooner had I finished that prayer than my father got up and left, saying he was taking a nap (I never recalled him taking a nap at ten o'clock in the morning.) So I called Vance. He told me he wasn't usually home then, but we set a time to get together at a restaurant, and I poured out my heart about my grandmother. After this, I felt closer to him.

Another student conference was coming up, and Vance asked if we could talk after the conference. I prayed and felt that whatever it was, God wanted me to respond positively. So one night, after the conference at Arrowhead Springs, on the lawn overlooking the lights of San Bernardino, Vance told me he loved me. I replied that God told me to respond positively. Poor Vance—I wasn't very romantic. He wasn't discouraged, however.

A summer ministry opportunity came up to go to Paris and work with international students. Several women from my campus—including my Swiss roommate, Simone—planned to go. Vance also planned to go, and Simone offered to drive us all around Europe in her father's car. Wow. I was excited! In my devotions, I came across a verse that captured my attention: "Through Him then, let us continually offer up a sacrifice of praise to God, that is, the fruit of lips that give thanks to His name" (Hebrews 13:15). My campus director asked me to talk about what I learned about this. So I prayed that God would make the verse real in my life the next week.

The next week, I met with my campus director and my supervisor. Both had reservations about my trip to Paris. I knew Vance wanted to go overseas, but it appeared God didn't want me to go now. Would I still praise God and accept His will? I found a letter written to Vance March 8, 1979:

I just talked to Susan last night. I can't believe what God is doing in my life! He took me seriously when I asked to learn about sacrifices of praise! Susan said that God kept impressing her that I should be on a beach project this summer under another Senior Woman to learn more about being a Senior Woman, that I needed to be excellent at it before going overseas, and that vision was my strength—so I didn't need a summer overseas. When she asked me what I thought, what could I say but how God had taught me about praising Him and that Greg had said the same thing, independently as far as I know, the very same day, BOTH of them, my authorities. Who am I to fight against God?

I thought this might be the end of my relationship with Vance, as God might lead us in different directions. That is when I knew I loved Vance. I felt very depressed about this and realized that a sacrifice of praise is a choice, not a feeling. Vance, however, didn't seem at all upset by the news. In fact, he said he was coming down the next weekend to take me out to dinner. In the middle of the week, I got a call from my parents. They wanted to know how I felt about Vance because he was coming over to see them. I could honestly say I thought I was in love with him. They replied that that was what they wanted to know.

I prayed and used the sound mind principle we had learned through Campus Crusade, based on 2 Timothy 1:7. One method of knowing God's will is through our minds. I made a list of the pros and cons of marrying Vance. This has been the only decision where I could not think of any cons. I was in love with him, we had the same calling, and my parents liked him. Everything said go. I bought a new dress and waited for the weekend.

So on Saint Patrick's Day, March 17, 1979, after a delicious dinner, Vance sat me down on a bench under a palm tree and a moon in the courtyard of the Hotel Del Coronado in San Diego and asked me to marry him. I readily said yes. We thought about getting married the following December, but the campus ministry discouraged getting married during the school year, as the staff would be so distracted. So we looked at August. Then a friend said we would just be on different assignments during the summer, so we might as well get married in June. Then my dad said he would like a June bride. June was less than three months away. We called the Family Ministry with Campus Crusade. They asked if we had any doubts, and we said we didn't. They told us we should get married.

Vance had to go to Mexico for a ministry outreach during Easter, but I was free to work on wedding plans, so I flew up to his hometown in the Central Valley of California to work on the wedding. I met his family, and Vance's sister-in-law—Sheri—took me around to pick out a cake, dresses, flowers, and everything else. We set up everything in one week. I could never have done this without Sheri, and I was happy with the preparations.

We had a simple church wedding. I wore a long cotton ivory gauze dress and a garland of flowers with trailing ribbons in my hair. I grew up in the hippie generation. I didn't change out of my wedding dress as we left on our honeymoon: driving through a fast-food restaurant for a snack and then on to the elegant Saint Francis Hotel in San Francisco. After two beautiful days, where we enjoyed crab salad and baked Alaska and other good food, we drove back to Vance's home to open presents and then traveled on to Yosemite for a week in a mountain cabin. We had a great time, and I learned during that week that three years earlier—before I knew him—Vance had asked people to pray Colossians 1:9–12 for him. Three years earlier, I had been impressed to pray Colossians 1:9–12 for my future husband.

After our honeymoon, Vance and I traveled to Minnesota for our summer assignment. In the fall, he would be Campus Crusade's new director at Cal State Fullerton. Our ministry held a training for new campus directors in Minneapolis. I think it must have been a new idea because the schedule for the women was minimal. Most of the women were new wives or newly pregnant. We all lived in apartments in the same complex and had a lot of fun getting to know each other. The women only had activities one morning a week. I remember taking walks along country roads and studying flower arranging. It was the perfect assignment for newlyweds. After our Minnesota assignment, we moved into our apartment in Fullerton and had fun setting up our first home. We had a very large carved dark wooden chair from Vance's family. I think it came from Europe by boat around the horn of South America. It looked like it came from a castle. Since the chair was the focus of the room wherever we put it, I placed it in a corner with mirrors and a potted plant. Vance sat there like a king during meetings.

Fall arrived, along with a full schedule of meeting new students at Cal State, starting Bible studies, working with student leaders, leading training meetings, and planning evangelistic outreaches. Vance and I bought a new gadget called an answering machine for our telephone so we could have one night a week alone.

So many students we talked with had already heard about Jesus. We wanted to go somewhere where people hadn't heard. So when the Christmas Conference came again, we went to seminars about serving in other countries. To divide and conquer, Vance and I went separately to different seminars representing different parts of the world. He came back very excited after hearing about the Middle East. "Isn't that where there is war?" was all I had to say. I knew little about the Middle East.

TURKEY

≋

We applied to a project in Turkey the next summer. To raise money to go, Vance spoke at a large men's meeting. I was the only woman and felt conspicuous in the audience. Before Vance spoke, a man stood up and pointed at me, saying that I was afraid I would die, and that fear is not from God. I was stunned and wondered how this man knew what I was thinking. I knew nothing about Turkey and had a picture in my mind of men in flowing robes with turbans on their heads, chasing us on camels while brandishing scimitars. I thought we would probably die. This was one more lesson teaching me to trust God. The next summer would be the biggest adventure yet and would lay the foundation for our future ministry.

The summer of 1980 arrived, and Vance and I found a special price on a plane ticket to the East Coast, where we were to attend cross-cultural training and meet the team we would travel to Turkey with. The specially priced ticket got us there early, so we spent our vacation seeing historical sites and staying with friends from Campus Crusade. Arriving early at the small college, we discovered there was only cold water in the bathroom. I thought this was probably the preparation for our summer trip, but we had just arrived before the college turned on the hot water.

The cross-cultural training was very helpful. We played a game called Bafa Bafa, where we divided into two groups representing two cultures. Neither group knew anything about the other. Each group received small plastic coins. Vance's group was individualistic—and the main goal was to trade and gain as many coins as possible. There were rules to the game, and everyone worked on their own. My group had a complicated social structure, with a patriarch and male elders. The main goal was to interact with each other and abide by the rules. Conversations started with giving a coin and asking how one's father was. Outsiders—especially men—had to gain entrance into the group, and the patriarch decided who was welcome.

Vance came to visit our group, and like everyone in his group, he knew nothing about our culture. He immediately went up to a woman and asked for her coins. The elders asked Vance to leave. He persisted in asking questions—trying to understand what the problem was. There was a lot of heated talking, and I saw the elders carrying Vance out of the room. Fortunately, nothing like that happened when we visited another culture. We often remembered our helpful training.

We met our team and flew to Athens, Greece. Everyone was so excited—we didn't sleep but stayed up talking. Vance was the only one who slept; he has always slept on airplanes. So when we arrived, we all had to take a nap, except for Vance—who went exploring. He remembers the feeling he had when he realized he could get lost and didn't speak Greek. We celebrated our first anniversary in Athens by going out to dinner and having moussaka. Athens was fun; we enjoyed seeing the Parthenon. Hearing about our upcoming trip to Turkey was not so fun.

We were the first large Campus Crusade group to go into Turkey. Less than one hundred Christians lived in this country of about forty million. Almost all the rest were Muslims. Turkey had a reputation as the graveyard of missionaries. The handful of missionaries in the country were under cover and had spent time in prison. The country was under martial law. We learned that if they put us in prison, we were not to worry but just work on our memory verses (we were studying the book of Acts) and someone would get us out within two weeks. We couldn't drink the water or eat anything not cooked or peeled, or we would be sick.

When we were still in Athens—as our team was having a Bible

study—someone asked me to read 2 Thessalonians 3:1. By accident, I read 1 Thessalonians 3:1, which says, "Therefore when we could endure it no longer, we thought it best to be left behind at Athens alone." We had a good laugh, as that was how we were feeling after learning about all the dangers in Turkey.

The plan was to gather addresses all over Turkey so Christians from other countries could mail in Gospel literature. It was difficult to get addresses, so our team would go on foot and by car all over the country, speaking addresses into tape recorders concealed in small bags that Turkish men and women commonly carried. We would walk in pairs and look like we were talking to each other while looking at the addresses across the street and saying them into the concealed tape recorder. Another team drove the car in the outlying areas of cities, recording addresses. Every night—in our hotel rooms—we were to transcribe those addresses into letters and mail them out of the country the next day. We were a team of about eight Campus Crusade staff. After a couple of weeks, college students would join us, making us a team of thirty.

It was time to leave for Turkey, and we boarded a large ship bound for the Greek island of Chios. This was an overnight ship, and as Vance and I were the only married couple, we divided up into men and women—sleeping in different areas of the ship. The next morning, everyone but Vance got off the ship on the island of Chios. They raised the gangplank while he was still aboard, and the ship prepared to visit another Greek island. I wondered when I'd see my husband again. He had been taking a shower and got off the back of the ship where the cars exited.

What I remember about the island of Chios was sun and warm weather, with men sitting around outside light-colored buildings. One was eating what looked like a raw squid—tipping back his head and dropping the squid down his throat. We didn't stay long enough to gather more impressions of this sunny Greek island.

Next, we boarded a small vessel and took the short trip to the west coast of Turkey. My first impression was of soldiers with guns and a feeling of oppression. That night in a pension—sharing a room with the only other woman—I felt waves of fear. I tried praying. It didn't help. Finally, I got up and went into the bathroom and read my Bible. The fear subsided, and I could sleep.

The project director was an adventurous person and gave us our first assignment. He divided us into groups and told us to find a bus and go to a certain town and get the addresses there. We couldn't speak Turkish, and the Turks didn't speak English. We had Berlitz books with Turkish words and phrases. Somehow, we did it. We got into a public van and found the town. I think we got into a government building where they showed us the blueprints of the town. Once we had the layout of the streets, we got the addresses. It amazed us that we had done this without knowing much. The next step was to rent two cars. Renting cars was an all-day process and involved drinking tea and having a conversation. We were grateful for the cross-cultural training. Our team was about to drive over fifteen thousand miles to help find one million families, who previously were beyond the influence of any kind of Christian outreach.

After renting two cars, we were off. In one of the first towns, our car took the central area, so we walked up and down the streets. We went in pairs—so we looked like we were talking to each other, but we actually read the addresses into our concealed tape recorders. Occasionally—when we were hurrying later in the project—we walked alone. This wasn't a good idea, as we looked like we were talking to ourselves.

The other car took the outlying areas. They came across rows of apartment buildings, so they dropped a man off at the beginning of the street. He walked into each building and read the names listed on the mailboxes into his tape recorder. Then the car picked him up, and they went on to the next street. Because there was martial law and unrest in the country, the police were on the lookout for anything unusual. A car dropping off and then picking up a man at every street was definitely unusual. A police car stopped our coworkers, and policemen with machine guns asked everyone to get out of the car. The police noticed everyone had tape recorders and wanted to hear what was on them.

We planned to transcribe the tapes every night and mail the

addresses out of the country the next day. We planned to have Turkish language lessons at the beginning of each tape and a Turkish language learning tape in an obvious place in the car. However, there was a pile of tapes with addresses on them in the car. I remember that only the European on our team had put the language phrases at the beginning of his tape. And nobody had rewound their tapes to the language lessons, like we planned to do if stopped.

The police picked the European man and tried to turn on his tape recorder, but they couldn't figure out how to work it. They gave it back and asked our friend to play it. So he rewound it discreetly and played it. The tape recorder told the police that today we are learning names and numbers. The police listened to the language lesson awhile. Then, they wanted to hear another tape. They went to the pile of tapes in the car, dug to the bottom, and picked up the language learning tape. The police told our friends to leave town the next morning, and an unmarked car followed our two cars until we were far out of town. We felt God's hand had protected us.

Soon after this—in a town that had been experiencing unrest— we felt uneasy. That evening, we ate dinner early. Turks usually eat after eight o'clock. We finally got our dinner and went back to the hotel. One man thought of going out for a walk but stayed to write a postcard. After we'd gone to bed, there was gunfire in the street outside—close to the restaurant we'd just had dinner in. All the lights went out in the hotel, and we gathered in one of our rooms to be sure everyone was okay. Again, we felt God's protective hand.

It was time to meet the college students and rent more cars. Our team of thirty would transverse Turkey but avoid the east, which was very dangerous; there were snipers on the road. We heard another mission group had gone to the east. I couldn't imagine their courage.

THE BLACK TONGUE

≈

W<small>E REORGANIZED AFTER MEETING THE COLLEGE STUDENTS AND</small> divided our group of thirty into cars. They assigned two young women, a young man, and Vance to the car I was in. We had the nicest route, which took us along all the coasts. We would travel to the Aegean Sea, the Mediterranean Sea, and the Black Sea. We also drove inland to a very interesting place with caves. We often followed the footsteps of Paul in the book of Acts and visited the sites of the seven churches mentioned in the book of Revelation. The history and ruins were everywhere, and it seemed nobody had discovered the tourist potential. We found Roman ruins just by the roadside.

One difficulty we faced was stomach problems from contaminated food and water. We ate in restaurants. The only way we could eat fruit we couldn't peel was to order a large glass of water, add a couple of drops of iodine to the water and drop the fruit in to soak for about fifteen minutes. In one restaurant, which we visited several times, the waiter began serving us fruit submerged in glasses of water. He must have thought it was an American custom. It seemed everyone got sick with diarrhea at some point, and we all lost weight, except for one person who was already too thin. God was gracious. Vance and I sent home a picture of us to reassure our families we were okay. However, we didn't realize how thin we were and how this alarmed our families.

Along the coast of the Mediterranean, one of the young women in our car had stomach trouble. It worsened because she didn't just stop eating, which usually cured us when we got sick. We left her in the hotel one day while the rest of us went out to get addresses. It was nearly impossible to call America, but somehow, she went down to the hotel lobby and got through to her mother. The connection must have been bad because she shouted, that she was sick. The English word for "sick" sounded like a bad word in Turkish. They told us not to say it but to use the word "ill" instead. We wondered what the hotel employees thought. Her mother thought she was speaking in code and was in prison. Many people prayed back in America. God answered prayer, and our teammate made a rapid recovery.

One of the lovely places we discovered was Hierapolis—a place of healing mentioned in the Bible. We had spent the day in one of the most dusty, difficult towns getting addresses and felt hot and tired. That evening, we stayed in a cheap government hotel beside the mineral baths of the ancient Hierapolis. Blooming oleanders surrounded a large natural pool of warm liquid that bubbled like Perrier water. Submerged everywhere were ancient columns and ruins. We sat on the ruins and relaxed in the bubbly water, amazed at the contrast with the dusty town, and gave thanks to God for the reprieve.

The next day, Vance got sick. He called me over to look at his tongue. It was black. Everyone was alarmed and wondered what strange, exotic disease he'd come down with. Just as we were thinking of finding a doctor, a student on our team came into the room and asked Vance if he had been taking Pepto Bismol tablets for his stomach. He had. We looked at the Pepto Bismol box and confirmed that the chewable tablets can create a black film on the tongue. We were all relieved, and Vance recovered after a few days of not eating.

THE ACCIDENT

≈

Most of the time, we drove on two-lane country roads through terrain that looked very much like rural California. Turkey, in fact, was gorgeous. You could almost picture the pirate ships that had sheltered in the aqua-colored coves along the mountainous Mediterranean coast. I will never forget swimming in water so clear that I looked far below to the floor of the sea. I could write pages about the loveliness of Turkey and sound like an ad for a tour agency. But we discovered that we needed to stay off the road at night.

One night, we got lost on a dirt road, trying to get to the town where our hotel was located. The road was under construction, with no lighting, and we often came to large piles of dirt in the middle of the road. Somehow, we found the town and didn't collide with a dirt pile. Another night, we were traveling along a country road, and a farmer's slow-moving combine appeared in front of us. Vance and I were in the back seat, and Vance—who grew up on a farm—recognized the shape of a combine. He yelled, "It's wide! It's slow!" I ducked behind the seat. I still wonder if God moved our car to miss that combine.

We had a romance in our group, and one night, when the couple went out for a drive, they collided with a slow-moving vehicle pulling gravel. Vance and I went to the hospital and found the woman going into shock. There weren't any doctors at the hospital at the time, so Vance went around gathering blankets for her. The doctors arrived and x-rayed her. As the only other woman on the team, I stayed by her side.

Both of our friends had hit the dashboard. The man had a huge knot on his forehead but recovered. The woman had hit her chest where there was cartilage, so it only bruised her. She would have broken ribs if she had been in a different position. The next day, there was an accident investigation by the police. It lasted most of the day, as officials interrupted their inquiries to kill an animal (I think it was for a feast they were celebrating). Somehow, everything worked out with the rental car company, and no one was seriously hurt. Thank you, Lord.

A funny driving incident happened while Vance was driving on a country road. A pair of donkeys were frolicking by the roadside, and Vance slowed down as they zigzagged across the road. It looked like a male donkey chasing a female. Then, unexpectedly, the female shot across the road in front of our car, and the male followed. We hit the male donkey and flipped him over. Fortunately, we were going very slow. The stunned donkey jumped up and ran off.

PEOPLE

≈

As OUR KNOWLEDGE OF THE TURKISH LANGUAGE WAS LIMITED, AND most people spoke little or no English, our interaction with people was superficial. Sometimes, when we were on foot, people invited us in for tea. We found almost everyone hospitable and helpful.

In one town, a man approached us and asked in English if we were looking for the church. Now, there weren't churches or Christians or missionaries at all in most towns. So we were very interested to know where the church was. He took us to an old ruined wall—all that remained of an ancient church.

We discovered that this was the site of the ancient church of Philadelphia, mentioned in the book of Revelation. The man spoke English and had become a Christian in another city. He said he was the only Christian in his town and believed the promise to the church in Philadelphia in Revelation 3:8: "Behold, I have put before you an open door which no one can shut." How we wanted to tell him what we were doing. The town he lived in was built in a logical order, and it was easy to get the addresses.

Another time, we stopped by the side of the road to photograph women working in the field in colorful baggy pants. One woman came rushing toward us calling out, "Hello! Hello!" She was from Australia and had married a Turkish man and now worked with the women in the fields.

Sometimes, we confused the local people; they must have wondered about the stupid foreign tourists. Our route led us to remote villages, and people stopped us to ask if we needed help finding our way. We usually said we were looking for Istanbul. Some roads we went down looked more like a goat path than a road.

In one neighborhood, we had to keep passing a house to go down all the different streets. A man living at the house noticed us driving by and asked where we were going. We told him we were looking for one of the main roads nearby. He told us to go down the street and turn right. We needed to turn left to get more addresses and then circle around by his house and turn left again. This happened several times, and each time, he emphatically motioned to us to turn right. After about the third time, he got into his car and led us to the right. Fortunately, we had finished with the neighborhood.

Another time, Vance was going in and out of apartment buildings, reading the names on the mailboxes. A man stopped him and asked who he was looking for. Remembering a Turkish man he had met in America once, he said, "Ismail Abaza."

The man asked if Ismail lived in that building. Vance said, "I don't know." Then the man asked if he lived in that city. Vance said, "I don't know. He lives in Turkey."

One morning, three of us ordered breakfast at a restaurant. Vance and the college student with us asked for eight-minute eggs, which we found are like our three-minute eggs. I asked for a twelve-minute egg, which is hard-boiled. The waiter looked perplexed but agreed. He came back with a tray of sixteen hard-boiled eggs, explaining in sign language that these were all he had. He thought I wanted twelve eggs. We ate a lot of eggs that day.

IMPRESSIONS OF TURKEY

≈

I WROTE IN A LETTER TO MY PARENTS:

This country is full of contrasts: desolate and green—old
and new—mountainous and flat. Our days are contrasts
too: incredible beauty in nature and hot, bumpy driving
in cities with old cobblestone streets. We see women
spinning thread, women dressed in the latest Western
styles and also in big, bright colored baggy pants with
long scarves; gypsy families camped in tents, adobe
houses, donkeys pulling carts loaded with bundles; men
in turbans driving tractors, and women covered with
scarves loaded on the backs of trucks, coming in from
the fields; herds of shaggy goats and sheep crossing the
streets—even in a big city; Turkish carpets everywhere
hanging up to dry; everywhere, men in clusters in tea
houses drinking tea and smoking cigarettes; finding out
that it only costs $30 per month to live in an apartment
but about $15 per day to drive our car, having the
electricity go on and off, squatting over Turkish toilets
that are incredibly stinky and dirty, not always having
hot water; seeing wild oleanders and olive trees all over

the hills with wild cyprus. If I was ever tempted to move to Turkey, I would build a house on the Mediterranean and hike to the high mountains and swim in the sea. It's California without smog or people.

And who could forget driving through city after city with no churches and no missionaries? We finally found a place where people had not heard about God's gift of salvation through Christ.

The time to leave Turkey was rapidly approaching, and our entire group of thirty gathered in Cappadocia, in central Turkey. Many strange volcanic cones dotted the arid landscape. In those cones and under the surface, ancient civilizations carved out a multitude of dwellings. The Hittites lived there, then other civilizations. During the early Christian era, they built thousands of churches and monasteries. Starting with the seventh century AD, Persians from the east and Arabs from the south raided the land. The local population built large underground cities out of the volcanic rocks to shelter in during the raids. These underground cave cities could house ten thousand people or more, going down many stories underground.

We saw air shafts, wells, living quarters, and churches. I will never forget the feeling of oneness with the ancient Christians as our group sang about Jesus in a cave church, with painted walls beautifully illustrating stories from the Bible. Our voices echoed from the rock walls as we lifted praises to God.

One of the theme songs of our project came from Psalm 91:

> He who dwells in the shelter of the Most High will abide in the shadow of the Almighty. I will say unto the Lord, "My refuge and my fortress, my God in whom I trust." For it is He who delivers you from the snare of the trapper, and from the deadly pestilence.

These words hit home as God delivered us from prison and disease. Finally, we drove across Turkey to the coast and boarded a boat for Greece. Out on the water, I could feel the oppression tangibly lift away. We flew to London, where we spent a few restful days feasting on

English breakfasts and taking in the beauty of green parks, as well as enjoying tourist sites.

Back in the United States, we helped recruit Christians to mail Gospel letters to the addresses we had collected. Many people from various places took part in this. Here is a summary of a few responses we received from Turkey:

One person read a letter sent to a relative speaking of the New Testament and God's word. They asked to receive the Bible correspondence course.

Another person expressed thanks for the letter and personal interest. They were surprised at first—wondering how we knew their address. They asked for the correspondence course about salvation.

A nephew of a man who received the letter was interested and wanted to discuss the things talked about in the letter.

Another person received the letter and said that if there is salvation, they wanted to know more about it.

God used this experience in Turkey to call us back to the Middle East, though we did not return to Turkey. It captured our hearts, and we would never be the same.

VANCE AND CAROL IN FRONT OF THE LIBRARY IN ANCIENT EPHESUS

CAROL NORDMAN

CAL STATE
FULLERTON

≈

Back in California, Vance and I plunged into the campus ministry at Cal State Fullerton. We told Campus Crusade we were interested in going to the Middle East again. They offered us a position on the island of Cyprus. However, they wanted us to come right away, and we had committed to be at Cal State Fullerton for another year. So they gave the job to someone else.

Our lives on campus were spent talking with students about God; we set up Bible studies and had large-scale evangelistic outreaches. Our group of seven staff and five student leaders discipled students, who discipled others. One girl I led to the Lord later became a missionary.

The student body president was a Christian, and I tried to encourage her in her faith. We set up a leadership dessert for women student leaders to present the Gospel, with the president as the emcee. We had a great response, as forty women came, twenty-seven of whom were officers of campus organizations. We met with several of them, and one woman and her husband attended church with us.

Later, Vance and I were looking for a place to take the students over Spring Break where they could have an evangelistic outreach. We spent a weekend as a couple in nearby Palm Springs and knew many college students went there over Spring Break. If only we could find local Christians, we could check on the possibility of bringing our students. As we drove down the main road in Palm Springs, we saw a store with a fish sign in the window. We stopped and asked the people inside if they knew any Christians who could talk with us about our plans. The business put us in touch with a church that turned out to have a desire to reach out to the masses of college students that descended on their city each spring; they had been praying for some Christian college students to come help them. The church offered to house our students.

During Spring Break, we met students on the streets as thousands filled the sidewalks. Our group talked with about one thousand people, and more than a hundred indicated decisions for Christ.

On campus, we held regular evangelistic meetings. Here is one comment from a girl who prayed to receive Christ with one of our students: "How wonderful it is to have Jesus Christ in control of your life. I want so much to serve Jesus in my life, and to listen and follow what He wants me to do. I had a great experience here; I can't express how touched I am."

After the campus year ended, we received our overseas assignment. We were being sent to Jordan to work in a Great Commission Training Center. I was bad at geography and thought Jordan was in Africa. We also didn't know much about the training center. But we believed God was calling us to the Middle East. Our staff and students gave us a going-away party, with a cake displaying a map of Jordan. We left for another summer of Bible classes and training in Colorado. Vance and I were both completing classes for a master's degree in Christian ministry and preparing to write a thesis.

INTO THE
GHETTO

≈

AFTER A SUMMER OF STIMULATING CLASSES AND SEEING OLD FRIENDS IN Colorado at Campus Crusade's Institute of Biblical Studies and Staff Training, we worked full time raising more support to move to Jordan. We needed $763 additional monthly support and $24,000 one time. This included a ten thousand dollar car. We also shopped for winter clothing for three years as we heard the clothes in Jordan were very expensive. As we presented our ministry to individuals, Bible studies and churches, the money came in steadily.

We stayed with Vance's mother in Merced, California. Mornings included time with the Lord and office work. Afternoons, we set up support appointments and met people to ask for financial assistance. Evenings held an average of two support appointments. We had fun meeting God's people and talking about our future ministry in the Middle East.

We had the finances we needed in time for the three-month cross-cultural training required by Campus Crusade's foreign-bound staff. They held Agape Intensive Training in Watts—an inner-city area of Los Angeles inhabited mostly by poor African Americans and Hispanics. They told us not to bring valuables, as crime was high. We lived with a local family.

Tuesday through Saturday mornings, we met for lectures, workshops, and paperwork at the Greater Cornerstone Baptist Church. The twenty-seven overseas candidates would minister in countries throughout Asia, Africa, Europe, and the Middle East.

Each week, the classes held a different emphasis:

- Weeks 1 and 2: Orientation and perspectives
- Week 3: Cross-cultural concepts
- Week 4: Practical training in Tijuana, Mexico
- Week 5: Values and culture
- Week 6: Phonetics (language learning)
- Week 7: International logistics
- Week 8: Interpersonal communication
- Week 9: Self-acceptance
- Week 10: Team dynamics
- Week 11: Language training
- Weeks 12 and 13: Termination and transition

We spent Tuesday through Saturday afternoons in the Watts area, telling people about Christ and leading Bible studies. This provided an opportunity to apply what we learned each morning in a cross-cultural situation.

Sunday, we spent five hours in church. Following Sunday school, worship service lasted three hours. Vance and I attended Mount Zion Missionary Baptist Church. E. V. Hill was the pastor, and what a dynamic pastor he was. Afterward, we had a big dinner with our host family. We had expected to live in a ghetto neighborhood—envisioning poverty, crime, and disorder. They assigned Vance and me to a couple who worked at Hughes Aircraft. Jerry and Doris's lovely apartment was in a middle-class black neighborhood. They were our age and a big encouragement. Doris spent hours Saturday evenings preparing a big Southern-style meal for Sunday. I'll never forget her luscious cakes and often thought she could open a restaurant.

Mondays, we rested and often enjoyed lunch away at the nearby beach in Marina Del Ray. The schedule and adjustments were intense, and I was often tired. I returned to writing in my journal during this time and recorded many of the things the Lord was teaching me. We made many adjustments while living in this new culture.

A Choice to Trust

≈

See, I set before you today life and prosperity, and death and adversity; in that I command you today to love the LORD your God, to walk in His ways and to keep His commandments and His statutes and His judgments, that you may live and multiply, and that the LORD your God may bless you in the land where you are entering to possess it. But if your heart turns away and you will not obey, but are drawn away and worship other gods and serve them, I declare to you today that you shall surely perish. You will not prolong your days in the land where you are crossing the Jordan to enter and possess it. I call heaven and earth to witness against you today, that I have set before you life and death, the blessing and the curse. So choose life in order that you may live, you and your descendants, by loving the LORD your God, by obeying His voice, and by holding fast to Him; for this is your life and the length of your days, that you may live in the land which the LORD swore to your fathers, to Abraham, Isaac, and Jacob, to give them. (Deuteronomy 30:15–20)

On January 21, 1981, I wrote in my journal:

> God set before Israel life and prosperity and death and adversity. God gives us a free choice. I see again the goodness of God. God wants to bless me, to prosper me—to give me a good life. It must be the devil who whispers in my ear, "If you love and serve God as a missionary, you'll have to grit it out, as a choice, and you'll be miserable and suffer and be deprived."
>
> How opposite this is of God's word. God says that when I love him and obey Him to serve as He commanded, He will bless me.... Lord, I've been duped, and I am not glorifying You because glorifying You means showing the world what You're like. I communicate fear that obeying and serving You is a sacrifice; that it will be hard and that overseas is risky in the Middle East. Because, inside I feel fear. I confess this to You, Jesus. Please forgive and change me, rearrange me. And use me to glorify You—to express to the world what Your word says about You; that serving You results in the abundance of all things—life and prosperity—blessing for me and my children as I love You by obeying Your voice (Your word says to go share with people) and by holding fast to You. My obedience shows my love for You. As a choice I now choose to believe Your word instead of what Satan and the world say. They lie! You are true! I choose to reflect Your image to the world— to glorify You and show them that serving You means blessing.

Looking back, this has been true. Prosperity hasn't necessarily meant riches and possessions, though God has always provided. But our lives have been rich and full of meaning and relationships.

MORE LESSONS
ON TRUST

≈

In February 1982, I sensed the Lord teaching me three specific things through the scriptures:

First, Romans 8:28 says, "And we know that God causes all things to work together for good to those who love God, to those who are called according to His purpose."

Even evil and bad things God makes into a blessing. The future holds nothing but blessings for me as I love God and express that love through obedience.

Second, Philippians 4:13 says, "I can do all things through him who strengthens me." Matthew 6:34 says, "So do not worry about tomorrow; for tomorrow will care itself. Each day has enough trouble of its own."

God gives me strength in every situation. I have the strength when I need it. Trying to deal with a problem beforehand results in nothing but frustration, fear, and grief.

Third, Proverbs 31:25b says of the godly woman, "She smiles at the future." Romans 12:1 says, "Therefore, I urge you, brethren, by the mercies of God, to present your bodies a living and holy sacrifice, acceptable to God, which is your spiritual service of worship."

Since God's plan holds only blessings, and he will give me strength to deal with anything when I need it, I look forward to the future with joy and a smile. My greatest desire becomes walking in God's will, for his will contains only blessings and strength to deal with anything when I need it.

These truths would soon be tested in the fires of circumstances. Three trials came my way.

During our training in Watts, my mother was diagnosed with a tumor in her intestine that could be cancerous. The doctor wanted to remove part of her intestine. I am an only child and knew I couldn't leave the country for a three-year assignment if my mother had cancer. My father was worried. Vance and I were scheduled to leave the country in just a few months.

Second, I developed a mysterious lump under my chin. A doctor told me this could be very serious and require an extensive operation.

Finally, the entire ministry in Jordan was closed, and our placement was up in the air. We had raised support for Jordan and studied all about Jordan. Now everything was uncertain.

Through the years, I've observed that after we step out in faith in a direction we believe the Lord is leading us, we are attacked with what looks like a disaster. It happens almost every time. If we give thanks and keep on walking, we see God step in. That's just what happened. I wish I could say I had faith with no worry. But there were sleepless nights and much crying out to the Lord.

On March 3, 1982, I wrote in my journal:

> Last night I woke up and couldn't go back to sleep because I was thinking, about my mother and about our placement. It's hard to leave things unsettled, Lord. I just want to jump right in and get it taken care of. But I say Lord, my eyes are on You. You must fight this battle for I am too weak, and the logistics of the future are beyond me. Thank you for this opportunity to trust You and to receive the crown of life; James 1:12; to endure under trial. You promise that if I do, I will be perfect and complete, lacking in nothing. So I won't look at the future for the time has not yet come for You

to deal with it. I'll only pray about it. My eyes are on You and I thank You!

Then on March 5:

I thought I'd record something I thought of and that I felt God spoke to me about. Last night at choir, a phrase in a song leaped out at me. "In the time of trouble, He will hide me." I feel like God is hiding me during this time emotionally, especially with my mother and going overseas and all. I have so much more peace and joy than I'd expected. It encourages me to ALWAYS be in His will even if it looks traumatic. Because, if I'm in God's will and the circumstances are full of trouble, God will hide me. Also, I thought of praising God. God is pleased when I praise Him. How I love to praise You Lord and I believe You release power through praise.

God resolved all three problems. My mother found an excellent doctor at UCLA Medical Center who had been a missionary doctor. He could operate removing no intestine. The tumor was benign. I saw the same doctor about the lump under my chin. He said it was a swollen gland and would just go down by itself, and it did. Finally, we were reassigned to restart the Great Commission Training Center in Egypt.

On April 1, I wrote:

We're going to Egypt! I'm excited, yes really excited to go, much more than Jordan. I really want to go, unlike when we were assigned to Jordan. I felt Your call but wasn't sure about the country of Jordan. I guess I feel a peace and a thrill about Egypt.

And on April 20:

Walking with God reminds me of Mr. Toad's Wild Ride [in Disneyland]. It often looks like we'll crash, but

God always rescues us. I can't dwell on the possibility of crashing or I will be full of fear and ulcers. Rather, I need to dwell on God and continue to walk in faith and trust that He will take care of everything.

EGYPT 1982

≈

THEY TOLD US TO PACK EVERYTHING WE WERE BRINGING IN BOXES, AND we finally finished seventeen large ones. My father wondered why we were taking so much and asked if none of these things were available for sale in Egypt. Then we received the news we shouldn't have boxes but trunks. Vance went to a local store and bought a lot of trunks. We still needed more, and he was too embarrassed to go back—so I went. The saleswoman talked about a man who had just bought so many trunks. I couldn't resist saying, "He is my husband."

Fortunately, friends came to help us repack, as we were so exhausted. Vance and I finally waved goodbye to our family and boarded the plane for three years in Egypt. Paul, one of the American Campus Crusade staff, met us in Cairo and brought us to his home in an old Peugeot station wagon taxi, which carried eight of our trunks standing on end on the roof rack. We breathed a sigh of relief when all arrived safely, after being carried up many flights of stairs on men's backs.

Egypt seemed as different from America as the Earth from the moon. People thronged the streets, horns blared, and the call to prayer beckoned faithful Muslims to pray five times a day. There was no place without noise, heat, and people. A few days after our arrival, we spent an entire day in the lobby of the Sheraton Hotel just because it was peaceful and cool. We wondered if we could handle living in Egypt.

CAIRO TRAM STATION

Then Kathy—Paul's wife—became sick with a high fever. I had to do the cooking for the four of us. Everything was from scratch, and I didn't know a lot about cooking. I felt sure I would make us all sick, as drinking water needed boiling for twenty minutes, and fruits and vegetables were either cooked or soaked in chlorine water and then rinsed with boiled water to kill germs. When Kathy found she was pregnant, she and Paul left for the States for better medical care.

Our ministry in Egypt was directed by a man named Mounir Faragalla. Soon after we arrived, Mounir had a heart attack. His friend—a cardiologist—was passing his home and stopped by to say hello. He came just as Mounir was having a heart attack and saved his life. Mounir lived in the coastal city of Alexandria, and we were in Cairo. Shortly after our arrival, Vance and I attended a staff conference. The Egyptian man in charge of the Cairo ministry didn't look favorably on foreign missionaries coming to work in his country. Things were looking pretty dark by this time.

With the national director needing heart surgery, Paul and Kathy leaving for the States, and the Cairo ministry leader disliking foreigners, we thought about pursuing Arabic language study in a different city that might be more hospitable. There was another American couple around our age working with our ministry in the city of Alexandria, about three hours north of Cairo by train. Traveling through the fertile farmlands of the delta to the Mediterranean coast, we felt like the sun came out. Even though Alexandria was another crowded city, the empty vista of the sea provided refreshment.

God worked in amazing ways to heal Mounir. Someone heard about his situation and connected Mounir with Oral Roberts Medical Center. Mounir and his wife Violet flew to the medical center in America for heart surgery. People were praying, and as the doctors prepared for the surgery, Mounir's heart miraculously healed without surgery.

Kathy had a healthy baby girl, while Paul worked with Arrowhead Productions and was trained in video. When they returned to Egypt, Paul went on to train Egyptians in video production and later became the director of Arrowhead Productions International. God used Kathy's illness to provide the training Paul would later use to touch the world.

The ministry leader who didn't want foreigners later left our staff. It seems we usually encounter strong opposition when stepping into a new assignment. Later, we went to Russia, and a coup began just ten days after our arrival. I would often think about Egypt and remember how God delivered us.

Daily Life
in Egypt

≈

I N ALEXANDRIA, WE MOVED IN WITH AN AMERICAN COUPLE UNTIL WE
found our own apartment. Our new home was in a nice part of town,
with a view of the Mediterranean. It was on the fourth floor but—as was
common—had no elevator. It came complete with French Provincial
furniture. The landlady was rumored to be a belly dancer. Our apartment
was furnished, but there was no seat on the toilet. Our landlady seemed
offended when we asked her about it, and we discovered this was usually
not included in a furnished apartment. Our neighbors upstairs were very
helpful and accompanied Vance downtown on the tram to get a toilet
seat. As a thank you, we bought them a box of candy. One day while
sitting in our living room, we saw something fall onto our balcony
from the floor above. It was the empty candy box. We learned throwing
garbage out the window was a common practice. This proved to be a
problem when hanging out laundry.

Windows had no screens, and clotheslines were strung outside
a window. I felt afraid reaching out to hang laundry while looking
down four floors to the street below. Fortunately, another balcony was
directly below our clothesline, in case I dropped something. Sheets had
to drape over several clotheslines. Unfortunately, our neighbors above
us had been in the practice of eating sunflower seeds and spitting out
the shells while looking out that window. Sometimes, sheets collected
spit-covered shells and needed rewashing.

Our building had a vacant lot beside it, and many people threw their garbage there. Stray cats found their food in the empty lot. One day, I got fish at the market and fried it. Something was wrong with the fish. I still didn't know a lot about cooking and asked Vance what was the matter. The fish hadn't been cleaned, and the insides were still in it. So I tossed the fish out the window to the cats below. At least they might like a fish dinner. In distress, Vance said we wouldn't throw our garbage out the window, so we hired a man to take it away. Shortly after, we looked out to see him throwing our trash in the vacant lot. Finally, we hired someone else who took it away on a horse-drawn wagon. We wondered if he took it to another vacant lot.

Shopping, cooking, and cleaning took up all my time. There were no supermarkets. I purchased food in the small, one-room stores and open markets. Fruit and vegetables were abundant, inexpensive, and delicious. Everything was in kilograms (equal to about 2.2 pounds), and numbers were written differently. I couldn't speak much Arabic and only knew the word for one kilogram. So I came home with a kilogram of everything. That was a lot of bell peppers for two people. Also, bell peppers and hot peppers were mixed together. I discovered this one day when the casserole I served was extra spicy.

SHOPPING FOR VEGETABLES

CAROL NORDMAN

Buying meat was a challenge. Sides of meat hung in the butcher shop, but I couldn't speak enough Arabic to say what part I wanted. Also, I didn't know enough about meat to know what I wanted. Meat always had come in a neatly marked package. So I went to the butcher and pointed to my leg. Success: I came home with a leg of lamb. I put it in the oven, but when it came out, it was covered with something hard. I called Vance again, and he informed me it was the hide.

I bought chickens live, selecting the chicken and watching as it was killed, and the feathers removed. I never got used to bringing home a warm chicken. They sold eggs in newspaper cones. One day, I got on a crowded tram with my newspaper cone full of eggs clasped in front of me. People were on every side of me; I think I could have lifted my feet and remained standing. Somehow, the eggs didn't end up all over me.

Most people bought food every day and carried it home. I tried to be more efficient and carry two food containers instead of one. I lugged home the groceries up a hill and then up four flights of stairs. I learned that this wasn't a good idea when my back went out, and I couldn't get up off the floor for a couple of weeks. This was the beginning of a disc problem in my back, which would gradually worsen over ten years.

Finally, we decided that if I would ever learn Arabic, we needed household help. One day, a woman came by our house, looking for work. We felt the Lord sent her to us.

Lila—our new maid—only spoke Arabic. As our language ability improved, we learned more about her. Lila was probably in her thirties, but we don't think she knew when she was born. She was superstitious, and if she had a dream or saw something on the way to work like certain birds, she considered it a sign that something bad would happen. Death terrified her and walking past a funeral would upset her all day. Lila believed when bad things happened, it was because she had done something wrong.

One day, she told us that her grandmother had died, and her building had fallen. She assured us that her grandmother was a *"seta tieba"* ("good woman") and said the doctor told Lila that her grandmother had died before the building fell. To say the building fell on her would show she was not a good woman because God wouldn't let a building fall on a good woman. On another occasion, Lila told us not to worry about a large piece of ceiling plaster loose in our kitchen because we were good, and there were angels on our shoulders who would protect us. As Lila observed our faith, she increased her efforts to be a good Muslim. However, she liked us to pray for her in the name of Jesus.

Lila took good care of our home, washing all the tile and wood floors on her hands and knees with rags and cleaning the kitchen with chlorine. I focused on laundry, shopping, and cooking, though occasionally, Lila cooked. We always knew when she was cooking because she used a couple dozen cloves of garlic in one meal.

At the time we lived in Egypt, most people washed their clothes by hand or had their servants wash them. We invested in the luxury of a European washing machine. It had about half the capacity of an American machine and took a couple of hours to wash a load. It was so gentle that once, when I put in a dirty folded cloth napkin, it came out folded and clean a couple of hours later. I finally understood why my Swiss roommate had said American washing machines tore up her clothes. We kept the washing machine going all the time—often day and night after we had kids. Lila kept saying we were so clean, as we were always washing our clothes.

Cooking became a challenge I enjoyed. I had several cookbooks, including *The Joy of Cooking* and the *Jungle Camp Cookbook* from Wycliffe Bible Translators. I pored over them for hours, devouring information on sauces, meats, homemade mayonnaise, and much more. We had a two-burner stove with bottled gas and an oven that cooked one temperature, with no thermometer, so baking was a challenge. At least my oven was close to 350 degrees and not 500 degrees, like another American woman's. She had to leave the oven door open to lower the temperature. I found I could put hot pots on the tile floor and managed well with two burners.

I mastered homemade mayonnaise in a blender I'd brought from America. One day, I got the spatula stuck in the whirling blade, and mayonnaise flew all over the kitchen. But the flavor was worth it all. Another time, I was cooking something sweet, and a swarm of bees flew in the unscreened window. Lila helped me get them out.

CAROL NORDMAN

I learned to make homemade mashed potatoes and white sauce and cheese sauce. I made macaroni and cheese from scratch with Gouda cheese sauce, topped with vine-ripe tomatoes and baked in the oven; it was awesome. Home cooking tasted better than store-bought meals. We roasted peanuts and ground them in our food processor for peanut butter. There was no brown sugar, but we learned to mix molasses and white sugar to substitute. Molasses needed boiling, and the impurities were skimmed off. In fact, drinking water needed boiling twenty minutes. Food eaten fresh—like strawberries—needed washing, soaking in a mixture of water and chlorine for fifteen minutes, and then rinsing with boiled water. Despite these things, we still had stomach problems. We joked that with all the effort it took to bring the food home, cook it, and then fight diarrhea, it was easy to keep our weight down. I learned to make some of our favorite Egyptian dishes, such as *kusherie*—made with fried onions, tomato sauce, lentils, and rice. Tomatoes were vine ripened, abundant, and cheap. I boiled them down for tomato sauce and soup. Wow, what flavor. Cooking was fun, even if I spent about four hours a day in the kitchen.

With daily life finally under control, we were ready to tackle serious Arabic study.

LEARNING ARABIC

≈

Full-time Arabic study began with three Egyptian language helpers: Ossama, Alet, and Amy. Amy prayed to receive Jesus with me. She was Ossama's sister, and I think they were from a Christian background. Sometimes, Amy had stomach troubles; they told us that was normal for summer. We heard of people with typhoid and hepatitis. Summer heat and disease seemed to go together. Amy and Ossama's home smelled sweet with the heavy scent of mosquito repellent.

We used Language Acquisition Made Practical, or LAMP: the study method we learned in our cross-cultural training. Our study cycle extended from 9:30 a.m. to 9 p.m., including four hours for cooking and eating. We began with a language text, such as, "Hello, my name is Carol. I am studying Arabic. This is all I can say. Thank you for listening."

We asked our language helpers—who were bilingual—to speak this text in Arabic into a tape recorder. Then, we taped them saying small segments, with pauses between the segments. We practiced saying these segments with the tape recorder until we memorized the entire text. Then we said our text to fifteen to thirty people. We developed a route—usually to shopkeepers. Van went first, and I followed closely behind. Often, we bought something from them and accomplished shopping and language learning at the same time. They corrected our pronunciation, and by the time we finished, we often sounded like natives.

Sometimes, this method could be embarrassing. People began laughing when I gave my text, until I found out I was actually saying, "Hello, my name is Carol. I am sick of Arabic, and this is all I can say. Thank you for listening." We gradually broke the sentences down and learned words and grammar. As we both learn by actively experimenting and both love to talk, this method was a lot of fun for us.

In the fall, I got a new language helper, Amal. She was a recent graduate from college in Egypt and was looking for a job in business. She taught me about Egyptian culture and language. I learned that most Egyptians think Americans are immoral from the American TV programs. She was surprised that Van and I had more traditional values. We were the first people she visited who were not relatives or close friends of her family. She said she trusted us.

Amal was a devout Muslim and often thought about God. She covered her head and wore long skirts and long-sleeve blouses. She usually prayed five times a day. She was surprised by how we prayed: asking for specific things, praying for other people, and claiming promises from the Bible. It also surprised her to hear we believed Jesus died. Her religion taught that it was Judas who died, and God took Jesus, who they considered a prophet, to heaven without dying.

When Amal was younger, she lived for ten years in Saudi Arabia. As a woman in Saudi Arabia, she seldom went outside her home. In fact, her only contact with the outside world was a drive in the car once a week and a shopping trip twice a year. She slept a lot from boredom. Upon returning to Egypt for college, she had many fears to conquer. In her classes, she felt so frightened by the number of people that a relative sat with her to ease her fears. When we met her, Amal was friendly and fun to talk to. Our marriage and happy relationship impressed her. We told her our faith in Jesus helped our marriage. She was curious but terrified whenever we suggested looking at the Bible.

Vance and I also took an Arabic class but felt we didn't learn much. Classroom learning just didn't seem to work for us in learning language. Once we knew enough to have a basic conversation, we kept talking and learning more as we went.

Evening at Our House

≈

While living in Egypt, I wrote this poem:

Cool breezes, billowing white curtains,
beyond-sky fading salmon into violet,
fading above darkening sea.
Quietly, we watch the change.
Shadows lengthening on polished wood floors
reflecting the sky.
Walls rosy with color.
Quiet the sounds of evening.
Breeze, sea, people eating, distant horns.
Lights appear winking on the water far across the bay.
The wind increases, the curtains sail.
Night begins, the city awakens.
A dog's bark and a child's voice announce coming activity.
The lull is past—the night begun.

LONGING FOR CHILDREN

≈

I GREW UP AS AN ONLY CHILD, AND THOUGH I HAD A HAPPY CHILDHOOD, I longed for a large family. When Vance and I married, I was almost twenty-seven. We knew we were going overseas, and people encouraged us to wait until I learned the language before having children. This made sense, and we thought this was wise advice. Yet I worried about the large family I yearned for. One night, while I was lying awake thinking about these things, a Bible verse came to mind. I sensed God saying, "This is for you." I couldn't remember if it related to children, so I got up and opened my Bible.

> Jesus said, 'Truly I say to you, there is no one who has left house or brothers or sisters or mother or father or children or farms, for My sake and for the gospel's sake, but that he will receive a hundred times as much now in the present age, houses and brothers and sisters and mothers and children and farms, along with persecutions; and in the age to come, eternal life." (Mark 10:29–30)

I shared this promise with Vance. "Are we going to have an orphanage?" he asked.

"I don't know," I replied, "but God will meet my maternal needs one hundred times as much."

After three months in Egypt, we thought about having children. I was almost thirty. I wrote in my journal on July 13, 1982:

> "I will instruct you and teach you in the way which you should go; I will counsel you with my eye upon you" (Psalm 32:8). This comforts me because it disturbs my spirit about when to have children. Because of the shots I took I didn't consider it safe till now. In mid-August we will go on malaria medicine for Pakistan, and it won't be safe again until January. (There was a staff conference in Pakistan for all the Campus Crusade staff in the area.) ... You will tell us Your will, and You will teach us the path You have laid out before us. Right now, I trust Your love for me. You have what is best for us. And I trust Your sovereignty and power to control and engineer everything for our good.... I thank You and praise You for Pakistan and malaria medicine. You can make me pregnant right now if that is Your will! ... Please work on my behalf. I lay my request before You and pray asking You grant it or give me peace and strength to wait on You joyfully and gladly accepting Your will as the best for us.

When the time came to take medicine to prevent illness for the Pakistan trip, it was too early to know if I was pregnant, though I suspected I might be. I had to decide. On August 26, 1982, I wrote in my journal:

> Father, You are the one I will listen to for guidance regarding this trip to Pakistan. When the time comes to decide, I am confident You will show me.... I have no peace in my heart about taking this trip. My decision now is not to go. Change my heart if You desire to.

We found traveling missionaries to stay with me in Egypt for a while. Then, I would move in with an American couple working in

Alexandria, since all the Campus Crusade staff were leaving for a month to Pakistan. On August 31, 1982, I wrote:

> I saw Van off on the train today, saw him go off to Cairo, then to Kuwait, Bombay, and Pakistan! I am excited for him and the other staff, and I lay them in Your hands to keep and protect and bring back safely. My eyes got teary as the train left. I'll miss Van. Yet, the peace in my heart soon returned. I claimed Your wisdom in this decision, Lord, and my heart confirms this is Your will for us. I wasn't sad but peaceful.... And then, on the tram, when I needed help about which tram to get on, the people were so helpful. That old man who has a daughter in America who helped me in such a kind way; it was like a touch of Your hand telling me, "I love you; I'm looking out for you!"

The only way I could contact Vance was by a telex. I went to a hotel and had one sent after I took a pregnancy test September 2, 1982 and had a positive result. I wrote that day in my journal:

> I'm so excited! I retook the pregnancy test today, and it was positive! I'm so excited, Lord. I want to tell the world.

Ministry
Begins

≈

Wᴴɪʟᴇ I sᴛᴀʏᴇᴅ ɪɴ Aʟᴇxᴀɴᴅʀɪᴀ, sᴇᴡɪɴɢ ᴍᴀᴛᴇʀɴɪᴛʏ ᴅʀᴇssᴇs, Vᴀɴᴄᴇ was in Pakistan for training with Campus Crusade staff from all over the Middle East. He asked so many questions, trying to understand the ministry in Egypt, that the staff teased him, saying he must be with the secret police. In December, back in Egypt, Vance sent the following in a letter to our family and supporters:

> After over one year of training (Biblical), raising support, more training (cross-cultural), packing, moving, settling in, more training (language), and more training (with all the Middle East staff), I'm finally getting down to what I came to the Middle East to do: TRAINING!

> To begin with, I will work with two of our Egyptian staff who are new. They are choice people but greatly need training. I am happy I only have two to train because I want to train them, not just teach them. By that I mean I want to influence their whole way of thinking. After finishing their training, I don't want them to have just heard how to develop a ministry of evangelism and discipleship. I want them to have personally experienced it, to understand it thoroughly,

have personal convictions about it, and be equipped to "train" others. Please pray that over the next six months, this will take place.

Vance learned many university students who had attended evangelistic meetings sponsored by the Presbyterian church filled out response cards. No one had contacted these students, so Vance visited them in their homes with Botros, one of his trainees. Vance spoke almost no Arabic, and Botros spoke little English. Somehow, they visited the students and saw many come to Christ. In the process, Vance learned more Arabic, and Botros learned more English.

Vance wrote in another letter about an experience with his other trainee, Samy:

> A couple months ago, I saw God work in a very unusual way. I was looking for opportunities for one of my trainees and I to do more evangelism. About that time, there was an evangelistic meeting held, and we got the names of twenty interested students to follow up. We wondered who to visit first, so we prayed, and chose a student named George. We went to George's house and found him studying to prepare for his third-year medical school finals. George is from a middle-class Coptic (Orthodox) Christian family, and like most Egyptian singles, he lives with his family. As my trainee shared the Four Spiritual Laws with him in Arabic, it became apparent that he was hungry to understand the Gospel. Since George is a medical student and most of his textbooks are English, I could answer some of his questions in English, which he recorded on a cassette recorder. We answered his questions as best we could, and he asked us to return the following week. We later found out that at the very time we came to his house, he had been praying that God would send someone to explain to him how he could have eternal life!

PROTECTION
AND PROVISION

≈

ONE EVENING, JUST AFTER I WALKED INTO THE BATHROOM OF OUR apartment, I stood at the sink, felt a breeze near my head, and then heard a loud crash. A ten-pound chunk of plaster and cement landed where I had been standing just a few minutes earlier. I looked up at the ceiling and saw exposed metal rebar. I could reach up and bend it with my hand. I felt watched over and protected yet shaken. We noticed widening cracks in the ceiling and discovered it affected four rooms. Our landlady said other parts would fall soon, and it needed extensive repair. This was not an uncommon thing in Egyptian buildings, which occasionally collapsed.

As we had been planning to take vacation anyway, this seemed like a good time to go. We were going to Cairo with a group of American executives arriving on a ministry trip. We would stay with them in a fancy hotel just below the Pyramids and tour Memphis and the big shopping bazaar. Then, we planned to fly to the nearby Greek island of Cyprus to relax and visit our Middle East ministry office. The time with the executives went fast. We saw a lot and answered a lot of their questions. Then I felt funny and went to bed, thinking it was just fatigue. I kept having stomach pains and threw up at six in the morning. Sometimes, fancy hotels were the worst places for getting sick. We flew to Cyprus, anyway. We asked friends to pray. It was only an hour's flight, and I made it with only some diarrhea on the plane. I felt better after we landed.

Cyprus is a lovely little island with hills like California, clean water, wonderful food, and great shopping. Some of our staff housed us and checked on vacation spots in the local mountains. The wife was also pregnant and due two weeks before me, and we shopped together for baby things.

While in Cyprus, my tooth hurt from where I had a previous root canal. This required a specialist, and they were hard to find. After talking with local dentists, we found they weren't trained to fix my tooth but could only remove a part. We mentioned to our travel agent that my tooth was bothering me. She replied her daughter had married a dental professor from New York. I had an abscess behind the root canal. He had to remove the root canal, fix the abscess, then do another root canal. Plus, I was pregnant. He had the shields to place over me when taking x-rays that other dentists didn't have.

It amazed me that the Lord had brought me to Cyprus just when my tooth went bad and led us to this specialist. People came to him from many surrounding countries. I discovered that God would provide for my medical needs in amazing ways many times—putting me where I needed to be with just the right doctors and medicines.

Preparing for
a Baby

~

One other American couple with Campus Crusade lived in Alexandria when we arrived there. Another couple arrived soon after we did. We all enjoyed each other and were about the same age. The two wives happened to be nurses who preferred maternity nursing. They were considering getting jobs in a hospital, so the three of us looked for a hospital for me to deliver our baby in. After looking at the two semipublic hospitals, we all decided I should go to the private hospital. I remember one hospital rented rooms for people to live in, with laundry strung to dry in the hallway.

When I asked Egyptians how good a hospital was, they told me it was well decorated. I didn't really care about the decorating. When I asked about a doctor, they told me he was from a good family. I learned that a nicely decorated hospital meant it was also clean and well equipped. If a doctor was from a good family, he had a good education. In Egypt, so much depended on your family and connections.

Vance and I visited the doctor who delivered at the private hospital. He was a professor at the medical school and had been in the United States. He also had ultrasound. Our neighbor's husband—educated in England—was the doctor who ran the hospital. The private hospital was more expensive, at about eighty dollars a day while the semipublic hospital was free, ten dollars, or fifty dollars per day, depending on what class you had. However, it was crowded and difficult to get the first class. The other classes had a reputation for fleas and other problems. We ended up paying about fifteen hundred dollars for everything, including a seven-day hospital stay. This was because we were foreigners and therefore charged double. However, our insurance covered this, and it was still so much less expensive than in the States.

Once we decided on a hospital and chose a doctor, I studied natural childbirth and assembled baby items. When I visited the hospital, they showed me the brass bed I would be in. They told me that women held onto the brass bars and screamed until knocked out with medication. One woman I knew thought she was dying when in labor because no one told her what to expect. I heard that in the villages, women may not know what part of her body the baby would come out of. I determined to learn the natural childbirth method and not use medication if possible. One of my doctor's patients had used this method, and he was familiar with it. Vance and I had a book from America and taught ourselves. At one point, we got stuck, and a book arrived unexpectedly from a friend in America that contained just the information that was lacking. We ended up giving one of our books to the doctor, who wanted to translate it for his patients.

In Egypt, the doctor held an exalted position. It wasn't normal for a woman to ask her doctor questions. In fact, doctors often addressed the husband, not the wife. When I asked a question, I could see the doctor's surprised reaction. Then, I thought he mentally reminded himself that this was an American, and he would answer me.

Going to the doctor's office was a new experience too. We often waited three hours to see the doctor. When I asked about making an appointment for the next visit, they didn't do that. So we tried going in the day before to make an appointment, and it worked. We only waited about fifteen minutes the next day.

Finding a crib was nearly impossible. Many Egyptians slept with the baby in their bed. I finally found a crib imported from Italy made of canvas, with an aluminum frame that folded up. We could travel with it in a car, and it doubled as a playpen. However, it didn't come with a mattress. I discovered there were special "mattress men" who made mattresses. So I visited one and bought a big piece of foam rubber. An Egyptian friend told me where to buy plastic, and I sewed a red, yellow, and blue plastic cover. I also sewed crib sheets and pads. A large vegetable basket made a nice Moses basket, and I sewed a pretty lining with yellow cloth and eyelet lace for when the baby was small.

Diapers posed another problem. Egyptians seemed to use three pieces of cloth, which sounded like lots of washing. An Egyptian friend said they stretched and got bigger and bigger until they could fit a man. Another friend preferred English terry cloth diapers. So I sewed terry cloth diapers, but the store ran out of white terry cloth, and the thick cloth was hard on my sewing machine. Blue, yellow, or orange terry cloth diapers were the choices. Finally, I wrote home to Vance's mother, who planned to come for the birth, and asked her to bring me some American cloth diapers. There were paper diapers in Egypt, but they were very expensive. We ended up only using them when we traveled.

As my due date grew near, I bought a nightgown for the hospital. One of my Egyptian neighbors said it wasn't appropriate, as it wasn't nice enough and looked lower class. So I went shopping with my language helper. I looked at a yellow nightgown but learned yellow meant jealousy. It was best to wear blue or white. I finally ended up with nice white and blue nightgowns. At last, I was ready, and we waited eagerly for Vance's mother and our first baby—which the doctor assured us would be a boy.

Winter in Alexandria was cold, especially inside unheated cement buildings. We were grateful for our heated waterbed, which was the warmest spot in the house. We wore wool and long underwear and bought a small heater. I was often sick with viruses. It was hard to know how much to rest, and I struggled with feelings of guilt when I couldn't work.

In January 1983, I wrote in my journal:

> I feel the nationals don't think I'm doing much, then I feel more under stress. Oh, deliver me from fear of what people think! Help me do what I know I can do, to go at the pace

I know is feasible and not feel guilty or afraid of what they think.

It seems my whole life, God has been removing fear and guilt and replacing them with his love and freedom. Another time during my pregnancy, I wrote:

Psalm 104:30 says, "You send forth Your Spirit, they are created." The creation in my womb is not just a scientific thing, it is you sending forth Your Spirit. How exciting to be involved with You in creation! I read in this Psalm how You created and sustain all the world and all creatures and provide homes for the creatures. Surely if You do that, You are able to sustain and nurture me and our offspring in me; for You have power to care for the whole earth. So, God, I look to You to care for me and the new creation inside me.

LEARNING TO
NOT SMILE :)

≈

I TOOK AT LEAST A YEAR TO LEARN NOT TO SMILE IN PUBLIC. I LIKE TO smile. I feel happier when I smile; it's usually contagious and makes others happy too. But in Egypt, smiling got me into trouble. It is inappropriate for a woman to look a strange man in the eye, to smile, or even to respond at all.

One day on the tram, a man said good morning to me. I am from California, where such a comment is usually only a casual remark.

I responded by repeating, "Good morning." That was a big mistake. The man then asked if he could be my friend. I responded that it was impossible, as I was a married woman. He waited awhile and asked again if he could be my friend. I again responded that it was impossible. When I exited the tram, he followed me off. Fortunately, Egypt is full of people, and I was not alone on the street with him. He was very polite and finally said he would leave me alone. But he had one request and asked if he could please kiss me. He made it sound like such a small request, and he would like it so much. It was funny.

I replied, "It's impossible," and walked off.

Apparently, he thought I was like the foreign women he watched on the television shows and in the movies. They did a lot of kissing.

On the way back, I went a different way to avoid running into him. So instead of taking the tram, I went out to the large road by the sea to catch a taxi. I needed to cross a busy street. I liked to stand by the tall police booth until they stopped the traffic, rather than trying to dodge the cars. I'd had a good experience with the policemen and felt protected by them. This policeman apparently enjoyed having a foreign woman near him and refused to stop the traffic. I finally had to walk to a different location and cross without his help.

That same day, another man followed me, speaking in Arabic. I didn't understand a lot of what he said. Finally, I turned a corner and said, "Goodbye."

I used to walk along the road by the sea when I was pregnant, as it had the longest stretch of unbroken sidewalk and was close to home. It amazed me how many men said something, trying to flirt with me when I was eight months pregnant. By that time, I had learned to ignore men, as the Egyptian women did. I used to count the number of men who tried to flirt with me on my walks. It was usually at least fifteen. Later, I learned that the prostitutes walked along this road.

I discovered that being married had no effect on men, but once I had a baby, men were no longer interested in me. After our baby was born, I went to the crowded beach with American friends and Vance's mother. A group of men lined up their chairs a few yards from our umbrella and sat down to stare at us. As soon as I picked up our baby, they made some disappointed remarks and left us alone. Being a mother is an honored role.

LESSONS IN PATIENCE AND PERSEVERANCE

≈

WHEN I WAS ABOUT EIGHT MONTHS' PREGNANT, VANCE AND I GOT OUR Egyptian driver's licenses. We had purchased a small red Fiat, which was a common car in Egypt. I remember being so scared to drive in Egypt that my knees literally shook. It was like an ice-skating rink. Cars wove in and out, along with pedestrians crossing through the moving cars and donkey carts. They passed within inches of each other. I gradually became comfortable with the lack of a rigid structure on the road and had trouble driving when I returned to the States.

On March 29, 1983, I wrote home to my parents:

> We had a busy day getting our driver's licenses. It's been quite an experience! We needed a medical exam, so Van asked the doctor across the street what to do. He told us to go to his hospital and give a written message to a certain nurse. We did and were given the papers showing we were in good health and had good eyesight. We never saw a doctor or had a test! Then, we had to get our landlady to register us and go to the police department to get a form saying we live here. Then today, an Egyptian friend took us to get our licenses. We couldn't have managed without him, going from one office to the next and getting different forms. It would have taken us days to understand the

procedure! We were there from about 9:30 to 12:30. We took a test where we each gave the meaning of three road signs. Then, we took the driving test. About seventy people watched as we drove a car around two corners and then backed up around the same two corners. So many people couldn't do the backing up part that I prayed for us as we waited our turn and analyzed their mistakes. We did fine! We decided going through tight places is more necessary to know in Egypt than getting on freeways. So we finally finished the process, but I was disappointed to find out our licenses are only good as long as our visas, then we have to renew them. Since we only have temporary visas, we have to go downtown every three to six months to renew our visas. This process can involve going back two or three times on successive days before we get our visas. The time we get on our visas is determined by the amount of money we change.

We were on temporary tourist visas for ten years. Van got to know the people in the immigration office. Since he looks like someone from the Middle East, they were sure he or his father was from Egypt or Lebanon or somewhere in the area. We didn't know of any relatives from the Middle East but were grateful he fit in so well. We learned more patience and perseverance in using the telephone. Vance's mother was coming to help with the baby, and we needed to call her in America and tell our friends in Cairo when she would be arriving. I wrote in the same letter to my parents:

> Last week we got up and left early, around eight in the morning, to call Van's mom and Cairo. You can't just call from a private line but must book a call in advance. Since we don't have a phone, it's just as easy to go to the post office where we can have them make the call then wait till it goes through. At the first post office we tried, something broke the phone system. We got our calls placed at the second post office. Van's mom

didn't answer, and we couldn't get the operator to let it ring longer (she walks slowly and takes a while to get to the phone). We got through to Cairo, but the hotel desk clerk hung up on us twice and we didn't reach our friends in the hotel (sigh!). So we decided to forget the post offices and try hotels, which also seem to get our calls through faster. They are more expensive. The post office is about $12 for three minutes, and hotels are $16 to $20 for three minutes (to the U.S.). The first hotel we tried couldn't phone Cairo because their system to Cairo was broken, or something like that. So we decided to go first class and go to the Sheraton. It's the best hotel in town and turned out to have cheaper rates than the other hotel. By this time, it was close to 11:00, and we were glad we had a car to go all these places! The Sheraton got us right through to Van's mom and to Cairo (though our friends still weren't in). Afterward, we sat in the Sheraton lobby and read and rested. It was so peaceful after such a morning! We finally got Cairo at night at another post office. We had an Egyptian friend with us which was good because there were at least thirty other people there trying to place a call. She knew the system and placed our call. We ate popcorn and talked to people and about thirty minutes later, reached our friends in Cairo. Our feelings run from frustration at how time consuming it is to live, to humor at how ridiculous it all seems. And, I hope we're learning to give thanks in it all too. But life is different, and the longer we live here, the more things we figure out how to do. And the more unknowns we run into. It's a constant learning process. I feel like our Arabic is improving. We can carry on conversations basically, but we still miss parts. The more Arabic we know, the easier it gets. We heard a funny joke. Jimmy Carter, Begin, and Sadat all died, and each had one request that could be granted. Carter wanted everyone in the U.S. to be happy and prosperous. That was granted. Begin wanted peace. That was granted. Sadat wanted a good telephone system. Unfortunately, that was impossible!

About seven years later, US Aid replaced all the phones in Alexandria with a state-of-the-art fiber optic system. We found that humor, along with a thankful spirit, helped as we learned to persevere and be patient with life and adjustments.

Amy Is Born

≈

I N MAY 1983, THE BABY'S DUE DATE CAME AND WENT. VANCE TOLD ME I couldn't have a baby within a week of his birthday, or everyone would forget his birthday and celebrate the baby's. His birthday is May 4, and the baby was due a week before. His birthday came and went. I prayed I'd go into labor on May 10 because our doctor was on a trip and would return on the tenth. On the tenth, he planned to induce labor. God answered that prayer, and Amy was born May 11, without being induced, a week after Vance's birthday.

We had a wonderful hospital situation. It was a mix of a hospital, a nice hotel, and a home birth. Our room had two beds (one for Vance), a baby bed, refrigerator, TV, private bathroom, and a sitting area decorated with pictures, flower arrangements, and modern furniture. Visiting hours were open, and they provided meals for me and one other person. The baby was with me from the start since there wasn't a nursery. Vance and his mother stayed all night when I was in labor, watching TV, helping me with the La Maze breathing, and eating. Vance ate lots of chocolate, which our Egyptian friends brought.

The next day, our two American nurse friends also came and helped. The Egyptian nurses watched this different way to give birth. I walked to the delivery room, followed by Vance, who looked like a doctor with his mask and medical shirt. He took pictures and audiotaped the delivery and Amy's first cry. All the nurses wanted their pictures taken. The labor was long (thirty hours) but bearable. It felt like climbing a mountain. I couldn't have hoped for a better delivery. Amy had lovely skin and a head full of dark brown hair. After I held her, they took her to Vance's Mom to hold. What a happy, proud Grandma.

Grandma had come with a load of baby items from a baby shower her friends gave her in America. She helped me give Amy her first bath and just helped in so many other ways as I rested. Her easygoing temperament, sense of humor, and practical nature made her such a pleasure to be around.

I remembered the verse the Lord had given me several years before Amy's birth:

> Jesus said, "Truly I say to you, there is no one who has left house or brothers or sisters or mother or father or children or farms, for My sake and for the gospel's sake, but that he will receive a hundred times as much now in the present age, houses and brothers and sisters and mothers and children and farms, along with persecutions; and in the age to come, eternal life." (Mark 10:29)

I wrote in a prayer letter just after Amy's birth:

> I feel Amy is part of my 100 times as much. I had an easy pregnancy and ideal delivery, surrounded by family and friends. Amy Joy lives up to her name, which means beloved joy. We pray she'll also have faith (in God), which is the Arabic meaning of Amy. She's easy to care for with a sweet, happy personality. Around the time I claimed my promise I wrote this song:

> Did you ever want to move in a direction
> and God said, "No"?
> He said, "Wait, child, for my timing,
> I want you to grow."

So reach out and learn,
there's so much to know.
Reach out and touch.
Reach out and grow.
God said, "Wait, child, for My timing."
He didn't say no.
His plan brings the greatest joy,
and He's never slow.
So reach out and learn,
there's so much to know.
Reach out and touch.
Reach out and grow.
People are hurting.
They're waiting to hear about the Lord.
Sitting and pouting
is something that you can't afford.
So reach out and tell them,
they're dying each day.
Reach out and love them,
show them the way.

As I waited on God, he fulfilled his promise in his time and way. Amy gave her life to Jesus at four years old, after hearing about it in Sunday school. She has walked with him since. Like the Arabic meaning of her name, she has the gift of faith, and we watch in amazement as she trusts Jesus, and he provides for her and carries her. Praise be to God for his faithfulness and love.

THE SPY AT CHURCH

≈

We ENJOYED THE FRIENDSHIP OF A FEW FOREIGN BELIEVERS IN AN English-speaking church in our city. We came from different countries, including Sweden and South Africa. Different men took turns preaching, until we had a full-time pastor. Our sweet fellowship became like family—especially for holidays such as Christmas. Also, several of us had children born around the same time.

A few English-speaking Egyptians and a Protestant Armenian family came to church. Everyone else in the Armenian church had emigrated to America. One year, a new Egyptian man appeared at our church. He seemed to enjoy listening to our conversations. It felt strange to be talking with a few women about subjects like shopping or babies and have this man walk up to the edge of our group to listen. We all believed he was gathering information for the secret police. We heard they sometimes paid people to do this. One day, he asked one of our American staff women to marry him so he could emigrate to America. The leaders of the church warned him never to do this again.

Later, he stuffed a note in the purse of our Egyptian-American secretary—offering her two thousand dollars if she'd marry him so he could emigrate. At that point, the church leaders asked him to leave the church, and that was the last we saw of him. I don't think we ever had another spy, unless he was much less obvious.

A New Home

≈

A quiet voice said to my heart, "It's time to move." Could it be the Lord? We were busy. This was no time to move. Then Vance said, "I think the Lord wants us to move." We talked about where we would like to move and picked an area of town. We drove down a street, and I pointed out a house. "There! That looks like what we want." It was an old Greek villa with a fenced-in yard. A fixer-upper with potential in a middle-class neighborhood. There was no sign it was for rent. We went back home. Within a short time, our landlady came to us with the news she had sold our apartment. We would have to move. It would be best if we moved in ten days. Vance found a real estate broker in the area we were interested in. The first place the broker showed him was the old Greek villa. The inside was more torn up than we expected, but it had potential. We took it.

We soon found the house needed many repairs, but our schedule was busy with ministry activities. I would take walks when the condition of our house became too depressing. We removed a truckload of garbage from the small yard. I picked up what I thought was an old rug and discovered it was the skin of a long dead cat. I shoveled out a pile of sand from the glassed-in back porch. Vance worked on the wiring and fixed the fuses. The hot wire and the ground wire were reversed because someone connected the transformer for our area of town improperly, which created problems. A repairman came to fix the broken windows. He knocked the glass into the house, then left the broken pieces in the living room. One day, the door fell off the refrigerator, and the broken eggs flowed in a stream across the floor.

Our living room had high ceilings with walls painted mustard yellow on the bottom; the top was paisley wallpaper, which was peeling off and hanging in limp strips. The floor was black and white squares of tile, and the furniture was covered with bright red cloth. Stuffing protruded in various places, and the curvy wooden edges were a bright gold.

I learned about patience. My schedule for fixing the house and God's schedule weren't the same. I sensed he was teaching me perseverance and to keep the dream of an orderly, nice home, even if it took time. I felt that if we could just get the kitchen and bathroom fixed, life would improve. The bathroom wall was crumbling. Each time we took a shower, more of it crumbled into the tub. The kitchen, painted a dark color, was caked with grease from years of neglect. There were no cupboards or shelves or hot water.

One morning after breakfast, I came into our front room to find men had been busy in the kitchen. Painters had arrived unexpectedly and gone to work. There in the living room was the entire contents of my kitchen, including the dirty dishes from breakfast. I took a quick glance at the situation and realized we couldn't live in the house without a kitchen and bathroom to use. So Vance, Amy, and I stayed at our office, which was in an apartment. Finally, we came home to a bathroom painted light blue with white trim. The kitchen was light and airy, with clean white walls stretching up to a high ceiling. We didn't even notice the piece of rebar sticking at an angle from the ceiling far above.

A carpenter came and made shelves for the kitchen, and we installed a hot water heater. Then a workman moved all the living room furniture to the front porch to recover and paint. Painters removed the living room wallpaper and painted the walls. Things were looking up. Next, we tackled the yard.

I considered our neighborhood. If we'd been in America, it would have looked like a dangerous part of town. But in Egypt, the street was safe, with upper, middle, and lower-class families interspersed in small apartments housed in tall buildings, two to eight stories above us. Most buildings were old and crumbling. Laundry, drying in the sun, fluttered from balconies. Neighbors looked down at the world below; small children peeked through balcony bars, and old men leaned on railings. Children of the poor families played on the streets among the cars and garbage; we had a big dumpster in front of our house that was always overflowing onto the sidewalk and inhabited by stray cats. The children wore ragged clothing. They had no parks or yards to play in. Their small overcrowded apartments often housed several generations of family members.

I determined to make a difference. I wanted to make one spot of beauty, one place of nature reflecting the Creator amid crumbling cement. It was a fight from the start. I soon found there were many enemies. Garbage filtered down from the apartments above or over the fence from passers-by. Sometimes, someone would miss the dumpster on the corner and toss something into our yard. I found everything from syringes, medicine, clothing, furniture, a chicken foot, and even a live duck. One neighbor, a tailor, was in the habit of throwing his fabric scraps out the window. These decorated our trees with brightly colored cloth hanging in long strips. Another enemy was the cats. They consistently dug up seeds I planted or sat on young plants. We also had weeds, including nettles. And, from the cats, we had fleas. Men regularly sprayed the house and yard for fleas and bugs.

I soon found an unexpected threat: plant thieves. I discovered that I shouldn't plant anything edible or any unusual flowers, or someone would steal them. So I chose lots of greenery and common flowers. Even some green plants disappeared. I learned that buying larger plants gave them a better chance of survival if a cat sat on them or a piece of garbage fell on them from apartments above. I studied the local plants to find which were the hardiest.

Gradually, a change came over our yard. People looked twice when they passed by. Poor children lined up at the fence to watch me planting—giving suggestions about dirt and water. I found little copies they had made with sticks in small patches of dirt. It seemed to be so unusual for them to see anyone plant something. I planted my favorite tree in the front yard—a fast-growing fern tree with bright red flowers. I hoped that someday, its brilliant green and red would brighten and shade the neighborhood. As the yard improved, the amount of falling garbage diminished, and the tailor even stopped throwing out his strips of cloth.

One day, a neighbor asked if she could store chairs in our yard, as she was having an engagement party in her home. At least, that's what I thought she said. I opened the gate to our small backyard and said she could. Later that afternoon, I looked into the yard and saw preparations being made for the engagement party. They lined the small area with chairs, and the garage door was the decorated backdrop for the engagement ceremony. That night, under the trees, many in the neighborhood gathered in our small yard for a community celebration. Loud music blared from a radio, and they served refreshments as the couple sat in large chairs against the garage door. They invited us to join in, and we mingled with the crowd. Our small yard was the largest facility available. Apparently, it was nice enough now for a party.

Another day, I was home alone with the children when I heard a strange noise in the yard. I looked out to find a man high in our palm tree, sawing off the fronds. I asked him what he was doing. He quickly apologized and climbed down. I said he could have one frond, but next time, he should ask me first. A few minutes later, I again heard a noise in the yard. I looked out to see a different man in the palm tree, sawing off fronds. A little less politely, I asked him what he thought he was doing. He also quickly apologized and climbed down. I went back in the house, only to hear the same noise a third time.

I lost my patience. "What do you think you are doing?" I demanded in Arabic. "This is my tree. Are you a thief?" The man thought I was crazy. I grabbed the end of the frond he was holding, shouting, "This is my tree."

I wasn't getting anywhere. The man thought I was ridiculous. I decided this was a situation a man should handle, especially in this culture. I went upstairs to my neighbors. The kindly Orthodox Christian couple had often come to our aid. The husband immediately promised to track down the offenders. A short time later, he returned with the news that the palm fronds were being used as decorations at a nearby wedding. I learned something new about the culture.

I also noticed we continually had fewer clothespins on the outdoor clothesline. One day, our family returned home to find three schoolgirls inside our yard, stuffing their pockets with clothespins. They saw us and ran to climb over the spiked wrought-iron fence. Two quickly got away, but the third, a girl of about ten, got her dress stuck on the spikes on top of the fence and could not move. Her legs were visibly shaking, she was so scared. Vance, intending only to scold her, talked to her firmly about not being a thief and gently helped her down. She pulled the clothespins out of her pockets as fast as she could and ran away. It amazed me that the neighbors had been watching the whole thing. I was sure they had seen the girls take the clothespins before we arrived. No one seemed very concerned. They did, however, like the firm rebuke Vance had given the girl without becoming violent. They objected to Vance calling the girls thieves as they insisted that children could never be thieves, because in Islam, a thief was a terrible person.

God led us to move again after problems with our landlord, and it was with some sorrow I said goodbye to that long-fought-over yard. We drove by the neighborhood later. The yard was not what it used to be, but it was still a green spot amid crumbling cement. Because of security, we didn't feel it was wise to speak openly to people around our home about our work, though everyone assumed we were Christians. I had hoped to create a spot of beauty as a visible witness and contribution to the neighborhood. The fern tree had grown immensely. Its bright green leaves and red flowers dwarfed the dumpster and reached up toward the balconies, where children peeked through bars and old men gazed down at the world below.

TRAINING

≈

WHILE SO MUCH WAS HAPPENING IN OUR HOME AND PERSONAL LIVES, the ministry pressed ahead intensely, like a boot camp, preparing young men and women for a lifetime of service. They spent mornings in class learning the theory and practical aspects of winning, building, and sending people for Christ. Classes, taught in English, had Arabic translation and structured notes in Arabic. Eventually, everything would be only in Arabic. Afternoon was the time Egyptians had their main meal at home, so we were off to be with our families. In the evenings, staff and trainees visited students.

The goal was the college campus. Since only students could enter the college campus, we visited students in their homes or dormitories. This involved traveling all over the city by car, bus, tram, or taxi. Trainees also spent time in checkout—going over the things they learned with their trainer. Each training cycle lasted about seven to eight months.

We had to be very careful to only work with the Christian population in our training. Witnessing to Muslims could cause foreigners to be expelled from the country, and the Egyptians could be imprisoned and tortured. Converting from Islam to Christianity could cause imprisonment, torture, and even death. Egypt's population at the time was about forty million, of which about 15 percent had a Christian heritage—mainly Coptic Orthodox. We found that about half of these cultural Christians indicated a personal decision for Christ when presented with the Gospel. Religion came from the family a person was born into. If your father was a Muslim, then you were too. If your father was a Christian, then you were a Christian. The culture was a group culture, and an individual decision was a foreign idea.

We had five Egyptians in our training cycle—three men and two women. One man discipled ten men, four of whom were new believers. His disciples were learning how to share Christ with others. Another man had a Bible study group with five students. The two women were helping other women understand their faith. Two of their disciples were new believers.

Our trainers were our American coworkers. They met with the trainees, helped teach classes, ran errands, and much more. Everyone took part in evening ministry. They encouraged mothers to go one night a week. We all worked hard, felt stretched, experienced spiritual battle, saw results, got tired, and felt encouraged. Life was full in every way.

TRIALS

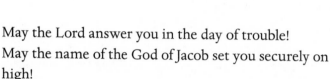

May the Lord answer you in the day of trouble!
May the name of the God of Jacob set you securely on
high!
May He send you help from the sanctuary
And support you from Zion!
May He grant you your heart's desire
And fulfill all your counsel. (Psalm 20:1–2, 4)

WHILE REPAIRS CONTINUED ON OUR HOME, THE MINISTRY GREW. VANCE carried responsibility that could have kept three or four people working full time. Sometimes, he barely had time to eat and didn't always even get a shower. He traveled to other countries to get advice about the training and how to be less busy. He needed an office manager, someone to oversee translating the nine months of classroom teaching, and an administrator. He also taught classes and had trainees himself.

In the spring of 1984, we discovered that our family was growing. We had hoped to have children close together so they could be companions, as we expected to travel a lot. The baby was due in November. We continued to have many guests, and one day, a girl broke out in a rash and fever while sitting at our table. The next week, I took Amy to the doctor and was in a large waiting room filled with mothers and children—many of whom had a rash on their face. I didn't sit down but walked around and tried to stay away from everyone. When I saw the doctor, he told me it was rubella. I knew rubella could cause serious birth defects. I didn't know if I'd had it as a child, which would have made me immune. Now there is a shot to prevent rubella, but it didn't exist when I was young. I couldn't contact my mother immediately and had to wait over a week to find if I was immune. I clung to Romans 12:2, choosing to believe God's will is good, acceptable, and perfect. We finally got through to my mother on the phone and found out I'd had rubella as a child.

We had another scare in August. Van's mother took a tour to Israel, and we met her there with Amy. We drove our car along the Mediterranean coast and left it at the Egyptian border. Then, we took a bus to Jerusalem to meet Van's mom. We had a wonderful time together and saw the sights of Jerusalem before heading back to Egypt. Driving home, Amy and I got a nasty eye infection. Both of us had an eye crusted shut with green goop. Our trip took us through remote parts of Egypt, and we spent the night in a hotel in a town with dirt streets. I knew we needed an antibiotic and that only certain antibiotics were safe for pregnant mothers. Our American nurse coworker had told me that any antibiotic ending with "cillin" was safe. We asked the hotel clerk if there was an eye doctor in town. He directed us to one, and we drove through the dirt streets to a residence. In the main room, they had set a clinic up with equipment to treat eyes. The Egyptian doctor gave us an antibiotic that ended with "cillin." Praise God. Amy and I both recovered after taking the medicine.

The next training cycle was fast approaching. Two Egyptians joined as trainers, and we had two secretaries plus others helping. Soon, the new trainees would arrive: two from Sudan, two from Jordan, one from Bahrain, and five from Egypt. Many Christian nationals continued to work on translating the curriculum. We felt a little awed by the privilege and responsibility of training Christian workers from so many places. As our ministry grew, our trials increased, but so did our deliverance.

One of our staff women led an English woman to the Lord. She had a small son and came to my home for Bible study. She was a sweet lady married to an Egyptian man. He worked in the shipping industry, and they had met in Japan. To our surprise, when they traveled to England, she ran away with their son. The husband had come home first, and she was to follow. She never returned, and he discovered that she had taken all her possessions with her. He had grown up in a village and, like most Egyptian villagers, knew nothing about how the home operated. He was helpless without her. He didn't even know where his clothes were in the drawers, as his wife had laid out his clothes each day. His mother came several hours on the train each week to cook for him.

He spent time at our home, talking and trying to understand why his wife had left him. We learned that other foreign women were unhappy in their marriages to Egyptian men and planned to escape in the same way. It was too difficult to leave while living in Egypt. The Muslim divorce laws made it nearly impossible for a woman to get a divorce, though it was easy for a man.

SARA IS BORN

≈

Life became so busy, I hardly had time to think about having a baby. In September, we had three conferences, two of which I went to. All required traveling. We also had two or three people staying at our home most of the time. This kept me busy cooking, washing, and talking to them. Along with it all, we had our furniture recovered, and the landlord built a garage in the backyard.

One day, an American man, Steve, showed up at our door. He had been working in another country with Campus Crusade. We didn't know he was coming, and he didn't know why our ministry sent him, but we told him he was an answer to our prayers for more help. Van planned to put him in charge of the office, which had grown to five secretaries, and a cook we had hired, along with buying food and handling finances. That would free Vance to spend time with his four trainers and two trainees. Someone else assisted with translation work. Van said we were keeping afloat, but there were leaks in the boat. The poor single trainees didn't have sheets and blankets at first. Two didn't have a closet, their shower and refrigerator didn't work, and only one burner worked on the stove. One young man ran out of food money; he told no one and just stopped eating. We found out and got him some money. Everyone had a good attitude, though.

Then, the cook got sick, and Van had to figure out how to feed about twelve people with hardly any notice. Despite these things, there was a wonderful spirit in the group. Then, we had an outbreak of fleas in our home. Amy and I were especially susceptible to them; she had at least seventy-five bites. We considered which sprays were safest. We spent the night away and took all our food from the cupboards. After the spraying, Lila—our maid—helped us wash everything. During this time, my contractions began.

On November 30 at 9:30 p.m., Sara Louise came into the world. She arrived naturally, exactly fourteen days late, just like her sister Amy. Our hospital was full earlier, and I would have had to go to another one farther from our home and not as good. We had also prayed for convenient timing since Van was away much of the time, and I was alone with Amy and no phone. Our hospital was a few blocks away so I could walk, but we weren't sure if there was room. Since we had planned to have the baby induced on November 30, Van was home and our coworker—who was also a pediatric nurse—was available to be with me. Her husband was available to take care of Amy. So it was very convenient for all of us. Also, we had one of the nicest rooms in the hospital, with an extra bed for Van, private bathroom, and sitting room for guests. My labor wasn't difficult or long. As with Amy, as soon as she was born, the nurse told us we had a girl but next time, it would be a boy. We told them we liked girls too.

Sara means "princess" and Louise means "famous woman warrior." We desired Sara to know the Lord and her identity as the King's daughter. Also, we prayed she would be a soldier for Christ. Sara was God's gift and part of God's promise to give us one hundred times as much (Mark 10:29–30). Sara—like her sister—came to the Lord at an early age and has walked with him since. She is a blessing to all her family and helps keep us all connected.

FAMILY, FRIENDS, AND ILLNESS

≈

Soon after Sara's birth, my grandmother on my mother's side passed away. I believe she was ninety-five. In her nineties, she had a change of heart, and I felt she came to know the Lord. Earlier, she didn't believe in an afterlife and disinherited me when I joined Campus Crusade for Christ. Before her death, she listened to Christian radio and attended Christian meetings held in the assisted living home where she stayed. She hummed hymns and became excited about what I was doing in ministry. Grandmother also put me back into her inheritance. Both of Vance's grandmothers and his uncle also passed away during our first term in Egypt.

We had a scare around Christmastime. I wrote home to my parents:

> I'm holding Sara now and Van and Amy are sleeping. I'm trying to tell Sara she needs to sleep in the afternoon with the rest of us, not in the morning. And, she needs to go to bed a little earlier than 2 a.m. But she hasn't caught on yet. Some nights she sleeps about 12 a.m., which is closer to our schedule. She's not really regular yet. Van has helped with things to let me sleep in the mornings or I'd never make it. It's surprising what we can do when we have to.

This Christmas was the flu Christmas. God gave me grace because it was OK, and we did OK. But, looking back, I wonder how, which showed me God gives you what you need when you need it! Amy, Sara, and I had colds, then both babies caught the flu. Sara scared us when her temperature reached 104.8 degrees. I had been taking it every two hours and giving her Tylenol. It was 3 a.m., and Van went to get a doctor while I followed Doctor Spock's book and gave her a wet rub with water. Doctor Spock is such a help. The doctor—from our local hospital here—said we were doing the right thing, and it was just the flu. Karin came by at 5 a.m. to check on us. That was the day before Christmas Eve.

Christmas Eve we had about fifteen people here for a party. But they brought the food and cleaned up. On Christmas, we had eight for dinner. Van made a turkey, dressing, and gravy, and I had baked two apple pies and heated frozen peas. Karin brought sweet potatoes, mashed potatoes, salad and, pumpkin pies. We also made wassail and brought out our cranberry sauce from Bahrain. Everybody helped, and it wasn't hard. The babies are well now.

Two weeks later, we were sick again with colds, and I wrote home on January 11, 1985:

We all have colds and Sara's nose is stuffy, so she isn't sleeping much. I suction it sometimes with a nose gadget I have for babies. It makes her really mad. It's cold and rainy here. It looks like it will be a wet winter. I'm using Amy's four dozen diapers plus the two dozen you sent, plus four dozen Mom Nordman sent. We can't hang diapers every day since it's raining.

Van put up more clotheslines in the backyard. He does the hanging up, and I put the clothes in the washer. Van gets up with Amy, makes breakfast and does the shopping. This week I took back the kitchen and am washing dishes and cooking more.

I continued the letter after two days:

My cold became laryngitis for two days. I rang a bell for Van and am resting more now. Sara is really growing. We haven't decided if we'll put an h on her name or not. Some people are staying with us. They have a girl Amy's age. I told them they could stay here but I couldn't take care of them. So I'm restraining myself and letting everyone else work. It's hard but I know they want it that way too. The wife is making curtains to cover our kitchen shelves. She's quite a seamstress. Our babysitter is watching both girls.

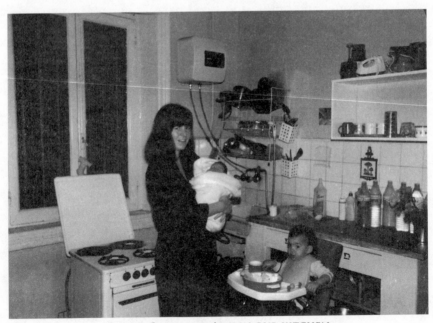

CAROL, SARA, AND AMY IN OUR KITCHEN

CAROL NORDMAN

Looking Back at Our First Term in Egypt

≈

As summer 1985 grew closer, we prepared for our first furlough. Through the challenges, we praised God for

- the five hundred college students who prayed to receive Christ during the previous two years,
- the healthy delivery of two beautiful girls,
- the opportunity we had to help our staff in the Middle East raise their own personal financial support,
- God's provision of an administrator when it seemed impossible,
- the fifteen new Campus Crusade staff we trained the last two years,
- our student training meeting which grew from four to forty college students the last year, and
- God's supernatural provision of our housing needs.

REVERSE
CULTURE SHOCK

≈

BACK IN AMERICA, I EXPERIENCED REVERSE CULTURE SHOCK. THIS CAME as a complete surprise, and I couldn't understand at first why I had such a hard time coming home. I found I had adapted to Egypt more than I realized and had trouble readjusting to the American culture.

We stayed with Vance's mother in Merced, California. Colleen—or Mom, as we called her—was an easygoing woman with a great sense of humor and a great love for her grandchildren. She had a woman staying with her who was a longtime friend of the family. Judy became like an aunt to our kids, and we all loved her. They welcomed the four of us into their two-bedroom home; there was an enclosed porch where Judy slept, and we all shared the bathroom.

I soon found I had forgotten how to use kitchen appliances, and it was too overwhelming to relearn everything at once. For a long time, I didn't use the microwave or the garbage disposal. Going to the mall was exhausting. I got halfway through it and had to go home and rest. There was just too much assaulting my senses. The grocery store was daunting. In Egypt, there were only a few choices for toothpaste, but in America, there were dozens. How was I supposed to know what to choose? What was the criteria? Did I look at the price or the quality or if it whitened teeth? I couldn't remember what brands of things I used to buy, and things had changed. I remember shopping with my sister-in-law Sheri and just asking her to make the choices for me about what to buy. Life was so complex. I could identify with another returning missionary, who entered a grocery store and cried.

America also felt cold and impersonal. People always surrounded me in Egypt—ready to help if I needed anything. When we attended our staff training in Colorado, I needed diapers for Amy and Sara. We were staying in dorms and didn't have a car. So, remembering a store several blocks away, I set out on foot. I soon found I wasn't sure of the direction and looked for someone to ask. There weren't any people on foot. Everyone was in a car. I looked for people in some office buildings and had trouble finding any. Finally, I reached the supermarket and found the diapers. But I discovered I had forgotten how to write a check. I saw a tall sign with the words "check cashing" on it. But when I got to the sign, there was just a machine. At last, I figured out how to buy the diapers and needed to make a phone call to get a ride home. But I had forgotten how to make a phone call on a pay phone. And things had gotten very complicated. It seemed I had to dial a million numbers to use the phone calling card. I felt so alone and confused.

I also felt anger toward American Christians. I didn't realize that I had made the missionaries I knew the normal standard for Christians. I couldn't understand what was wrong with the Christians who lived with obvious sin in their lives and didn't have a passion for evangelism. I wanted to shake them and wake them up from lethargy.

America felt plastic after seeing so much poverty and oppression. It seemed like a plastic mold had settled over the streets, making the roads and curbs and landscaping so perfect. The real, uglier world must be underneath.

I learned that these feelings were reverse culture shock. Gradually, I readjusted to America. Each time we returned, I experienced some of this, but it decreased until I could travel back and forth without such a dramatic reaction. Also, I felt a little of what someone coming from a foreign country must feel, and I'm grateful for that understanding.

ON THE ROAD

≈

PEOPLE OFTEN ASKED US HOW WE ENJOYED OUR "VACATION" IN AMERICA. Furlough is not vacation. We spent a month in Merced, visiting family, churches, and supporters, two weeks in Colorado at Campus Crusade's staff training, one week in Houston, visiting supporters and a supporting church, and just over a month in Los Angeles, visiting family and supporters. We took a week of vacation.

Though the fellowship was wonderful, traveling with two in diapers was a challenge. Sometimes, we felt traveled out and peopled out. I wrote in my journal toward the end of our furlough:

Dear Father,

If I complain, I complain against You who called me to this lifestyle. Sometimes, often, it's hard to be always moving and busy and changing. Sometimes Van and I get short with each other. We get tired, feel pressured.

It's been quite a while since we had a relaxed, fatigue-free evening together. Well, we did rest some yesterday! But there are goods and bads of our lifestyle. It is a privilege though not always easy. But sometimes I think the normal Christian life should be easy and comfortable. But You said the opposite. The righteous have many afflictions but are delivered (Psalm 34:19). Those who want to be godly will be persecuted (2 Timothy 3:12). We are in a battle, and the normal Christian life is full of troubles and pressures. But You give us peace and strength in the middle of it all. Help me remember <u>this</u> is normal!

INTO THE FIRE

≈

Wᴇ ʀᴇᴛᴜʀɴᴇᴅ ᴛᴏ Eɢʏᴘᴛ ꜰᴏʀ ᴏᴜʀ sᴇᴄᴏɴᴅ ᴛᴇʀᴍ ᴀɴᴅ ꜰᴀᴄᴇᴅ ᴀɴ ɪɴᴛᴇɴsᴇ spiritual battle that lasted about a year. While doors remained open for ministry and the Lord sent more staff and a maid to help, we felt attacked on every front. Our staff team experienced troubles, our girls had illnesses, and some American missionary friends of ours were imprisoned—falsely accused of working with the Children of God (which used their wives as prostitutes as an incentive to join their group). I wrote home to my parents on November 1, 1985:

> We've had lots of uncertainties, moving in and out, guests, and minor illnesses. First, Sara had diarrhea and got on an antibiotic. Then, Amy got flea bites (lots), a fever, and the bites got infected (big sores). I kept her in pants and kept antibiotic cream on her. Then we packed up the house and moved to a hotel for a night to spray the house (for fleas). Then we unpacked. Then Amy got a boil with a big hard spot three inches across. We started her on an antibiotic as the doctor was gone that day. When we saw him, he said it wasn't serious. So that cleared up. Then we had one day notice we were going to Cairo for a few days. So I packed up again. We did have a good time seeing friends. Then we got back, and Sara got a fever. She has a throat

infection and is on antibiotics. Now her fever is gone, but she's still got a cold. She acts a lot more perky. That plus everything else, we've had a house guest almost since we got here, we had our bathrooms repainted (good but messy). I finally unpacked the last suitcase today from when we arrived.

I know you heard about the Americans who are being detained. They go to our church. One was at a dinner party we attended the night before they were taken. They were taken from their homes at 2 a.m. and taken to Cairo in the back of a pickup truck and put in prison. The children went without food, water, or diapers for a day. Then, the wives and children were placed in a hotel under house arrest and the husbands kept in prison. Only one wife had been allowed to pack. Two had babies and small children. The prison situation isn't so great. The wives got some money to their husbands, and they use cigarettes to get the guards to let them use the shower and toilet and to put a light in their cell. Friends are sending them food and providing the wives with money. They are charged falsely and will probably be deported. Anyway, it shook us all up to say the least. We're planning to pack a bag in case we need to leave suddenly. We have connections with Egyptians that should help us if we get in a situation like that. And, of course, the American Embassy is working on the situation.

Then, one of our CCC women from the U.S. had to leave, as she had signs of an impending heart attack. That left her roommate—a single girl—alone. Then, the owner of her apartment kicked <u>her</u> out! So now she's with a family staying in their living room. She has a good attitude, though. Then, there were problems in the work over the summer that are still being resolved.

Boom! Boom! Boom! I really sense the war going on. So please pray for us here. I don't want to scare you, but I want you to know what's happening and that we're still here and doing OK in it all.

After our American friends were held for a month, they were released to return to their homes before being deported. I wrote home in a prayer letter:

"Beloved, do not be surprised at the fiery ordeal among you, which comes upon you for your testing, as though some strange thing were happening to you." (1 Peter 4:12)

Sometimes I forget we're living in a world at war with God. It is normal to experience conflict. It helps to be reminded of this when difficulties arise.

WHAT IS THE ROLE OF A MOTHER?

≈

I BECAME A MOTHER AT THIRTY AFTER WORKING FOR CAMPUS CRUSADE for Christ for eight years. I always had a written job description. Now, I looked around at other mothers in ministry and saw they seemed to approach motherhood differently. I felt confused and wrote in my journal:

> Dear Lord,
>
> I feel so emotional about what _is_ the role of a mother? Does it vary based on her personality? Her children? Other things? Is it to disciple her children? Or is it to disciple her children and work outside as well? Maybe some can. Or is it to have children and have others assist in discipling them? It seems to vary even among committed Christians. We are torn between family and ministry. I like the idea of concentrating on my family, but I feel guilty that I'm not out more. But, I'm happy at home. Oh, help me Jesus! What is right and wrong? Or are there no absolutes here?

In Titus 2:4, the older women are to "encourage the young women to love their husbands, to love their children, to be sensible, pure, workers at home, kind, being subject to their own husbands, so that the word of God will not be dishonored."

Young women are to be working at home, concentrating on loving husbands and children. The Bible says this should be my focus, so this is right to be my focus. The result? "The word of God will not be dishonored." It brings glory to God. This is what You said, Lord. My culture doesn't agree!

I also considered how Jesus trained his twelve disciples. He ministered to the twelve but also had a larger ministry teaching and healing. He didn't leave the twelve at home but took them along in his larger ministry. They constantly observed what he did. I took this as a model with our children and tried to include them in our larger ministry. Having events and guests in our home was an easy way to include them—especially when they were young. Later, family mission trips were wonderful ways to minister together.

The Lord answered my prayer for direction as a mother, and I've found that family and ministry are not in conflict as I follow God's calling.

SUFFERING
FOR CHRIST

≈

DURING OUR THIRD TRAINING CYCLE, FOUR YOUNG MEN FROM NORTH Africa, Abu Ali, Hosni, Mustafa, and Ahmed, joined us. They had all previously been Muslims and came to Egypt to attend our training center. I need to give background about the situation for Christians in North Africa and in Egypt.

North Africa has been mostly Muslim for many centuries. It was very dangerous to be a Christian, except for foreigners. In contrast, Egypt has had a Christian community since the beginning of Christianity. Most Egyptians were Christians when Islam began in the seventh century. Shortly thereafter, Muslims invaded Egypt and pressured people to convert to Islam—often at the threat of their lives. Christianity has been on the defense ever since. Despite fourteen centuries of persecution, about 18 percent of the population of Egypt were Christian when we were there. Many were cultural Christians and did not have a personal faith in Christ. All but a small percentage of the Christian population were Coptic—an Eastern Orthodox branch of the church. We had freedom to work openly within the Christian community, but as I mentioned, sharing Christ with the Muslim population could cause deportation or imprisonment.

Christians in Egypt had freedom but were treated like second-class citizens—discriminated against by radical Muslims in education and employment. Muslim radicals often caused unrest with Christians. Sometimes, they burned churches. The government's response was to station poorly trained and ill-equipped guards at churches. The situation was better than in North Africa, where there was even less freedom and a training center such as ours would have been impossible.

Our four North African trainees enjoyed the training center. Toward the end, they had to renew their visas. One Saturday shortly after they renewed their visas, someone called Vance and asked where the trainees were. Since it was a weekend, we thought they had gone camping or were visiting another city, which they often did on the weekends. One of our Egyptian staff went to their apartment, and the secret police took him away, beating and threatening him, telling him not to tell our ministry what had happened. Despite his fear, he went immediately to our national director and told him that the North African trainees had been arrested. God used this to develop the young Egyptian staff member, who later became a leader in our ministry. So began the greatest trial we faced in Egypt.

We didn't find out until years later some details of the four North African trainees' six-month ordeal in prison. After learning of their arrest, our director contacted the police. They told him that they had sent the trainees back to their home countries. We contacted people in their home countries, but no one had seen them. The police held the four North Africans in Alexandria for three days, beating them, not allowing them to sleep, and constantly interrogating them. It was another two months before our director learned that they were moved to a maximum-security prison in Cairo. It was the same prison where members of the Muslim Brotherhood, involved in the assassination of President Sadat, had been. They were treated badly in the Cairo prison and faced dangers from the Muslim Brotherhood, who hated them for being Christians. Brotherhood members constantly attacked their beliefs and tried to force them to turn back to Islam. The conditions were terrible in the prison, as they were in small cells with many other prisoners. They had no beds to sleep on and only a hole in the floor for a toilet. The food was bug-infested beans, and they drank contaminated water. After a couple of months, our ministry could get money and gifts to them to help with their imprisonment, but even some of that did not reach them.

About three months after they were arrested, our ministry hired a lawyer, who went and met with them. Their situation improved some after that, and they were allowed out of their cell to bathe and shave. They could also purchase items in the prison canteen and receive some new clothes. Their lawyer assured them he would have them out of prison soon, and they put their hope in him. After several court appearances, nothing seemed to happen, even though their lawyer pointed out the illegal nature of their imprisonment and how their imprisonment was creating bad press outside the country.

Abu Ali later told us that they became discouraged and realized that they had stopped trusting the Lord for their deliverance and were instead trusting in the lawyer. They saw that their suffering was a normal thing for believers and that it wasn't anyone's fault.

Our friends began to pray and recite scripture together and even sing in the prison. When all the efforts of the lawyer had failed, there was increasing pressure from outside Egypt. Two American congressmen wrote to President Mubarak about their situation, and Amnesty International listed them as prisoners of conscience. One day, about six months after their ordeal began, the police came to their cell and told them they were leaving. They took them to a deportation center, and after some time, they boarded an Air France flight in handcuffs, which were removed after they were shoved into their seats. The flight left, and they were free.

Abu Ali, the leader of the group, later said that they learned a great deal from their time in prison. God was with them. They learned to pray, and prayer was food to them. They learned to love and forgive even those who put them into prison. They learned what liberty means. In Christ, they were free, even in prison, because they learned to have no desire for sin. And they learned to be free when they had nothing.

The following was written by Paul Read, one of our coworkers in Cairo:

What I Have Learned in the World

I have learned what it is like to be confronted by the CIA and told to quit meddling in international politics.

Two Moroccans and two Tunisians were arrested in Egypt with no charge. The only thing against them was that they had converted from Islam to Christianity. Americans close to them left the country for fear of arrest, and no Egyptian wanted to get near them for the same reason. Somehow it fell on me to send them food in prison (Egyptian prisons didn't feed prisoners) and get a lawyer to represent them.

For months I sent them food, clothes and roach spray through intermediaries and haggled with an Egyptian lawyer over court appearances. (He was paid too much for doing nothing.) At home I hid anything that might incriminate me in case I got a midnight visit from the Secret Police. After six months of several court appearances and an international landslide of letters to the Egyptian government, the four were still nowhere near being released.

Then one day, Vice President George W. Bush came to Cairo. I got a call from an assistant to VP Bush (HOW did they know I was involved? I thought I was careful to stay under the radar!). The assistant said that Bush had given an ultimatum to Pres. Mubarak: release the four, or no more US dollars for you! The four were released and deported within the week. They now live in France.

A couple of days later the US Embassy calls and says to come meet with someone. I go, and it's the CIA. They had a file on me two inches thick. The man scolded me and told me to stay out of government affairs. He yelled at me and made me feel like a criminal. I was interfering with negotiations between the US and Egypt. Then he calmed down and said, "That's the official government position, but if you need any help in the future, just give us a call." And he smiled.

OUT

≈

AFTER THE TRAINEES DISAPPEARED, AND OUR EGYPTIAN DIRECTOR learned the police had taken them, he asked the foreign staff to leave the country so he wouldn't have to worry about us while he dealt with the situation. I didn't think about needing to pray. Prayer just came naturally—and it was heartfelt. Our other American family had three children, and the wife expected to deliver a baby at any moment. Another team member was a nurse, and together, they plotted out hospitals on the escape route, in case the baby came. We all got out and met on the nearby island of Cyprus, where the baby was born. We found apartments and thought about what to do next.

We weren't sure if we could return to Egypt, so Vance and I spent our time investigating other possible locations for the training center in Cyprus and Paris. Vance's mother, Colleen, joined us in Paris. Our family stayed with the staff in Paris, and one day, I went downstairs to take a nap with Amy and Sara. When we came back upstairs, Vance and his mother had decided to go to Morocco the next day. They went to meet the American ambassador, who was a believer, to see if he could help get our North African friends out of prison.

Unfortunately, he could not help—telling us it was all he could do to help the American believers in Morocco; it would appear suspicious if he asked about Moroccan nationals in another country such as Egypt. Colleen—always adventurous—had a wonderful time in Casablanca. Finding we had time on our hands, our family finally took some needed rest and vacation. Colleen had always wanted to see Europe in a convertible. After a couple of weeks living in a Paris hotel, where she only ate croissants, she was ready to return to an English-speaking country. So we headed for Great Britain.

We made a strange traveling group, as Colleen needed both knees replaced and couldn't walk far. Sara—at a year and a half—was still in a stroller, and Amy—at three—walked at a slow pace, holding onto the stroller. The only person who could handle the luggage for us all was Vance. He was also the driver and had to navigate using the opposite side of the road. Colleen didn't exactly have a convertible but enjoyed the sunroof of the car she rented for us all. I sat in back between the girls in two car seats and just felt grateful to be somewhere safe and peaceful. As the green countryside of England rolled by, I felt the stress and fatigue from the events in Egypt lifting.

Dale and Jewell, who had directed the ministry in Houston, now lived and ministered in London. They had a place for us to stay, and we enjoyed catching up with them and their two children. Then we traveled on to Bath, where my Swiss roommate from San Diego worked with Campus Crusade. She found us a furnished apartment, where we stayed happily for about a week, exploring the city. Then we traveled west, staying mostly in the countryside in bed-and-breakfasts, and drove through Wales. Catching the ferry to Ireland, we found a furnished house in a suburb for about a week and relaxed with the local people. I felt right at home with so many redheads in these countries of my ancestors.

Finally, it was time for Colleen to return home. Vance, Amy, Sara, and I stayed in the Paris apartment of a Campus Crusade staff member traveling out of the country. We also drove to Germany to visit ministry supporters who worked in the military there. This was during the time of the Chernobyl nuclear accident, when a radioactive cloud floated over parts of Europe. Gratefully, it didn't float over us.

The four trainees still languished in prison, but we heard there was hope for their release, and our Egyptian director felt it was safe for us to return. Vance believed this was what we should do. For the first time, I disagreed with him about our future direction. I wrote in my journal on July 18, 1986:

> As I think about the future and the good possibility of going back to Egypt, I feel stressed. I was just so glad to leave—like a bird set free. I didn't feel that way before when we left, just this time. I guess we were in a strong battle. Anyway, when I think about going back, I feel weak. Thank you for the scriptures You reminded me of, Isaiah 61 and 62 and Psalm 139. The hope of Isaiah 62; what I will be like in the New Jerusalem. I feel so weak now and realize my sin and failure and vulnerability. But then I will be righteous, glorious, a crown of beauty, a royal diadem. God's delight will be in me! He will rejoice over me as a bridegroom does a bride. And Isaiah 61:3: Jesus came to give me "the mantle of praise instead of a spirit of fainting." And "so they will be called oaks of righteousness, the planting of the Lord, that He may be glorified." And Psalm 139:5: "You have enclosed me behind and before and laid Your hand upon me."

> So I am encouraged by Your word. You met me in my point of need. You didn't want to go to the cross, but You were obedient and were blessed for it. I don't really want to go back to Egypt, but I will trust You leading Van, and I will be obedient. And I sense such a comfort—a warm trust in You. You are my Father, and I can trust You! As a little girl snuggles in her Daddy's arms and feels warm and safe, there is that with You. So I don't just go alone to that unknown, unsure place. I go in Your arms, and You will be my strength where I am so weak.

I came to the Middle East to see You do a miracle—even as You did in impossible Houston. So why should I give up now that I realize my weakness and must trust You? The song I wrote then (in Houston), "As a drop of foam rides a mighty wave, so my soul is thrilled as I ride on God's power." That was a little wave—a little miracle. This is a big wave—a big miracle. I lean on You, Lord. I am waiting to ride on that big wave of Your power that will thrust forward Your kingdom.

I go as a lamb as part of the Lamb's army. I go as a lamb—weak—among wolves. And by accepting to die—by dying to myself—my own desires—I conquer by following Your example, who accepted to die physically. I can accept to die in many aspects. If physically, You will give me grace for that too. But now it is to my own flesh—my own desires—even my own physical health if I experience stress. By accepting to die, I conquer.

RETURN TO
EGYPT

≈

After you have suffered for a little while, the God of
all grace, who called you to His eternal glory in Christ,
will Himself perfect, confirm, strengthen and establish
you. (1 Peter 5:10)

ALL WENT WELL ON OUR TRIP BACK TO EGYPT AND RETURN TO OUR
home. Shortly after—in October—Van left for a two-week trip to
Thailand. An Egyptian staff woman came to stay with me and the
girls. We spoke Arabic, and I even dreamed in Arabic. However, we
both were fearful and imagined there were spies watching us from
the auto body shop across the street. We had a visit from Violet, our
Egyptian director's wife, who assured us everything was okay.

The second week, my Egyptian roommate got sick with a fever
of 103–104 for three nights in a row. Her mother came and stayed
several nights to help. Then Amy got a fever of 103 and had diarrhea.
Fortunately, the doctor was just a few blocks away. He gave her several
medications to treat an intestinal infection. The next day, Sara got the
same green diarrhea and visited the doctor. Then Van returned, and
we all recovered.

Finally, on November 5, 1986, we wrote home:

Yesterday afternoon at 1 p.m.—after six months and eleven days in prison—Egyptian police put our four North African trainees aboard an Air France plane for Paris.... You may be wondering if we are being shrewd as serpents by returning to Egypt after these problems. We want to assure you our decision was taken after much prayer and counsel. We aren't involved in anything wrong here, and even though the authorities know who we are and what we are doing, no attempt was made to discourage us from returning. In fact, these problems have brought things more in the light—which is a better safeguard for us.

The international pressure put on the Egyptian government for violating a human rights agreement by putting our trainees in prison gave us all more boldness. Also, we had come through the fire and were no longer as fearful. Our small foreign church had more of a sweet spirit of unity after the imprisonment and deportation of our American friends the year before. All the trials had a purifying effect. Most dramatic of all was the spiritual growth of our four North African trainees, who had endured terrible conditions and abuse.

The year after we returned to Egypt was fairly quiet. We had two memorable events. First, a new family member was on the way. We had wanted another child for a while, and this time, I wanted a boy. The other big event was the arrival of a new family to work with us. Ray and Gail would become lifelong friends; they had a girl Amy's age and a boy Sara's age. We took a trip to upper Egypt together—taking turns watching all four kids so each couple had time alone together. I think I was about five or six months' pregnant. We boarded the train for Cairo and then switched trains to upper Egypt. We had a sleeper train, where the individual rooms converted into bedrooms; the seats changing into beds. There was even a small sink in each room.

The children had so much fun together in their special rooms. We didn't get much sleep, as the tracks were bad, and the train swayed a lot. They also made announcements on loudspeakers that interrupted our sleep. But it was all worth it to be together and to wake up in the morning to see banana groves and the banks of the Nile River. The green belt along the Nile River was narrower here, and the sandy desert stretched just beyond.

Finally, we arrived in Aswan, home of the Aswan Dam that holds back the Nile. We stayed in a nice hotel and took turns watching the children. We all rode in a horse-drawn buggy and visited ruins of the ancient Egyptians. The people in Egypt love children. It amazed them to see a couple with two four-year-olds, two two-year-olds, and a pregnant wife. They wondered how we did it. At one nice restaurant, the waiters were happy to see us all come. Even though we made a big mess, the waiters always welcomed the children.

On the train trip back to Alexandria, Vance and I did something that caused some nervous moments for Ray and Gail. Ray had stomach problems (a common occurrence in Egypt). He wasn't feeling well at all. The train stopped for an hour in Luxor—a famous tourist sight, with many ancient ruins. Vance and I had never been there and decided there was time to take a brief taxi ride and get the overall view of Luxor. Assuring Ray and Gail we would be back before the train left, we called a taxi, took Amy and Sara, and left the luggage with our friends on the train. We had a great time, but when we returned, only the rear door of the train was still open. We got on, and the train left soon after. But Ray and Gail didn't know we were on the rear of the train. All they knew was that the train left, and they had two small children, all the luggage, a sick husband, and a limited knowledge of Arabic. They were not happy when we finally made it to their section of the train. Fortunately, they forgave us, and we have enjoyed their friendship since.

TESTINGS

≈

WHEN WE ARRIVED HOME IN ALEXANDRIA, WE FACED CHALLENGES. I wrote home on June 24, 1987:

> I've slowed down some this month. I was tired after our trip to Aswan and as soon as we got back, we faced three semi-crises. It seemed the realtor wanted us to move out of our house (the contract expires in September); the police wanted to see Van; and our maid wanted a substantial raise. I prayed a lot about all three and sensed the Lord telling me this was a trial He wanted us to go through, and we should stick it out, and it would all come out okay. It turned out the realtor was the one causing problems—probably because he gets money every time he puts someone new in a house (so it pays to change tenants). The owner seems quite happy with us, and he is the one with the authority. And since the dollar value has increased about 40%, we gave Lila her raise, and she's happy.

The following, written by Vance, tells of his encounter with the secret police:

> The Egyptian government had an agent in the secret police office of our city whose job was to spy on the

Christians and intimidate them. He would call in pastors and other Christian leaders and try to get information from them. If they didn't cooperate, then he would think of ways to harass them, such as taking their identification card so they would have problems conducting official business. I don't know how much ability he had to incarcerate people, but he was definitely feared by the local Christians. He had told our director that he wanted to meet with me. Our director wanted to be with me if there was a meeting, so he invited the officer to have coffee with us at a private club, knowing this would make the officer uncomfortable since the officer wasn't a member and was from a lower class.

Some time later, when our director was out of town for a couple weeks, I received a notification from the secret police to meet with him. After receiving the notification, I spoke to some missionary friends, who gave me some advice on talking to him. I then went to the American Embassy to inform them that I had been called in. I also wanted to tell them who I was and what I was doing in the country as a precaution to him claiming to the embassy staff I was doing something I was not. Some other missionaries had been arrested a couple years prior, and the police claimed they were working with a group they had arrested for distributing pornography. The consular officer I should have met with was out of town, so I met with the administrator, instead. He was a pleasant person and told me to report back after my interview.

My appointment was in the evening, and when I showed up at the secret police office, I was sent to a large, dirty, and dark waiting room with about two hundred people waiting in it. I sat there for an hour or so. It seemed they wanted everyone to sit and sweat before their meeting. I had brought my Bible with me, so I spent the time reading. After an hour, they took me into the main office and had me sit in the hall. One of the secret police officers who walked by while I was waiting looked familiar. I realized later that I had seen him several times working in the immigration office. He was evidently involved in collecting information there, though I doubt he ever shared it with those working in immigration. I was forced to wait another thirty minutes in the hallway. I passed the time silently singing Christian songs; one in particular stands out: "In Moments Like These, I Lift up a Song to the Lord." When I was finally ushered into the office of the officer, I was surprised to see that he shared his office with three others. Somehow, I determined that they were responsible for keeping track of Palestinians living in Alexandria. He had an old gray steel office desk, and I sat at an old steel chair in front of his desk. I realized at that point that he wasn't a very important officer. He didn't speak English well and asked if we could speak in Arabic. I told him my Arabic wasn't very good, and I preferred to speak English. I had made it a practice of never talking to officials in Arabic to make sure I didn't inadvertently say something that could be misunderstood. My pronunciation was very good, and people often thought that my Arabic was better than it was. This had the added benefit of discouraging officials from asking much of me.

He began asking me general questions. I remember the first question he asked was about when I came. It wasn't clear just what he was asking (When did I first come to Egypt? When did I return from my most recent furlough?), so I asked him, "When did I come from where?"

My friends had advised me that if I asked for clarification of the questions, it would give me time to think and answer them more easily. I found this to be true, as the first thing that came into my mind when he asked a vague question was what I didn't want to tell him. After a few more clarifying questions, he indicated he wanted to know when I had come back from Cairo, where I had been when his initial invitation had come. He then asked me why I was in Cairo, and I made the mistake of saying to see a friend, which led him to ask what friend I had seen. I didn't want to mention one friend I had met there, so I mentioned the name of another friend, who was working officially with the Presbyterian Church and whom it was also known worked with CCC. (My friend was unhappy when he heard I had mentioned his name, but nothing came of it.) He also asked about other staff working with CCC, but I kept asking for clarification, and it ended up that he was asking about someone who had left and not returned.

On a couple occasions, he asked me questions I didn't really want to answer, but about that time, he would get interrupted, and I just let the question pass. From his questions, it became clear to me that he had a lot of information, but he didn't know how to put it together. His lack of just a basic understanding of how a church operated kept him from putting information together in a meaningful way. He seemed to assume a church operated like a mosque, which it doesn't. He also didn't have any understanding of how missionaries or mission agencies worked, either. The whole interview probably only lasted about 30 minutes, after which I went home. A few days later, I stopped by the embassy to give a report on my meeting. This time, I met with the officer who normally handled things like this. She was a career diplomat, an American woman who was married to an Egyptian Muslim. She asked me about my involvement with the four North Africans who were imprisoned and began accusing me of causing problems with the Egyptian government. Then she began defending the Egyptian authorities for their actions.

This made me mad, and I gave her a piece of my mind and told her she needed to be more concerned about human rights and stop making excuses for the Egyptian government's atrocities. After all, she was supposed to be representing the United States. I am very sorry to know that we have such people working in our embassies. It was clear to me that if I had a problem, she wouldn't go out of her way to help, and only pressure from my congressman would make her act. Unfortunately, I am afraid this is too often true overseas. After this meeting, I was never asked back by the secret police, which I took as a sign that I had done a good job of not telling him anything useful.

AMY'S DECISION

≈

AMY WAS ALWAYS A GOOD LITTLE GIRL. EVEN AS A SMALL CHILD, SHE WAS compassionate and gentle and concerned about people's feelings. As a baby, she conveniently slept through the night soon after birth. Vance and I would take her in a carry cot out to a restaurant, and she slept through the meal. We took her to church—and she concentrated on the pastor while he preached. He said it felt strange to look out in the congregation and see a baby staring at him. I even wondered if Amy really had a sin nature until one day, when I saw her push another little girl.

Then—when she was just three and a half—Amy told me while we were at home that she had asked Jesus to come into her heart. Surprised, I asked where she had heard about this. We thought she was too young to understand and were waiting until she was older to talk about it. Amy told me she learned about this in Sunday school. I inquired where she was when she asked Jesus into her heart, and she told me she was there on her bed.

Then I asked, "So where is Jesus now?"

She replied that he was in her heart.

Amy continued to grow closer to Jesus through the years, talking to Him, singing, and writing poetry. She never turned away (though I'm sure she had to confess some sins). Her gifts of childlike faith, encouragement, and serving have grown and developed through the years.

On November 26, 1986, I wrote in my journal:

Dear Father,

Thank you for Amy's profession—saying she asked Jesus into her heart. I feel not afraid that I can face the future because I know she will spend eternity with You. Help me teach her and help her to grow.

Amy has lived up to her name Amy Joy—which means beloved joy. In Arabic, Amy is short for Imen, which means faith. Love, joy, and faith are all so characteristic of Amy today.

DECISIONS IN GERMANY

≈

I N MARCH 1987, VANCE AND I TRAVELED FOR ABOUT A WEEK TO GERMANY to meet with our Middle Eastern director and international vice president. We would discuss moving the training center to Paris. Vance didn't think this was a good idea and worked long hours preparing a proposal to keep the training in Egypt. After our time in Paris the previous summer, we felt that Egypt was the better choice.

I was excited to get away alone with Van but hesitant to leave Amy and Sara. I prayed and got counsel from other mothers who had traveled, then decided it would be okay if the trip lasted less than a week. So, leaving the girls in the care of Ray and Gail, Vance and I flew to Switzerland then traveled overland to Germany. I had always wanted to see Switzerland, and though it wasn't the Alps, it was still beautiful.

Our meeting was near the Black Forest of Germany. We stayed with some of our staff and enjoyed the lovely scenery. At the meeting, Van presented his proposal. At the end, our international vice president said he went into the meeting determined to send us to Paris but ended the meeting convinced that we should return to Egypt. It was a pivotal decision that paved the way for the future growth of national staff in the Middle East.

SISTERS

≈

LIFE IN OUR HOME QUIETED DOWN, AS WE NOW HAD A SEPARATE apartment for our training center. So we had fewer ministry activities in our home, though we still had a lot of guests. I spent three to four hours a day in the kitchen, preparing food for our family and guests. I worked to create a homey atmosphere with good food and nice decorations. It was fun. Lila took care of cleaning the house, which made everything else possible. Amy and Sara—at four and three years old—were a joy. I wrote in letters home:

> Amy and Sara play together all day. They don't stay around where I'm working as much but go all over the house playing imaginary games. They don't play as much with their toys except as props in their games. Often one girl is the mommy and one is the baby, or mommy to a doll. Playing with sand is cooking. They set the table and serve strawberry soup (?) They seem happy and usually play well together with an occasional squabble where they need a referee.

> Amy discovered mud pies yesterday on her own. Today she and Sara were outside, baking "cookies." Van said I should get some mud in a container for them to play inside with, as we live in a city, and lots of people walk by our yard. In Egypt, people from good families don't let their children play in the mud.

Sara is great at mechanical things. She loves taking things apart and putting them together, pushing buttons and understanding fastenings and how things open and close. Maybe she'll be an engineer. She has a sense of humor and loves rough play and being active. She also likes to take charge, and when the girls play house, Sara is usually the mother!

They also play with crayons, pencils, play dough, tempura paint, puzzles, and games. Sara is especially good at puzzles and building things. She is very precise.

On the Fourth of July, we went to a party with Americans. I think Amy was happy to be around so many English speakers. We found her going up to total strangers and talking. We had never seen her so outgoing.

When we visited the island of Cyprus, Sara loved swimming. I wrote home:

When it comes to most physical activities, she has good coordination and pushes her little body to the limit of what it will do. I think she has the makings of a good athlete, which is fun for me as I love sports. Sara has always been slender and athletic. Amy's getting long and leggy. Amy loves to talk and is always pretending to be someone or playing pretending games. She gets Sara involved, and they play together for hours—house or doctor or traveling somewhere—using all sorts of things for props. They are pretty attached to each other. They get into some mischief. I don't know if I told you about Amy making a honey sandwich on the toilet (It was pretty sticky when I sat down on it!) or the day I found them on the front porch with the hose, pretending they were swimming (with their clothes on), or the time Sara got into Van's file drawer and was having a good time reading financial papers. (Now she is a CPA! Even at three she was interested in offices.)

Amy and Sara were very interested and involved with preparing for the new baby. I wrote home:

Amy and Sara have lots of questions such as how the baby gets out. Sara thought they would cut open my stomach. Sara is always interested in mechanical questions about how things work. They insist they are both having babies too. They're also fascinated about the idea of marriage. The other day, Sara said she was going to marry Daddy. I told her Daddy was already married. She asked who he was married to. I told her, "Mommy." She looked surprised then understood. I think it's the first time she realized it. I guess she forgot though. Today she said she would marry Mommy. They both fight over who is going to marry Matthew— their three-year-old playmate. Sometimes it's solved by Matthew having two wives.

AMY AND SARA HAVING AN EARLY MORNING SNACK
OF PITA BREAD AND WATER IN THE KITCHEN

BARRIERS

≈

AN ARTISTIC WROUGHT-IRON FENCE SURROUNDED OUR TINY YARD—separating us from the busy street just steps away. In so many ways, we were separate from the outside world. For ten years, we renewed our tourist visas. We were unable to get a visa even to work within the Christian population; any evangelism to Muslims could cause expulsion from the country, especially any evangelism to their children.

Just a few yards from the window, street children peered through the iron fence—interested in the foreign family living in their neighborhood. We relied on our Egyptian Christian friends to know how to navigate in the culture. They told us not to associate with the street kids or let our children associate with them. So existed yet another barrier.

Then, there was the concept of class. As foreigners, we were in the upper class and expected to act upper class. All this felt strange because I'm not upper class, and as an American, I don't agree with the concept of classes. So many barriers separated us from our neighbors, many of whom lived in tiny apartments with several family generations.

I wrote in my journal:

> I have such a burden—a heavy feeling for those suffering people around me and such a feeling of helplessness to help them. I see the children standing

at the fence, wanting to play with my girls; children in rags, playing in the garbage; children who never see lovely things, like gardens, except for ours; children who eat a fraction of the meat and protein mine do; children I can barely communicate with and if I could share (Jesus) with them, I feel I might risk our being here; children the Egyptian Christians say I shouldn't let my children play with, Christians I respect, for the health and safety of my own children. And I want to SHOUT, "How can we help these people?" What can I do? It's hard. I'd either like to be removed from seeing them or be doing something to help them. It's frustrating. Dear Lord, please show me what to do!

THE SECRET TO HAPPINESS

≋

Being outdoors rated first on an interest test I once took. I love nature, physical activity, and art. Sometimes, I marveled at God's grace that enabled me to live contentedly indoors much of the time in Egypt. I wrote in my journal:

> I'm longing for creation and the freedom I knew of being fit and running and hiking through God's glorious world—the physical feeling, the sights, sounds, smells.

> I lifted this to the Lord, and I remembered Joni (Erickson). She is confined to her wheelchair. She realized that it's OK not to like it; that it won't always be this way! It is temporary. She would rather be in her wheelchair and know Christ than be out and not know Him.

> I would rather be in God's will and live in a crowded city that looks like a ghetto than live in Yosemite or another national park or be able to jog or hike through nature consistently.

I thought of our government. We want people to pursue happiness. But the way to find happiness is not to pursue it, it's forgetting yourself—to be absorbed in something outside yourself—in following the Lord. The selfish thing is to pursue what I want, to be outside in nature, but it is not the way to true happiness. How deceived we are by what we've been taught and raised with. True happiness comes from denying self, taking up your cross, and following Christ.

Someday, I would like these things in heaven, Lord.

I didn't have to wait until heaven. Now we live on the California coast, and I walk regularly on the beach, see magnificent sunsets from our home, enjoy a lovely garden, and have become a painter. God has given me the desires of my heart.

TIMES OF REFRESHING

≈

IN MY SIXTH MONTH OF PREGNANCY WITH OUR THIRD CHILD, WE TRAVELED as a family to Jordan for five days and to the island of Cyprus for about three weeks. In Jordan, we visited former trainees and were so encouraged. They showed us a diagram of their disciples who were discipling others. We heard stories of steps of faith they were taking and how God was doing amazing things. I'll always remember sitting on a vine-covered porch and sharing a Jordanian meal from a large round platter piled with food. As usual in the Middle East, people loved our children. Our friends had fun taking Amy and Sara bumper car riding. Some young people were going to Petra and the Dead Sea. I wanted to go but didn't think it was wise in my pregnant condition, as we would have to ride a long way on a donkey. The son I carried would grow up to spend a college semester studying in Israel and Jordan, visiting Petra and floating in the Dead Sea.

We traveled on to the island of Cyprus for vacation and an area staff conference. I have always enjoyed Cyprus with its beautiful beaches, mountains, Greek food, and great shopping. I wrote home:

> Cyprus—as always—was beautiful. We had a furnished two-bedroom apartment next to the sea. When we looked out the window, we saw the sea, boats, and

water skiers. Many mornings we just walked across the street and swam. We could see little fish around our feet. We usually went in by 10:30 or 11, showered, ate lunch and took a nap. Then we got up and went out to dinner, ice cream, and computer games or a kiddie park. Some days we shopped the sales or went to the zoo. We also enjoyed the time spent with our friends.

In a different letter, I wrote of the upcoming conference:

Soon our schedule will be a lot busier. Van's doing some speaking and trying to help people get settled in as they arrive. I've been trying to help with childcare. We have twenty children coming with fifteen four or under. I have a real burden for the mothers, who are mostly off in isolated countries with little input. I hope this conference will be refreshing and restful.

After a restorative trip, we returned to Egypt, where our maid—Lila—had prepared for our coming. I wrote home:

It's always nice to get home. Lila had the house clean, had watered the yard and houseplants, and had a complete meal prepared and frozen. Also, she made hibiscus drink, bought and chilled a watermelon, and bought and cleaned some vegetables for us. It made coming home very nice. She's been so good to us.

THE HOPE OF THE RESURRECTION

≈

An ETERNAL VIEW PUTS EVERYTHING IN PERSPECTIVE. ONE OF MY favorite Bible passages is 1 Corinthians 15. I wrote in my journal:

Dear Father,

I love You! I come to You, Your child. Thank you for the hope and victory of the resurrection! I like 1 Corinthians 15. The reason we take risks and suffer and toil is, the resurrection (verse 58). It is not in vain (toil). We work steadfastly, immovably in Your work, Lord, because of the resurrection, what we will be, an imperishable, glorious, powerful, spiritual body, bearing the image of the heavenly. Our toil is not in vain. It has a reward. Steadfastly continue, train and raise godly children, continue in the ministry God has given us.

P.S. Please show me what to do about the fleas and deliver us from them and please fix our phone. Be our husband and father while Van is gone. I need and love You.

CRITTERS

≈

W E SOMETIMES ENCOUNTERED ANIMALS AND BUGS IN OUR GROUND-level villa. We had no screens, and flies were common. Occasionally, I ran into a stray cat in the house. The most alarming time was in the middle of the night, as I was on the way to the bathroom. I think the cat was just as shocked as I was when we ran into each other.

One day, I set some frozen chicken out to defrost on the kitchen counter. I returned to find the entire chicken missing and a stray cat sitting in the window. I looked him in the eye and asked, "Did you eat my chicken?" He just looked back at me and licked his lips. Eventually, I located the remains of my chicken under the refrigerator.

Although we didn't see a lot of cockroaches, they were around. We had a small water heater on the kitchen wall, and when we removed it, we discovered a cockroach nursery full of swarming baby cockroaches. We regularly sprayed for fleas and always had flies.

I tried to keep things off the floor because Amy especially liked to put things in her mouth. One day, I noticed something black in her mouth and scared us both when I screamed. It was a large beetle. After examination, it looked like it had been dead for a while. Another day, I killed a spider and then couldn't find it. Sure enough, I found it later in Amy's mouth. Somehow, she survived all this. Our worst experience was when she got a stomachache after eating a leaf off a tree outside. We went right to the doctor, who said she would be okay and told her sternly to not eat any more leaves.

Finally, I have to tell the rat story. This happened before the children were born. We were visiting American friends, and the wife and I were in the kitchen cooking. We had preheated the oven when the bottom door of the oven where trays were stored opened slowly by itself. We watched in horror as a huge rat came running out of the hot oven. We screamed and jumped up and down—trying to get out of its way. Our husbands in the other room couldn't imagine why we kept screaming until the rat raced into their room and dashed around the perimeter. The men took off in pursuit with a broom and emerged from another room singing a funeral dirge with a large dead rat in the dustpan. That was the only rat I remember seeing during our time in Egypt. Later, when we didn't live on the ground floor, we didn't see as many critters, and the only problem was the flies.

PETER IS BORN

≈

THE DUE DATE FOR OUR THIRD CHILD'S BIRTH CAME AND WENT—
following the pattern of Amy and Sara. I had several false labors, and
once, we went as far as taking Amy and Sara to our friends, Ray and
Gail. When the doctor sent us home, we went out to a movie. Ray and
Gail said it was a tricky way to get a babysitter. Finally, after about ten
days, the doctor induced labor. Amy and Sara had both been exactly
fourteen days late, and I wonder if things would have gone naturally
if we'd just waited a couple of days. The labor wasn't too bad, just
intense.

I can't remember if it was with Sara or with Peter, but the doctor—
also a professor at the university—heard about inclined labor tables and
tried it out on me. The only trouble was, he used a slanted vinyl table,
with no handles or any way to hold myself on. Trying to keep from
sliding off the slippery table while going through the most difficult
part of labor was just too much. I insisted they lay the table flat, and
it soon was.

As soon as Peter was born, the nurses celebrated—stripping off
their gloves and sterile clothing—even though I still needed cleaning
up. One person said that I had my boy and wouldn't be back again.
My status immediately went up. They now called me "The mother
of Peter," or Om Botros. *Botros* is the Arabic word for "Peter." Since
there is no P sound in Arabic, people would call him Beeter, so we told
our Egyptian friends he was Botros. We chose the name Peter after

Vance's father, who went by the name "Pete," even though his name was Elmer.

After we brought Peter home, I was changing his diaper one day when Lila happened to be in the room and was surprised that we really did have a boy. She thought we were just too embarrassed to admit we'd had another girl.

SUSTAINED IN SICKNESS

≈

The Lord will sustain him on his sickbed and restore him from his bed of illness. (Psalm 41:3)

I CAN'T REMEMBER BEING SICKER THAN I WAS WHEN PETER WAS THREE months old. Our family traveled to Cairo and then flew to the island of Cyprus for a staff conference. In Cairo, I came down with a fever. Once we arrived in Cyprus, I went to a doctor and received medicine that didn't help. The fever grew worse and even with the maximum amount of fever-reducing medicine, we couldn't get it below 104 degrees.

Everything seemed hazy as I lay in bed with Peter next to me. He was an easy, laid-back baby and seemed thrilled to have Mom available all the time. Drinking hot milk didn't bother him at all. Lynn—one of our coworkers who also was a nurse—often sat in the next room and kept checking on me. I thought I must be very sick for Lynn to be sitting in the next room. I went to a different doctor and got antibiotics. I had strep throat and tonsillitis. The fever lasted six days, and when I finally recovered, my friends at the conference gave me a big welcome. They had been praying. Even though I was so sick, I was never in distress and always felt cared for. God answered prayer, sustained me, and restored me.

ISAAC

≈

SACRIFICE AND DEDICATION CHARACTERIZED MOST OF THE TRAINEES who came to us. We often felt humbled and challenged by their willingness to risk their lives and health to reach their people. Isaac, a father from Sudan who left his wife and children for nine months of training in Egypt, was no exception.

We received the following letter from Isaac:

Dear Vance and Carol Nordman

I greeting you in the name of Jesus Christ our Savior. How is your daughters Immi and Sara? I hope they are well.

I am very sorry because I never wrote to you, maybe when you receive my letter you will amaze, and say that where I have been long time! Now I can tell you what happen with me.

I say to you more than eight months I was working with team of translation in our own language [New Testament] beside my work discipling others. I will never change my line or vision in order to fulfill the great Commission in Sudan. Now my ministry is better, praise the Lord. I train last year, and this year,

I train hundred and ten person to reach others using
4.L [Four Spiritual Laws]. And fifty of them now in my
group Concepts Booklets [The Transferable Concepts,
a Bible study course] We ask God to bless them.

Isaac had a large ministry reaching thousands of people in Sudan.
After years of fruitful work, we heard Isaac died of hepatitis in a hospital
in Sudan. Coworkers believed he had been intentionally mistreated
because of his influential ministry.

How privileged we felt to know such godly, joyful people like
Isaac. Any difficulties we experienced seemed so small in comparison
to their sacrifices.

PANIC ATTACK

≈

SOMETIMES, I HAVE TROUBLE OVERESTIMATING MY LIMITS. SOMETIMES, it's a matter of trial and error—especially in new situations. On May 3, 1988, I wrote home:

> Van is in the office late tonight. He's preparing for his traveling. He'll be gone one half of May and most of June, though he'll be in and out every ten days or so. I'm not having anyone stay with us this time. The children are old enough that they like to talk to me, and sometimes it's more stressful having someone else trying to talk to me too. I enjoy having evenings to myself too. We have neighbors upstairs if I need them and a phone and friends.

Amy was almost five, Sara three and a half, and Peter six months. I didn't expect that they would cut our phone off, and I didn't realize how tired I had become.

After Van left—and the phone was off—we were all in bed for a nap when I thought, *All the door handles and locks were up high. The girls couldn't reach them. What if something happened to me and they couldn't get out of the house?* There was no phone. My body became sweaty, my heart pounded and I, well, I panicked. Fortunately, I gathered up the children and drove across town to the home of missionary friends. The wife was home. She sent me to bed and watched my children. I slept and later realized just how tired I had become.

I learned several things from this unpleasant episode. First, I can't go it alone. I need others, and I need to accept help, especially from other believers. Second, Vance and I reevaluated his travel schedule. After talking with other families where the husband traveled, we determined he would travel no longer than two weeks at a time, with some time in between trips. He was handing over more of the Egyptian training to our staff and traveling to other countries in the area, helping them with training. Eventually, we would decide that if Vance was planning to travel a lot, I needed to be somewhere where I had more support.

I have never had another panic attack, thankfully. And I'm learning, through the years, that needing help from God and from others is not a bad thing. I am just a limited human being, and I need to accept my limits. As I depend on God's strength and allow others to help, together we are strong.

THROUGH A CHILD

≈

SOMETIMES, GOD SPEAKS THROUGH A CHILD. I SAW HIM SPEAK THROUGH Amy.

There wasn't a lot of grass in our city of Alexandria, but there was a place called the Sporting Club that had grassy fields and a playground. It was like a country club for the rich. Foreigners could also use it. In one corner were stables, and we paid a man to take the children on a horse around a ring.

One day at the Sporting Club, Amy saw a woman on the playground and wanted me to meet her. I could hardly see who was in the playground, as the grassy field between us and the playground was large. Amy kept insisting I talk to the lady.

As we reached the playground, my children ran to play with the woman's children, and I introduced myself. She told me her story, and I listened in wonder. She was a Catholic European who had married a Muslim Egyptian man. She couldn't tell her children about her faith in Jesus, or her husband's extended family would take them away from her. So she told them Bible stories but changed names and places. She planned to tell her children all the facts of the stories after they were old enough to keep it secret. I felt that our talk encouraged her, as she seemed to have little contact with Christians. I left amazed at God's leading. God would use Amy in the future in this way, and she still listens to his voice and follows him.

THE WEDDING RING

≈

Sometimes, God's care for the details of life amazes me. I saw this care when it came to Vance's wedding ring. He used to take off his ring when he washed his hands and sometimes put it in his pocket. One day—after a trip to Cairo—he realized he didn't have his wedding ring. We couldn't remember when he lost it and asked Lila if she had seen it. She was very offended, thinking we assumed she had stolen the ring because we asked her. We tried to reassure her we weren't accusing her of stealing.

Sometime later, we took another trip to Cairo—driving on the desert road and stopping at a roadside restaurant. We sat outdoors at one of the many tables scattered in the desert sand. As we had our meal, one waiter excitedly asked to see the ring on my finger. He examined it and hurried off. He soon returned with a female coworker, who was wearing Vance's wedding ring. The etchings are the same on our rings and the waiter had noticed it. Apparently, Vance's ring had fallen out of his pocket into the sand when we had stopped on our previous trip. The waiters found it in the sand. They graciously returned the ring—happy to have found the owner.

Vance lost the ring another time while we were on furlough in the United States. He thought he had left it in the bathroom at a campground in Arizona. We gave up all hope of seeing it again when, about a year later, back in Egypt, a visiting friend from America handed us the wedding ring. We finally solved this mystery by talking to Van's mom. Vance left the ring in the bathroom cupboard of the travel trailer we borrowed from the Nordman family. A cousin's wife found it when she was cleaning the trailer and gave it to Vance's mom. When Vance's mother learned about our friend coming to Egypt, she sent it with him to us. Vance doesn't take off his ring anymore when he washes his hands. And we are very grateful that God cares about the small things.

Perfect Timing

≈

In July 1988, things weren't going so well in our home in Egypt. We had given the landlord's son money to pay the phone bill. He pocketed the money and claimed we had never paid him. As a result, the phone bill was unpaid, and the phone permanently turned off. It had taken years to get the phone in the first place, as phones used to be very difficult to get at all.

Then, the ceiling in one room dripped water out of the chandelier, and a lot of plaster fell off. Since it was not uncommon for whole ceilings to collapse, this was very serious. The neighbor upstairs claimed the water was from our house—not his—even though we had no water in that part of the house.

We planned to leave for furlough in September and didn't want to move in July. Then the solution came when another missionary family left temporarily, and we moved into their home until our furlough. We packed everything except what we would travel with and stored the rest in a room below their home. So we were ready to go when the news came in August that Vance's father had passed away suddenly. We could make it back to the States on time for the funeral and be with the family. Looking back, we saw how all those unpleasant experiences in our home in Egypt had forced us to pack up early and be ready to go to America quickly. God's timing is always perfect.

SYRUP OF IPECAC

WHILE WE WERE IN THE STATES, WE SAW GOD'S PROTECTION OVER Peter, which led to protection for another child back in Egypt.

Peter learned to walk at Grandma Nordman's house in Merced. He loved to walk around the living room, holding the furniture for balance. When he came to Grandma's coffee cup with a small amount of cold coffee and milk in the bottom, he would indulge in a swig (I think Grandma left it just for him). Peter has been a coffee lover ever since!

One day, Peter came upon a purse and got into a bottle of salt tablets. We quickly discovered he had eaten a number of them and called poison control. This was a dangerous situation, and they advised us to search the neighborhood for syrup of ipecac. A lady across the street had some, so we gave it to Peter and sent him outside in the yard, where he wandered around until he threw up the salt tablets.

I decided that I would carry syrup of ipecac with me from then on. When we were back in Egypt, one of our trainees called from the hospital, saying his small son had swallowed something poisonous, and he was at the hospital. No one at the hospital knew what to do. Vance went to the hospital immediately with the syrup of ipecac and saved the boy's life. The hospital staff wanted to know what we had given him; hopefully, they have saved more lives at that hospital.

When I was a child, I swallowed a bottle of pills and had my stomach pumped. I hope this trend doesn't continue to future generations. We are all grateful for God's protection and for leading us to syrup of ipecac.

ON THE MOVE

≈

MISSIONARY FAMILIES KNOW FURLOUGH IS A VERY MOBILE TIME AND not vacation. We got the idea to haul a trailer while visiting supporters. We'd park in front of the home we were visiting, and when it was time for the children to go to bed, the kids and I would just go out in the trailer. Peter celebrated his first birthday on the beach in Southern California. We picked up a cake and drove the trailer down to the beach. Having a stable home for the kids made everything so much easier. After visiting supporters in Los Angeles, we drove the trailer to Phoenix, Arizona, where my parents had moved.

Visiting Grandma and Grandpa McMahon was a lot of fun. We stayed in their house, and Grandpa made up a game of "pick up the crumbs" to keep the carpet clean after meals. He made it fun—and the kids liked to play it. Grandma and Grandpa lived in Sun City West—a city for seniors. There was a recreation center with a miniature golf course, bowling alley, ping-pong, and a swimming pool. We all had a good time.

During our year in the States, Vance spent a month at Campus Crusade headquarters, finishing his master's degree. We also flew to Houston and visited friends and supporters. So life was full of travel and change but also full of fellowship with good friends and family. Finally—in August 1989—we were ready to return to Egypt, which had become our home.

FAITHFUL IS HE WHO CALLS YOU

≈

B ACK IN EGYPT, I WROTE IN A PRAYER LETTER:

> This week I found an old journal I'd kept eight years
> ago. What fun it was to read about our first experiences
> in Egypt! I was reminded of God's faithfulness in my
> life. God called me to work with Campus Crusade.
> Then He led Van and I together and brought us to
> Egypt. In answer to prayer, He gave us three wonderful
> children. I realized that He will continue to be faithful
> to help us fulfill our calling in the ministry and to raise
> our children.

> When we left Egypt last, I felt like something had to
> go. The combination of living in Egypt, having Van
> travel, and three small children seemed too much. But
> gently, steadily, God worked in my heart during our
> year in America. It was Egypt we were called back
> to. Van's job didn't change. I came back in faith—not
> knowing how I would manage.

Right away I felt blessed. We found a beautiful home, our maid returned three days a week (for only $40 per month!), and we found a fruit and vegetable store that delivers to our door. Also, we have an excellent babysitter who comes twice a week. Life in Egypt seemed much easier.

Van didn't have to travel nearly as much as I'd expected. We have been able to take some local trips with him, which has been so good for the children. Their lives are enriched by exposure to people from many countries and by visiting historical sites of ancient civilizations. These trips are also excellent for deepening family relationships.

I do feel God has met our needs according to His riches (Philippians 4:19). His faithfulness in the past will continue in the future—even if I can't see how it will happen.

A Place to Play

≈

Our third home in Egypt overlooked the city of Alexandria. High above the bustle of cars and the tram, we lived on the eleventh and twelfth floors, with an inside staircase between the floors. On the eleventh floor was a large living area, dining room, kitchen, office, and bathroom. We also had a balcony open to the sky as large as the living room and another balcony the size of a bedroom. On the twelfth floor were four bedrooms, a bathroom, and an open living area. One bedroom had a room-sized balcony with a roof above, and two bedrooms had small balconies. But there was no yard or a nearby park for the children to play in. Downstairs, the street was as busy as downtown New York. I wondered how to provide a safe play space for three small children.

I had seen an Egyptian movie on TV about a family with a small child. The little girl ran around the apartment and then to the balcony. In one horrifying instant, the child tumbled off the balcony onto the street below. These images etched themselves in my mind. Our balcony walls were only about four feet high. The windows also had no screens, and a climbing child could easily fall eleven or twelve floors to the street below.

Vance and I enjoyed the challenge of childproofing our new home to make it safe for our little family. Gardening has always been a favorite hobby, and I had found a nursery in the city. We placed pots of sharp cactus along the walls of the big outside balcony and window boxes of thorny cactus in the open windows. We had the opening in the covered upstairs balcony closed off with a chain-link fence from the balcony to the roof so the children could play on that balcony unsupervised. That balcony and the bedroom connected to it became the playroom.

Somehow, we got the idea of building a sandbox in the playroom balcony. I will always remember driving our little Fiat downtown to a store that sold sandbags and having them piled into the trunk. I didn't realize how heavy sand is and soon found myself with a flat tire. Vance wasn't with me, but I felt the Lord caring for me. Just when the tire went flat, I was driving by a tire store. They fixed the tire, and I drove home with the load of sand. In Egypt, the buildings have a man called the Boab. The Boab lives at the bottom of the building to watch it and to help tenants with things like carrying groceries. Even though he used the elevator, our Boab complained profusely about having to take so many bags of sand to the twelfth floor. He couldn't understand why this crazy foreign woman wanted bags of sand in her home.

Amy, Sara, and Peter, then five, four, and one, enjoyed their home in the sky. Each morning, Amy woke up early and sat on her balcony, listening to the call to prayer and the noises of the city and watching the sun rise over miles of buildings. Our home became a center for meetings and social times for the Egyptian and foreign staff members. All the children went upstairs to the playroom, and the adults met in the living room below. One rambunctious little boy loved playing around the edge of the big balcony. Soon I heard him howling with pain and crying about the big piece of cactus in his hand. Unfortunately, he left the cactus on Amy's balcony, and the next morning, instead of peacefully watching the sunrise, she found cactus embedded in the arch of her bare foot.

So no children fell off balconies. Many children enjoyed the playroom, sandbox, and the big balcony. I thank God for providing for the children in unexpected ways.

THE ZOO

≈

ONE OF OUR FAVORITE RECREATIONS AS A FAMILY WAS A VISIT TO THE Alexandria Zoo. In 1958, they built a beautiful zoo in Alexandria, but by the 1980s, it was in a sad state of disrepair, yet still a fun outing. We could feed the animals and get close to them and have a casual conversation with the zoo workers. A fun zone with a rickety-looking Ferris wheel and kiddie rides was always a treat, though I felt unsure about the safety of the Ferris wheel. We spent under ten dollars for the family to visit the zoo. This included entrance fee, ice cream, drinks, kiddie rides, and tips for the men who let us feed the animals. I usually packed a lunch, and we ate by the bird pond, where there was an open-air restaurant.

How can we forget giving carrots to the giraffe? At first, he took them from our hand, but over the years, as he aged and drooled, we had to leave his carrots on the fence and stand back to avoid his slobbery drool. There is nothing like gazing into the open mouth of a hippopotamus five feet below and dropping food onto his tongue or standing right next to a seal and holding a wet fish. But we had to be careful of the lion cage. The bars were spaced far enough apart for an escaped child to extend an arm into. The zookeepers enjoyed making the lions roar for the crowd.

You can see a video of the zoo at the link below, including feeding the giraffe, hippopotamus and other animals, walking in the cages and also seeing the lions, just like we did in the 1980s.

http://www.youtube.com/watch?v=Q673sxnXP6A

AMY FEEDING THE GIRAFFE AT THE ALEXANDRIA ZOO

TOURISTS?

≈

ALMOST NINE YEARS HAD PASSED SINCE WE FIRST ARRIVED IN EGYPT ON tourist visas. Although we worked under the Presbyterian Church in Egypt, we never could get a missionary visa. Finally—in January 1990—we visited Egypt's most famous tourist sites.

Peter was two, Sara five, and Amy six and a half when we attended the first annual student winter break conference in Luxor, Egypt. Over sixty staff and students came from all over Egypt. Two staff from one of the largest Campus Crusade campus ministries in the United States came as the main speakers. Other ministry leaders came from the States as well. Our family met the Americans in Cairo, where we saw the pyramids and went for an hour-long camel ride. (I have not learned how to ride a camel without getting a raw bottom. There must be a trick!) Then we boarded the sleeper train for the fourteen-hour trip south to Luxor.

I oversaw childcare for ten children, and we all had a wonderful time. We studied the life of Joseph, learned about hieroglyphics, and looked for them on the walls of ancient tombs. We had so much fun with all the students, who loved being with the children. As our large group crossed the Nile on a ferry and left the narrow green valley to explore ancient tombs on the edge of a vast desert, the students took care of the children. They loved to carry the kids on their shoulders and entertain them. We felt like one big, extended family. Other days we marveled at huge columns in rows at Karnak and enjoyed a sound and light show and visited King Tut's tomb and coffin.

At the end of the conference, we had many encouraging comments by the students. Our faith was strengthened, friendships were renewed, and finally, Vance and I could say we had visited Egypt's most famous tourist sites on our tourist visas.

RANDY

≈

WHAT AN AMAZING GROUP OF PEOPLE SERVE AS OVERSEAS MISSIONARIES. In our city in Egypt, we had three organizations represented by about fifteen missionaries from the United States and Europe. We all attended the small international church, and the missionaries took turns preaching, until the Lord provided a full-time pastor after several years. There was an abundance of little girls Amy and Sara's age, along with other children. Birthday parties were always happy, noisy events in this close community. There were no big issues in these families, like rebellion or divorce. Usually, those things made it too difficult to stay on the mission field.

One family I highly respected had served in the area for many years. They had a large family, and one day, I heard some difficult news. Their thirteen-year-old son, Randy, died in a skateboarding accident. I guess I identified with Randy, partly because he had red hair. I had known him since he was seven, and his sisters often played with Amy and Sara. I went by myself to Randy's memorial service downtown. At least two hundred people were there—both foreigners and Egyptians. I found myself moved to tears and left the building sobbing uncontrollably; I walked around downtown until I felt composed enough to call a taxi.

But I found the knowledge that Randy had recently given his life to Jesus comforted me. Then we heard the most amazing story: A family of Europeans who were part of our mission community were back home in Europe. The wife had a dream a week before Randy died. In her dream, Randy had died from a skateboarding accident and she saw him all dressed in white. She hadn't wanted to say anything and alarm Randy's family—so she hadn't told them. We were all comforted with the thought God was in control and that Randy was with the Lord.

MANILA

≈

IN THE SUMMER OF 1990, AROUND SIX THOUSAND CHRISTIANS—MOSTLY
Campus Crusade for Christ staff—came from around the world to
Manila, in the Philippines. The purpose was to provide vision, training,
and practical experience to reach a city for Christ. Our family arrived
early to prepare for the Middle East delegation, which included twenty
Egyptians, ten Sudanese, nine Jordanians, six Lebanese, thirteen
Americans, and twenty-two from other countries.

From the beginning, we and others felt the spiritual battle. The
organizers had many odd problems. We were no exception. But we also
enjoyed many comforts. Our family had a real house with a walled-in
yard. It was the home of missionaries on furlough. Two maids even
came with the house. One did laundry. Our clothes disappeared from
the laundry basket and returned clean, folded, and ironed. The other
maid was a Bible school student and took care of everything else. Every
morning, we awoke to find breakfast on the table, which included
fresh pineapple. The Philippines had big malls and chain restaurants.
Sometimes, it felt like America, except for the weather. It was always
warm, and violent rainstorms often hit suddenly and then disappeared.
Life was everywhere. It seemed every inch of ground had plants or
bugs or something living.

Amy (seven), Sara (five and a half), Peter (two and a half), and I
spent happy days exploring. I brought home every kind of fruit from
the grocery store I'd never seen before to try. The maids told us what

they were. We studied plants and pressed them between waxed paper. We visited museums, and the children played in our yard in the warm rain. The girls took ballet lessons with Filipino children. People spoke English. Living in the Philippines was fun.

Sometimes, I got to visit the big meetings and hear from great Christian leaders. Mostly, I was with the children. With no cooking or housework, we learned about and explored the world around us. Even with the many problems we saw God deliver us from, our family had much to enjoy and appreciate during our summer in Manila.

Our family arrived in the home of missionaries on furlough late at night. We excitedly explored the two-story house, complete with rooms set up for children. Loud exclamations brought Vance and I hurrying to a child's room. Our kids had discovered a giant black beetle. It was late, and we were tired; we found a glass in the kitchen and just placed it over the beetle. The next morning, we realized it had been long dead and probably belonged to one of the children on furlough. This was the beginning of our experiences with insects in the tropics.

I found a book on tropical bugs and decided it would be a good idea to read up on them. So I was feeling alarmed from the book when I opened the door to our bathroom and there—in the sink—loomed a huge centipede. In my mind, it was a foot long, with thousands of wiggling legs as it reared up from the sink. I screamed and slammed the door. Recovering, I opened the door, and it had disappeared. That was worse. Where did it go? In the hamper? Under the sink? I carefully searched, unsuccessfully. Vance thought perhaps it had gone back down the drain, and he sprayed insect poison in that direction. I left a jar and a wooden spoon by the sink. Our house maid said we shouldn't worry. If we got bit, we should just go to the doctor and get a shot so we wouldn't get sick. Out in the jungle—where she was from—they were bigger and swam in rivers. Ugh! About a week later, I discovered the centipede again in the sink; I quickly killed it with the spoon and deposited it in the jar. It was only three inches long and about as thick as a pencil.

Cockroaches loved the humid climate and scurried on our floors at night. Every night, the housemaid dusted the concrete patio outside with cockroach powder, and every morning, we awoke to her sweeping up the dead roaches. There must have been hundreds every morning. One day, Amy and Sara were swinging in the yard when they saw a huge spider. Amy said it was gray and fuzzy, with a body as big as a hand. The housemaid came and hit it with the stick end of the broom but couldn't kill it. She finally chased it away.

One day, a huge moth about five inches across perched gracefully in our tree—displaying beautiful wings. We took pictures and then got out paper and drew pictures. We also enjoyed the chameleons on the inside walls of our home. They were so interesting to watch as they changed color to match their surroundings.

The peskiest bugs were the mosquitoes. Amy and Peter were most susceptible and ended up with about one hundred bites apiece. I had to take them to the doctor and get a special cream I applied to each bite several times a day. This was a long process but kept away infections. They are still sensitive to mosquitoes. We learned a lot about insects that summer, and I felt grateful that I usually lived in a dry climate without many bugs.

About a week after we arrived in the Philippines, my lips tingled, then slowly, my face swelled on one side until even my eye was swollen shut. We went to a local clinic, and the doctor put me in the hospital. He was concerned that my throat would swell until I couldn't breathe. It wasn't safe to spend the night alone in the hospital. I can't remember why exactly. Our housemaid who was the Bible college student went the second mile and stayed with me in the hospital at night and took care of our family by day. I am so grateful the Lord sent her to help us.

For three days, I went through many tests to discover the cause of the swelling. Drinking castor oil to clean out my bowels was the worst. I now appreciate the suffering of young children who used to drink castor oil as a punishment or a tonic. It is so greasy. It felt like swallowing something that should lubricate a car. The swelling subsided by itself, and the cause remained a mystery. They finally sent me home with a syringe I could use to inject myself if the swelling returned and I couldn't breathe.

One day, when we were visiting a new church, the swelling returned. There I was, with one eye swollen shut. I kept telling people I didn't normally look so strange. Then, I discovered that when I ate a mango, my lips tingled. I remembered I had eaten mangoes both times before my face swelled. I love mangoes but have stayed away from them since, and the swelling has never returned.

Amy, Sara, and Peter enjoyed playing with children in the play areas of fast-food restaurants. Then, they encouraged us to meet the parents. That was how we met Ellen. As we sat and talked, we told her about Jesus. She prayed and gave her heart to him right in the restaurant. Ellen gave me her husband's card. He held an important legal position in Manila.

Another time, we were shopping in a grocery store. Amy saw an American woman and encouraged me to meet her. I discovered her name was Anne, and she also worked on the staff of Campus Crusade but with executives. As I told Anne about Ellen, she suggested Van and I invite Ellen and her husband to an evangelistic dinner for executives and government personnel. Ellen and her husband came to the dinner, saw his boss and several coworkers there, and enjoyed it very much. A lawyer was sitting to my left, and he had a lot of questions. While Ellen watched, I shared the Four Spiritual Laws with him, and he also prayed to receive Christ. What a chain of events began with our children encouraging us to meet people.

In July, a 7.8 magnitude earthquake struck the city of Luzon. In Manila, Vance, Amy, and Sara were visiting friends of ours in an apartment building. Amy remembers being in the bathroom washing her hands when the water from the sink moved back and forth. They all ran outside. I was shopping in a bookstore with Peter, holding books, an umbrella, and him. The room shook, and the ceiling made strange noises. I knew I had to put something down and remember thinking, *Put down the books, hold on to Peter.* There was nothing to get underneath, so we followed everyone else downstairs and onto the street. People were everywhere. Later, we heard almost one thousand people had died in a mountain resort, where the people ran outside a building and thought it was safe, so they went back in. Then the building collapsed.

I think it was the next day that the children and I went to a local mall. We arrived early, and the mall was still closed, so I got a newspaper to read. On the front page was an apology for the small size of the paper. The offices of the newspaper were near the seacoast, and they thought there might be a tidal wave. Vance was at the conference, also near the coast. Fortunately, the tidal wave never came.

That summer, we had a terrorist threat against Americans. We all stayed home for a few days until the situation improved. Our ministry sent young people coming from America to a Thailand mission trip instead of coming to the Philippines.

Later, we had to move from our house and stayed awhile in a hotel. I was with the children when I heard gunfire outside. We were about four floors above the street. Down below, I watched what looked like a movie scene. Gunmen were holding up an armored car, and people everywhere lay flat on the ground to avoid being shot. The gunmen removed a sack from the armored car and threw it into the trunk of another car. Finally, the thieves drove off, and people got back up. Egypt felt much safer than the Philippines. That summer, amazing things were happening in the many ministries, and there was also a lot of opposition.

God was at work bringing many to himself in Manila. Every day, our Egyptian delegation had to walk down a street by the port to get to the hotel where the conference was held. Prostitutes also were on this street, looking for business. This distressed our friends until our women talked to the prostitutes about Jesus. At least one prostitute came to the Lord through an Egyptian student.

All the delegates had ministry assignments in different parts of Manila. One Sudanese disciple of Vance's came home every day from sharing his faith exhausted, but with a big smile on his face. He drifted off to sleep every night, telling his roommate of all those he saw pray to receive Christ that day. Hosni, one of our North African friends who had been in prison in Egypt, shared his testimony and gave an evangelistic presentation in a college classroom. He saw many indicate decisions. One group of our delegates had to ride in the back of a jeep—breathing exhaust—in the crowded Manila traffic for an hour and a half to get to their campus. After a couple of days of this, they complained and asked that their campus ministry assignment be changed. Their leader encouraged them to trust God with this situation. Later, Vance arranged another campus for them, but they said they were so encouraged by how God was using them they wanted to keep their campus, despite the difficulty getting there.

In August, at the end of the project, our family took time to relax. We stayed at a resort on the coast recommended by friends. Nestled in a tropical paradise, we had our own small house on a bluff, overlooking the ocean. We called for a jeepney—an elongated jeep with seats on both sides open to the air and covered with a roof. The jeepney took us wherever we wanted to go in the resort. Amy and Sara rode horses, we all swam in a saltwater pool fed by a waterfall, and we strolled along the ocean, looking down at sea crabs and long skinny fish with bright green noses and tails. I lay in a hammock under a coconut tree, gazing up at coconuts and across the ocean to distant mountains covered with lush vegetation. We saw a man fishing with a net and then a snail three inches long. Flowers bloomed all around, and lush vines with leaves three feet long wound up a tree.

For lunch, we relaxed in a restaurant open to the sea on one side and drank coconut juice—served in the coconut. A cage of parakeets kept us entertained. One day, we took a ride in a glass-bottom boat. Vance, Amy, Sara, and I snorkeled near the boat—amazed at the colorful coral, starfish, and tropical fish. I will never forget this refuge of beauty and rest. God has refreshed us many times in life beyond what we would have asked for, proving again the truth of His promise, "Come to me, all who are weary and heavy-laden, and I will give you rest" (Matthew 11:28).

God's timing isn't always what I would choose. I like everything ready ahead of time, with extra flex built into the schedule, just in case. More than once, things have come together just in time. I hope that eventually, I can learn to relax when this happens and trust that God has everything under control.

At the resort, Peter came down with an ear infection, and it was almost time to fly back to Egypt. On the day of the flight, we were in a mall in Manila, and I saw a sign for an ear clinic. They couldn't help us but recommended another clinic. Taking a taxi, our family stopped at the clinic on the way to the airport. We discussed where Peter and I could stay in Manila if the ear infection prevented him from flying. I didn't like the idea of being left behind in the Philippines. While the rest of the family waited in the taxi, I hurried Peter into the doctor's office to discover a long line of patients. I appealed to them—saying I had to catch a plane—and they graciously allowed me to go in next to see the doctor. He examined Peter and said he was okay to fly. We ran out of the office, jumped into the waiting taxi, rushed to the airport, and, with great relief, all got on the plane.

Our flight plan to Egypt took us through Germany. We arrived early in the morning and had time before our next flight, so we took the children to a park where they could run around. I sat on a bench watching Peter play when a German lady came up and talked to him. He was two and a half. He patiently listened to her go on and on in German. When she finally left, I heard him muttering to himself as he walked by that he only spoke English.

A Change
of Plans

≈

Back in Egypt, Vance and I lay in bed one night, talking about the future. The training center was staffed mostly by Egyptians, and the curriculum was translated and being taught in Arabic. We knew neither of us were good managers. Our strengths lay in setting things up until they were running well. From tests we had taken with Campus Crusade and from experience, we knew once things were going, it was best to turn them over to a skilled manager and put our energy into beginning something new.

That night as we talked, we asked ourselves what we would do if we could do anything we wanted. We both agreed that we'd like to set up another training center. Training young believers to reach their own people with the Gospel was so rewarding. We felt like the apostle Paul, planting ministries. We wondered where in the world a new training center might be needed. Campus Crusade had already established training centers in so many countries.

Then an idea occurred to us. Vance had made a new friend when he was buying bread in a fancy new bakery in Alexandria. This friend was unusual because he was Russian. Mikhail Gorbachev had instituted glasnost and perestroika ("openness and restructuring" in Russian) in the USSR. So in 1990, there was more freedom for Soviet citizens to interact with Westerners, and it was possible for us to get to know our new Russian friend. We enjoyed dinner with Vance's friend and his wife and wondered if there could be a need to set up a training center in their country. Things were changing. After seventy years of atheistic oppression and being cut off from the rest of the world, could the doors finally be opening? We would check it out on our next furlough. We never expected the unusual chain of events that soon took place.

> The mind of man plans his way, but the LORD directs
> his steps. (Proverbs 16:9)

In the fall of 1990, Vance planned to visit the States for a month of meetings to work on standardizing Campus Crusade training curriculum for new staff worldwide. Also, my parents wanted to visit us in Egypt for their fiftieth wedding anniversary in January. As we prepared for these events, news broke out of an impending war in the Arabian Gulf. Though we were far from the Gulf, we were still in the area, and the situation looked unpredictable. My parents thought it best not to come to Egypt, and Vance didn't relish leaving his family. Finally, we decided the whole family should go with Vance to America so he could attend the meetings and we could celebrate with my parents.

All went along well in America, until we got ready to return to Egypt after Christmas. During a routine test, the doctor found a growth on my cervix and sent it for a biopsy. But the results wouldn't be back until after we had returned to Egypt. Then I got sick with a fever. The doctor thought it could turn into a brain infection. I lay there in bed, with the departure time fast approaching. We had unchangeable tickets. Our pastor came and anointed me with oil and prayed for healing. The airlines refused to change our tickets. Finally, we put the family in Vance's brother Clay's motor home and drove from Merced to the San Francisco airport. I lay on a bed in the back— still with a fever. Vance planned to show me to the airlines and ask if they wanted me to fly in that condition. On the way to the airport, we got a call that the airlines had agreed to change the tickets. Back in

Merced, problems related to my health quickly vanished. The growth was benign, the fever went away, and I felt fine.

As we prepared to leave for Egypt on our new departure date of January 8, we encountered another roadblock. We received a fax from the office of the international vice president of Campus Crusade, asking us to delay our departure until after January 15. Then the Gulf War began, and our leadership stopped us indefinitely from returning to Egypt. Fortunately, the airlines agreed to reschedule our "unchangeable" tickets to some indefinite time. We wondered what the Lord had in mind for us next.

OUT OF THE CAVE

≈

I'VE FOUND THAT GOD GIVES US GRACE TO DO WHAT HE CALLS US TO DO. Egypt was not an easy place to live. Physically, life just took more time and effort. Culturally, the Middle East differs greatly from the United States. And as Christians, we were under surveillance and lacked many freedoms we take for granted in America. Yet we were happy and content in Egypt. It felt like home.

During our unexpected stay in America, our family visited nearby Yosemite National Park. We bicycled in Yosemite Valley, with soaring granite cliffs towering above us. Waterfalls fell from high above down steep rock faces. We attended church in a little chapel nestled among the pines. I believe God used the message that morning to speak to my heart. I can't remember the scripture, but the illustration remains imprinted upon my mind. We can compare life to hiking up a mountain. Partway up, we find a cave and rest. We felt tired and God provided that cave to rest in. But we aren't meant to live in the cave. We need to go out and finish climbing the mountain. There is a great view from the top. I felt like we had become comfortable living in Egypt. Everything was set up and running. We had a nice house with lots of helpers. We were resting comfortably in a cave. But God was calling us to come out to climb the mountain again. We sensed a new challenge ahead requiring us to trust God for grace.

RUSSIA?

≈

W HEN WE RETURNED TO THE STATES TO ATTEND THE CONFERENCE, WE had arrived a few days early so we could celebrate Thanksgiving with family. Vance contacted a friend in the International Training Office to see if there was a possibility of us helping start a training center in Russia after our term in Egypt was completed. He told Vance he happened to be traveling to Austria in a few days to meet with a staff team that, to our surprise, had moved into Russia the month before.

When Vance went to the training conference in Southern California, he talked with our friend, who had returned from talking with the Russia team. They said there was a need and asked if we could come as soon as possible. At this point, we told them we could not, as we had another year to finish our term in Egypt; however, once we were unable to return to Egypt due to the Gulf War, we decided to look into moving to Russia.

So, Vance and I planned a trip to Moscow to check out the situation and talk further with the team that had recently moved there. We also needed to know more about the living situation and schooling for the children. We left the children with Grandma Nordman and flew to Moscow just in time for Easter.

PROVISION
IN ZURICH

≈

GOD'S PROVISION OFTEN COMES IN UNEXPECTED PLACES AND UNEXPECTED ways. In San Francisco, the night before the plane trip to Moscow, I got sick with a sinus infection. We flew the next day to Zurich, Switzerland, and my ears were hurting as the airplane descended. I decided I had to do something before flying the next day to Moscow. It was evening, and the possibility of finding a doctor looked slim. We asked at our hotel, and to our surprise, they directed us to a nearby ear clinic that was still open. Then, we had the problem of language. Again, God provided when we met an Arabic speaker who helped us navigate the clinic. The problem turned out to be wax in my ears, which they quickly removed. The following day, we flew on to Moscow, and my ears were fine. We couldn't have imagined an evening ear clinic near our hotel with an Arabic speaker to help us. God has continually provided medical care when we've needed it.

MIRACLES IN MOSCOW

≈

W<small>E NEVER EXPECTED TO HEAR</small> "C<small>HRIST IS</small> R<small>ISEN</small>" <small>IN WHAT</small> P<small>RESIDENT</small> Reagan called the Evil Empire. Vance and I grew up during the Cold War—taking cover under our desks in school during drills in case Russia attacked America. Russia was an atheist country, and they persecuted Christians. Russia was the enemy.

When we arrived in Moscow in April 1991, the snow had melted, and everything was damp, brown, and barren. Huge blocks of dreary-looking apartment and government buildings lay in organized masses among evergreens and leafless trees. The American team director picked us up from the airport in a Russian Fiat, and we drove through the city's streets. We noticed colorful banners across the streets and asked what they said. He sounded amazed as he told us they said, "Christ Is Risen." He had lived in Russia for several years and this was the first time he had ever seen a Christian holiday officially recognized. More incredible still was the Christian concert to be held in—of all places—the Kremlin, the seat of the atheist, Communist government. We attended the concert, which was also broadcast nationwide on television, and listened as Bill Bright, the president of Campus Crusade for Christ, told the audience about Christ, who died for them, and gave people an opportunity to receive him.

Later that week, Vance and I joined a couple of the staff to follow up a new Christian at Moscow State University—one of the top universities in the USSR. We attended a Christian jazz concert put on by the Campus Crusade Music Ministry. We then visited a meeting of about one hundred students gathered at the university. They met weekly to sing Christian songs, hear a study on John's Gospel, and join in discussion groups. God was moving in great ways in Russia, and the doors were swinging open after being tightly shut for seventy years. After seeking the Lord in prayer, Vance and I felt God leading us to step through the open doors and set up a new school to train national staff from the USSR.

A Letter from Vance to Our Children

≈

July 1991

Dear Amy, Sara, and Peter,

I love you very much, and I want to give you the best life possible. I am convinced that the best way I can do that is by being obedient to God's leading in my life. Several years before you were born, your mother and I each individually chose to give up our own personal ambitions and to give our lives wholly to Christ.

> If Christ be God and died for me there is nothing too great that I can do for him. (C. T. Studd)

We don't see this as a great sacrifice but are convinced that there is great reward in following Christ in this life as well as the next. Our experience has also proven this to be true, as God has blessed us so much. One of these blessings has been you.

"He is no fool who gives up what he cannot keep to gain what he cannot lose." Jim Elliot

When we left America for Egypt several years ago, your mother and I were in agreement on our call and realized that there would be sacrifices we would have to make if we lived outside America. We have also found benefits from living overseas, not only for us but for you as well. Now we are moving to Moscow in the USSR. Unfortunately, you were not involved in our decision to follow Christ nor to live outside America. Nor are you having a say in our decision to move to Moscow, although one of the main reasons we made this decision was that we thought it would be better for you.

You are probably too young to understand what is happening in the USSR today. The next 10 to 20 years will reshape the face and heart of Russian society, and we have the privilege of influencing the outcome of this change. Any sacrifices you will make will be investments in a new Russia and will mean that millions of people who never heard about Jesus will have a chance to. There will be thousands and thousands more people in heaven when you get there because you lived in Moscow.

You are growing up now. It is no longer just Mom and me moving to a new country. This time, we are all moving. We want to go to Moscow as a family working together to tell them about Jesus. I am praying that you will see that God isn't calling your mom and I to go to Moscow but that He is calling you to go to Moscow also and that He has a plan to use you to bring His love to the Russian people. You may have to make some sacrifices, but whatever you give up, God will return to you one hundred times over (Mark 10:29–30). If it is hard for you sometimes, remember that Russia and the whole world will be a better place because of what you are doing.

I love you very much,
Dad

Moving to the Soviet Union

≈

W E HAD ABOUT THREE MONTHS TO RAISE SEVERAL THOUSAND DOLLARS and get our family of five ready to move to the far north. Moscow has about seven months of snow each year. Our family had never lived with snow. I remembered visiting a Russian school in Moscow where the young children were discussing the month of May in English. One little girl said, "In May, the sky is blue." I wondered, the sky isn't usually blue? I would discover it wasn't. We were going to a different climate than sunny California and Egypt. They advised us to purchase winter clothing before traveling to Moscow, but where does one find winter clothes during the summer in central California? God provided all the funds we needed, and I found catalogs that had winter clothes on sale. I thought of buying maroon-colored down coats in several sizes for the children. Peter and the girls could wear maroon and pass the coats down as they outgrew them. Poor Sara would later bemoan her unmatched outfit of a maroon coat, aqua scarf, and bright red hat.

Apartments in Moscow were tiny, and they recommended bunk beds, which were unavailable in Moscow. Vance built a shipping crate so we could send the bunk beds and other items by sea. He built it on a trailer for towing a car, which we parked in the driveway of Grandma Nordman's house. We brought everything we planned to ship to the front lawn to pack. The neighbors watched these interesting events, and Judy laughed when she saw our large pile and smaller crate. But Vance is an efficient packer, and it all fit. Finally, we drove to the port in San Francisco with the ominous letters "USSR" stamped conspicuously on both sides of the crate on the trailer. As the crate left on its way by boat to the USSR, we prepared to fly back to Egypt to pack and say goodbye.

Emotion rose inside me as we prepared to leave Egypt. I felt much more attached than I'd realized and leaving was agony. I wrote this poem in July 1991:

Grieving

Grieving, grieving, grieving.
Packing up and leaving.
Leaving to others the work we've begun,
as a father passes his work to his son.
Of their world we are no longer a part,
but we'll carry their love along in our hearts.
The memories are too many to count,
and packing to leave, I feel sadness mount.
It's sadness mingled with joy for I know,
that as we part, it's so we'll both grow.
As we step out in faith, the adventure goes on,
and we press toward the goal, and the prize and the dawn,
when we'll see the Lord's face, and he tells us, "Well done."
In that home there's no parting,
we're together as one.

We filled July 15 until August 10 of 1991 with packing and goodbyes in Egypt. The staff gave us a going-away party and a beautiful silver platter. They felt they were sending us out as their missionaries to Russia. Then, just as we were ready to fly north, all the children caught the chicken pox. Amy had it the worst, and we spent some itchy days.

Finally, we were ready to go on August 14 and took our thirty-two pieces of luggage—which were mostly boxes—to the Cairo airport. Amy was eight, Sara six and a half, and Peter three and a half. Amy and Sara helped push the luggage carts piled with our boxes. We could only see the moving luggage carts as the piled boxes hid the little girls.

We were flying on the Russian airline—Aeroflot—on a plane that had just arrived from Ethiopia. They didn't get the message we had arranged with the airline to bring thirty-two pieces of luggage. They doubted they would all fit on the plane. Finally, we checked all the luggage and prepared for the flight, hoping that all our boxes would arrive with us. Moscow is only a four-hour flight north from Cairo. We passed over countries we'd never flown over, and the climate changed from a hot, dry desert to a cool, rainy forest. It was with mixed feelings we said goodbye to our home of ten years.

EIGHT
EVENTFUL DAYS

≈

THE FIRST DAY

O UR FAMILY STEPPED OFF THE PLANE IN MOSCOW AT 8 P.M. ON AUGUST 14, 1991, my father's birthday. The process seemed so easy. As we waited at the baggage claim area, unsure whether our luggage had arrived with us, they surprised us when our thirty-two pieces of luggage were the first items to appear on the carousel. We packed our bags on several luggage carts. The customs agents waved us and our carts past the x-ray machines normally used to check incoming luggage. We entered the Soviet Union—a Communist country—with no problems.

The handful of Campus Crusade for Christ staff in Moscow had arranged a bus to take us and our luggage to our new apartment. Officially, we entered the Soviet Union under a new cultural program set up by Gorbachev as part of his Perestroika program. A cultural exchange cooperative invited us and found apartments for us.

Moscow was full of wide, tree-lined streets and few cars. Huge, dreary high-rises with thousands of small apartments rose in semicircles around central areas containing a few functional-looking stores, schools, and other public buildings. The structures reminded me of those on a military base. Our apartment, on the seventh floor of a massive rectangular building on the outskirts of Moscow, was conveniently located near Leninsky Prospekt, a major Moscow boulevard leading from the outskirts of town to the Kremlin. We found ourselves and all our luggage quickly stowed in a furnished two-bedroom apartment. There was a closed-circuit radio in the kitchen that played only an official government station.

I looked out the window one evening and was surprised to see fireworks. We all enjoyed the show and wondered what it was all about. Later, when we asked our Russian neighbors what the occasion was, they said they didn't know but thought it was probably some military holiday. We ended our first night after finding beds for the five of us; we slept, full of new impressions and curious to explore.

THE SECOND DAY: FINDING FOOD

On the second day, our family unpacked a few boxes and piled into a taxi for a five-hour shopping trip. The total cost of the taxi for five hours was six dollars. We visited a foreign store and bought three small bags of food for eighty dollars. Then we visited the *rynok* (open market), where we purchased fruits, vegetables, cheese, a beef roast, smoked ham, honey, and other items. We filled up the taxi trunk and spent less than twenty dollars. We learned to avoid the foreign markets as much as possible.

The rynok was fun and resembled a local farmer's market. We all enjoyed the free tastes of different cheeses and honey. Because of the long winter, they pickled many vegetables for preservation. People especially seemed to take pride in their pickled mushrooms. Though they were never my favorite, I still enjoyed them. With the apartment stocked with food, we went to sleep, looking forward to exploring our surroundings the following day.

THE THIRD DAY:
EXPLORING THE NEIGHBORHOOD

The handful of Campus Crusade for Christ staff living in Moscow were spread all over the southern half of the vast city—so our family explored our neighborhood on our own. Our contact with our fellow staff was often limited to the telephone. We assumed we could not live close to each other because renting apartments was such a new thing. Most Russians waited for years to get an apartment. Our sponsors were renting apartments from the residents who then had to find other accommodations—generally with relatives. Under Communism, they strictly regulated contact with foreigners. However, with the new policies of Mikhail Gorbachev, glasnost and perestroika, things were changing. As a result, they allowed our team to live among the general Russian population.

Outside our apartment building, we discovered the post office and—to our joy—an Arab sandwich restaurant across the street. The clerk at the cash register only spoke Russian, but fortunately, the cook was from Syria and spoke Arabic. We could speak to him in Arabic, and he translated for the clerk. We knew little Russian, and few people spoke English, so we were happy that at least we could purchase familiar fast food nearby. I had studied Russian in college, and that helped. Local stores didn't seem to offer much, and for a long time, we wondered where people got their food. Many people had food sources at work and root cellars in the countryside, where they stored the vegetables they grew themselves during summer.

Our children were most excited about what lay across the street from us—a vast park filled with birch and pine trees. They left landscaping to nature in Moscow, which gave it a natural beauty. Meadows with wildflowers, birds, and butterflies, and acres of trees, surrounded the massive utilitarian apartment blocks. They filled the forest park with trails and surprises. Around a corner would be a playground or wooden bridge or a wooden playhouse to climb on. Squirrels and birds entertained us. We could easily get lost—especially off the trails. In winter, these trails turned into cross-country ski trails and walking trails. My favorite thing is being outside in nature, so Moscow was turning out to be a lovely place for me.

THE FOURTH DAY: GORKY PARK

On the fourth day, our family took the bus from outside of our apartment building two stops to the subway. Then we traveled about five stops on the subway to a huge park called Gorky Park. It contained two lakes and was so big we only saw half of it in three and a half hours. The children had a lot of fun riding on carnival rides, bikes, and horses. We ate shish kebabs and ice cream, and tried barbecue beef with Russian bread, gingerbread, and fruit juice. Amy will never let me forget telling her that the bags of colored fluff she insisted were cotton candy were pot scrubbers. I guess I had seen pot scrubbers that looked like those colored, square bags, probably in Egypt. We discovered later that Amy was right. They contained cotton candy. The cost of the day, including transportation, rides, and food for the entire family, was less than five dollars.

THE FIFTH DAY: CHURCH

Our fifth day in Moscow was a Sunday, and we visited the international church, which had several hundred people attending weekly. It was truly international, as people from many countries met to worship. Especially noticeable were the Africans, who had a passionate love for Jesus. African students had received college scholarships to study in Moscow, and for many, it was their best chance to get a college education, even if they didn't believe in Communism. As a result, there were a number of African Christian college students. In the past, these students could not attend the church because it met in the US Embassy compound. The Moscow Protestant Chaplaincy was established after negotiations between Roosevelt and Stalin. Stalin had agreed to grant a visa for a pastor and promised to give the church land on which to build. They never fulfilled the second promise, so the church had to meet on the embassy grounds. This made it difficult for many non-Americans to attend. During Mikhail Gorbachev's changes, the church could move outside the embassy to the international school, and Christian college students were freer to worship openly. We not only had African Christian college students in attendance but also African diplomats.

Later, I wrote home on September 28, 1992:

> We enjoy our international church here—there are about 500 people I'm guessing—from all over the world. There are many Africans. Recently the church has taken on a new ministry to help Somalian refugees who have come to Moscow with nothing. About one thousand refugees have contacted our church for help with food, housing, and medical care. There have been thousands of dollars donated for help with this, but the need is so much greater. Our church also provides hot meals for over one thousand senior citizens in Moscow daily and donates food to foreign students studying here. We really enjoy the church, as it has a finger on the pulse of human need here—and there is such a variety of people who go there. We meet missionaries from many groups as well as embassy people, military people, businesspeople, etc. Van helps teach Junior High Sunday School.

At different times, I taught Sunday school and especially enjoyed singing in the choir. I will never forget all walking to the front of the church in a line to receive Communion. It felt like heaven, with so many races and nationalities all worshiping together. The Africans were especially passionate. At the end of the service, we all joined hands and closed with an African song.

Church in Moscow felt like a foretaste of heaven, with people from everywhere gathered before the Lord. It blessed us to be a part of the body of Christ during those historic days in Moscow.

The Sixth Day: The Collapse Begins

On Monday, August 19, 1991, we awoke to the news on BBC Radio that the Kremlin had announced that Mikhail Gorbachev was unable to perform his presidential duties due to illness. It sounded like a political illness to Vance, so he immediately called our director in Moscow, who hadn't yet heard the news. We then called Vance's mother to let everyone know we were fine and were happy to find the international phone lines were up. Looking out our window, everything seemed normal in our neighborhood, with people boarding buses for work as usual. We had prearranged for a taxi to take our family shopping downtown to buy fur hats for the winter. We were surprised when the taxi driver showed up on schedule. He didn't speak English, and when we tried to ask about the coup, he shrugged and said, "nyet problem." With a little apprehension, we went downstairs and piled into the taxi, headed straight for the center of town and the Kremlin.

Our concerns rose as we reached the bridge crossing the Moscow River near Moscow State University. On both sides of the street, at the entrance to the bridge, was a tank. Driving over the long bridge, we saw tanks on the opposite end, also guarding the bridge. The street we were on—Profsoyuznaya—headed straight for the Kremlin. We felt more apprehensive the closer we came to the Kremlin but were relieved when the taxi driver turned on the main ring road that circled the inner portion of the city. After driving halfway around the inner portion of Moscow, he again drove in toward the Kremlin but stopped after a few blocks. We realized at that point he had intentionally taken us the long way to avoid driving by the Kremlin. After all that, we found that the hat store was closed.

Vance and I discussed returning home and canceling other errands, but our children reminded us we had promised to take them to McDonald's for lunch. Things in the city seemed calm, and McDonald's was on our way home, so we proceeded to what was the largest McDonald's in the world. Located in a very large two-story section of a larger building, a line of people two blocks long stretched in front. But the line moved quickly, and within thirty minutes, we were ordering. The prices were in rubles, and with the very favorable exchange rate, we could afford to buy the kids anything they wanted. After Big Macs, milkshakes, fries, and apple pies for the five of us, the total bill was around five dollars. McDonald's serves the same food all over the world, and it always made us remember home when we ate there. While we were waiting in line, we met some Americans on a short-term mission trip, who had just arrived in Moscow from an outlying town. They were on their way to the airport to leave. It was good to hear planes were still flying. We all wondered what would happen next.

THE SEVENTH DAY: THE COUP CONTINUES

Tuesday, August 19, 1991, Vance met with our Campus Crusade country director to visit the US Embassy for the purpose of registering our presence in Moscow. We did this when we were in Egypt but hadn't registered since we arrived in Moscow. Considering the current situation, it seemed prudent. They could not drive directly to the embassy because the Garden Ring Road we drove on the previous day was blocked; people had parked buses and trucks to close the entrances to the highway. Some Garden Ring Road underpasses were closed off as well, preventing driving on the Ring Road. Parking the car after driving over the same bridge with the tanks that we had driven over the day before, the men then took the subway. When they arrived at the embassy, there was a long line of Russians waiting outside to apply for visas—which was not an unusual sight. However, the embassy lay on the Garden Ring Road, and there was no traffic at all that day on the wide, six-lane avenue. Americans could enter the embassy through a separate gate without a line.

Everything buzzed with activity. When our men registered, they asked if there were any plans to evacuate Americans. The embassy staff they spoke with knew of none. It wasn't clear to Vance if they even had a functional warden system capable of contacting all the Americans who had arrived since they had instituted glasnost. The embassy personnel were surprised to hear the Garden Ring Road was closed, saying it was open when they drove to work that morning. Just as Vance and our director were leaving the embassy, a large crowd of people marched by on Garden Ring Road, chanting "Yeltsin! Yeltsin!" As the crowd passed by the US Embassy, the leader shouted on his megaphone, "Hurray for America! Long live President Bush" (George H. W. Bush, forty-first president of the United States). It was something Vance never—in his wildest imaginations—ever thought he would see.

Although our director had told all the staff to stay away, he suggested they walk to the Russian White House or parliament building—which was only a few blocks from the US Embassy. It was a beautiful summer day in Moscow, and people were milling around as though they were on a Sunday stroll in Gorky Park. Several tanks were parked outside the White House, modern Soviet tanks and loaded for battle. These tanks had been sent the day before by the coup leaders to arrest Russian President Boris Yeltsin, who was leading the resistance to the coup. But after meeting with Yeltsin, the general leading the tank force had chosen to switch sides, and now the tanks and their special forces soldiers were protecting Yeltsin.

The barrel of the main gun and the machine gun had flowers taped to them. Vance also noticed on a tank he walked by that people had placed fruit and other foodstuffs on the back of the tank for the soldiers. There were even children climbing on the tanks. Believing this would be a once-in-a-lifetime opportunity, Vance climbed up on the tank. From the top, he had a good view of people as far as he could see, strolling in the area surrounding the White House. The men then took the subway and noticed that people were reading fliers posted on the walls of the subways by Yeltsin supporters. Our director called all the staff together the next day to pray for the situation and then drove Vance home.

The next morning, we learned that three people were killed during the night, when a crowd of civilians had attacked tanks trying to break the barriers at a Garden Ring Road underpass near the US Embassy.

THE EIGHTH DAY: THE END OF AN EMPIRE

The next day, the handful of Campus Crusade for Christ staff in Moscow met at our director's house to pray. The staff children played in another room while the parents prayed. We arrived just before ten in the morning and were anxious to see if there was any news on CNN. CNN in English had been available in Moscow for some time, but we needed a TV with a UHF tuner to watch it. Only our director had such a television. Despite the coup, CNN had continued to broadcast from 10 a.m. to 10 p.m. from the main Moscow TV station tower. We waited and watched the show as 10 a.m. approached, wondering if CNN was still on the air. Then at ten o'clock, the station came on as usual.

We watched the hourly news summary, filled with information about the coup in Moscow. After watching CNN for fifteen minutes, we prayed. At the top of each hour, we would watch the news summary and then go back to our prayer meeting. We planned to pray until three o'clock and then go to a storage facility, which contained thousands of Bibles, and pass them out in the street so the Bibles wouldn't be confiscated if the coup succeeded. At 3:00 p.m., we ended the prayer meeting and turned on CNN again for one final time. We heard there were rumors that the coup leaders were fleeing the city. Our family had the youngest of the children, and we felt it best to return home with them and not join our team in the Bible distribution. We took the subway home and, upon arriving, turned on the television. We didn't understand what was being said but could see Yeltsin was on TV, and it seemed obvious the coup attempt had failed. We later learned that the coup leaders had driven down the main street from the Kremlin to our area of town on Leninsky Prospekt on their way to a military airport to fly out of Moscow. The coup was over, and so was the Soviet Union.

PREPARATIONS

$\approx$

With the fall of the Soviet Union, there was a period of uncertainty and a lack of central control as the various republics adjusted to the new political situation. There was also a time of great optimism that a more open society and free markets would bring people the prosperity and freedoms of the West. As a result, a great opportunity opened for missions. Vance and I offered Russian Bibles to our neighbors and friends we had made in the neighborhood. Everyone gladly accepted the large black Russian Bibles we offered them. Our neighbor Slava, a leader in the Soviet Academy of Science (he and his wife Luda later became close friends), proclaimed as he left our home with a Bible that he was going home with his treasure. Another man—a local avant-garde artist—stayed up all night reading his new Bible. His wife Vera also became a close friend of mine.

Vance and I began preparations for life and ministry in Moscow. We needed to buy a car, get Amy and Sara into school, learn Russian, and set up the training center to train our new Russian Campus Crusade for Christ staff. Meanwhile, the Russian government was in disarray, food was hard to find, banks ran out of money, and the Mafia appeared in many places. We felt like we were living in the Wild West.

By the spring and summer of 1992, missionaries flooded into the area as though there was a gold rush. The new Russian staff we were to train had come from the efforts of many short-term mission trips to the universities of the Soviet Union by Campus Crusade staff and students during the time of Gorbachev. Before the changes instituted by Gorbachev, they didn't allow Christians to attend universities. Many new believers came out of these atheistic universities, and we would have the privilege to prepare some of them to work full time to reach their own people. So many opportunities lay open before us.

Educating children is always a big consideration for overseas missionaries. When Vance and I traveled to Moscow several months before moving there, we visited a school to get an idea of what it would be like to have our children in a Russian school. The plan was to put the children of the CCC staff in a Russian school and hire two teachers to teach English and American history. When we visited the school, they gave us a third-grade reader. In the inside flyleaf, written in Russian, were the words, "Lenin lived, Lenin lives, Lenin will live." However, after the fall of Communism, they removed this from the textbook.

After arriving in Moscow, the Russian school that the staff had arranged for us to put our children in gave our ministry one of their classrooms for our use. The Russian school was a large multistory building for children from kindergarten through high school. They gave us the only available room, which had been used for military science and wasn't heated. On the walls were posters about war—such as how to throw a grenade. I picked up a gas mask as other parents covered the posters with white paper to prepare the room for our ten children. Sara, six, was the youngest, and the oldest girl was fourteen. Two young teachers would arrive soon from America.

The plan was to study with the Russian students for some classes and with our American teachers for the classes only they could teach. School began at 8:30, with tea and snacks served for all the school, and ended at three o'clock. After school were activities, including dance for Amy and gymnastics for Sara. Before the American teachers arrived, we put our children in classes with the Russian students full time. This resulted in some confusion, which we laugh about now.

Amy and Sara had been homeschooled, so this was their first experience in classrooms. Also, our children didn't speak Russian, and the teachers didn't speak English. The first day of school, all the

CCC parents and students met with the principal in her office, and then they took the children to their classes. When they returned home from their first day at school, the girls said they had enjoyed it. Only later did we discover that they had left their classes to find the other American students, who also left their classes. Then together they wandered the halls and had a good time. The Russian teachers didn't know what to do because of the language barrier. We had to explain to Amy and Sara how school operated. So they stayed in class, though Sara wasn't happy because every time she wrote something, the teacher would remove the pencil from her left hand and place it in her right hand.

We were all relieved when Patti and Laura, our American teachers, arrived. However, things didn't work out as we had hoped. The Russian school kept changing the timing of the various class subjects, so it was impossible for us to schedule times for our children to study with the Russian students. Some teachers also didn't return from their summer homes before school began, so their classes were just not offered. We set up a one-room school with our two American teachers teaching all the subjects for all grade levels. Our children had Russian tutors for Russian language study and only had P.E. with the Russian students. Despite the bumpy start, our little school grew and became a blessing to us and many others.

Vance and I began by studying Russian using the Language Acquisition Made Practical (LAMP) method we had used in Egypt. We memorized phrases and practiced with twenty people—usually strangers. We both love to talk and meet people, so this method worked well for us. I remember standing about a block away from the post office one day, asking people where the post office was. One lady stopped, saying that she spoke English, and told me where the post office was.

I replied, "I know where the post office is. I'm just practicing speaking Russian."

I often made a mistake when answering the phone. When someone asked for the owner of our apartment, instead of saying in Russian, "She no longer lives here," I would say, "She no longer lives." As soon as I hung up, someone in the family would tell me I had said our landlady died. I still love to speak Russian when I have the opportunity, though I never learned enough to be fluent.

Purchasing a car in Moscow was an adventure. First, the selection was very limited. There were no car dealers or used car lots. The only ways we knew of to buy a car were to purchase from the Soviet auto manufacturer or import a car from abroad. Having lived in Egypt for ten years, we knew the advantage of purchasing a local model so we could find people to repair the car and get parts locally. A young man who had been serving as a private taxi service for us helped Van purchase the car. He lived in a dormitory for working people. It was like a college dormitory with a community kitchen on the floor. All the residents had their own room but shared the bathrooms and kitchen.

Local residents who wanted to purchase an automobile from the Moskvitch manufacturer went to their office and placed their name on the waiting list. Several years later, when their name came up on the list, they returned and waited in a long line to purchase the automobile (for a relatively inexpensive price). Foreigners who wished to purchase automobiles for hard currency (dollars) could show up with the money and drive away with a car the same day. Financing was not available for foreigners. We purchased the same car one of our other staff had—a Moskvitch 2131. It was like our car in Egypt but a little larger, to accommodate our growing family (see photo at http://en.wikipedia.org/wiki/File:M2141s_aleko-f.jpg.)

After determining that the going price for this car was five thousand dollars, we needed to get that much cash to take to the dealership. Vance had a gold American Express card we could use at the Moscow American Express office to write a check for up to three thousand dollars and receive cash. Getting enough cash for the transaction required two trips. Vance always felt a little uneasy, realizing people must know all the foreigners were going to the American Express office to get cash. Taking two thousand dollars with him the day he planned to purchase the car, he had a friend drive him to the American Express office, where he got another three thousand dollars. Leaving the American Express office with a little trepidation, Vance jumped in the car, and they headed for the Moskvitch dealership—hoping no one was following them.

After arriving at the dealership, they ushered Vance in immediately to a private office, where they completed the transaction, and he happily turned over the five thousand dollars in his pocket. They took Vance to pick out his car in a multistory parking garage with a car elevator. That week, the dealership was filled with white cars. The color available depended on what color the factory painted that week. He noticed about three different colored cars set off to the side. Inquiring about the red Moskvitch, they informed him that the motor was bad on that car. There were also a couple of blue Moskvitchs, one of which was set aside because of a bad battery. He asked if he could purchase that automobile; they replaced the bad battery with one from another car, and the blue car started on the first try. Vance then returned home with our new blue Moskvitch 2131 hatchback. The car came with a set of tools (which should have warned us) and three free trips to the dealership in the next several months. It took all three trips before the car was running properly and all the nuts and bolts finally tightened. It seemed the factory only finished the car well enough to drive it off the lot.

AN OFFICE
FOR GCTC

≈

AFTER SEVERAL MONTHS OF LANGUAGE LEARNING, WE BEGAN preparation for the training center, where we were to train our future Soviet Campus Crusade for Christ staff. In Russia, they officially called the ministry *"Novia Jeesen"* (New Life). Office space was very difficult to come by, even though there were many unused and underused buildings. Basically, you had to find a government enterprise willing to rent you some rooms. We wanted to be near Moscow State University and found the best option was to rent a couple of rooms permanently at the University Hotel across from the campus. The hotel offered us two rooms to use for offices and said we could use part of the dining room for classes. Vance met with the director of the hotel to complete the deal. He was a very obese man with lots of rings on his fingers and seemed to be like a king in the hotel.

We had the beds removed from the rooms and remodeled them as offices. The dining room was being repaired, but they told us that we could use it as soon as they finished it. It was not ready by the time the training cycle began, so Vance had to give up his office for a classroom. We were there for a year, but they never finished the dining room. After we moved to another location, they finally opened the dining room as a casino. A couple of years later, we read in the paper that someone gunned down the hotel director in front of the hotel. He had run afoul of one of the Russian mafias.

When we realized the hotel wasn't working out well, Vance sought other options. He mentioned it to our neighbor, Slava, who said he would check on a local institute where he had contacts. Slava secured office space at the National Academy for the Economy just a few blocks from our home. It was a prestigious institute directed by Abel Aganbegyan, who was the adviser to Gorbachev on the economy during the Perestroika reforms. The institute also held Yegor Gaidar's economic institute. Gaidar served as Boris Yeltsin's first prime minister. In fact, the offices we rented were in Gaidar's institute building. The Lord provided above and beyond.

THE PEOPLE'S
PARADISE

≈

W<small>E LIVED IN THE OLD SOVIET UNION FOR SEVERAL MONTHS BEFORE IT</small> was officially dissolved on December 25, 1991. Growing up having to hide under our classroom desks in grammar school to prepare for a Soviet attack, we never dreamed that we would one day live in the country Ronald Reagan had called the Evil Empire. When we traveled to Turkey the summer of 1980, Vance and I remarked as we looked north from the southern coast of the Black Sea, "Just imagine, the Soviet Union is just across that sea. This is probably the closest we will ever come to it."

It surprised us how bad things were when we moved to the Soviet Union. The problems were not the result of recent economic problems but had been bad for many, many years. The building we lived in looked like it belonged in a ghetto, though we were in one of the best parts of town, with broken windows in the entrance and a general state of disrepair. Our building, originally built for rocket engineers, was typical of all the buildings in Moscow. We heard stories from Russian friends of how their ancestors had suffered in the gulags and under Stalin. The car most Russians drove—called a Lada—was 100 percent an Italian Fiat. It even had the same model number. Here was a country that put the first man in space but didn't design their own cars or keep their buildings in repair.

On a visit to Saint Petersburg to look for office space, we faced another surprising revelation. After the Russian Revolution, the rich had to move into one room of their large apartments, and they put different families in the other rooms. We had seen this in the movie *Doctor Zhivago* but always assumed this was a temporary solution but found that people were still living that way seventy years later. To purchase a large apartment suitable for an office in St. Petersburg, our realtor would find smaller individual apartments for each of the several families living in the apartment we were interested in. The shared home had only one kitchen and one bathroom for all these families to share, and the families did not like each other or their living conditions.

Communism had not made life better for the people of Russia. One of Vance's Russian language teachers—the wife of a Russian military officer—remarked to him one day that she could understand how an American or a British person could believe in Communism. It is a very good sounding philosophy, but a Russian would have to be a fool.

NEW FRIENDS

≈

VERA

A COUPLE OF MONTHS AFTER ARRIVING IN MOSCOW, I TOOK PETER TO the playground to play in the snow. My back had been bothering me, so I lay down to rest on a snow-covered bench while Peter played. Vera, a Russian woman about my age, saw me in the playground and introduced herself in English. She saw me in the playground and assumed I was not Russian since I was wearing waterproof snow pants and lying in the snow on a bench. She also came to play in the snow with her son, Yuri. Vera—lovely, tall, and blonde—spoke fluent English. As we talked, I found she had studied physics in school and learned English. She told me she had been prepared to work as a teacher in an African country that the Soviet Union planned to colonize.

Vera later told me that Communism had never made sense to her, so she studied physics, which made sense. She also told me she believed in God and was baptized quietly in a bathtub a few years earlier when the Communists were still in control. A relative living abroad sent her a children's Bible, which she had been reading. Her mother was a committed Communist Party Member, and her father had served in Russian assignments overseas. So Vera did not feel she could be open about her faith. She became a good friend, and we met together to study the Bible.

LUDA

We met our neighbor, Luda, through her husband, Slava. In Moscow, there are seven months of snow. We had to learn many things about cold weather, such as what to do when your car door lock freezes. Slava showed Vance how to use a hot water bottle held against the car door to unfreeze the lock. Vance borrowed Slava's hot water bottle often, as we didn't know where to find one. On Vance's birthday, Slava gave him a hot water bottle. Slava and Luda became our good friends, and we spent pleasant times together in their apartment over tea. Luda taught me how to make Russian Easter bread (*kolitch*) and color hard-boiled eggs by boiling them with onion skins. She arranged the brick-colored eggs around the round loaf of kolitch for Easter. Luda also told me about the time an escaped cockatiel flew into her kitchen window. It spoke Russian.

I started a Bible study for ladies in our apartment, and Luda joined us. I remember going over the Gospel again and again. Somewhere along the way, Luda understood and gave her life to the Lord. She worked as a typesetter for a Russian government publishing house. When Vance needed a secretary, he asked Luda to come work for him in our training center. However, Luda couldn't touch-type—only hunt-and-peck. Vance offered her the job on the condition that she first learn to touch-type. She agreed and learned in just a few weeks. Soon she was typing the curriculum for the training center.

The trainees learned how to do evangelism, follow up new believers, start Bible studies, and much more. As she typed the notes, Luda grew stronger in her faith. She became a mother figure for our trainees. If they had a headache, they went to Luda, who had aspirin for them. Her nurturing personality and gentle spirit made her a perfect mother. She continued as a secretary for our ministry even after we left Russia.

IRENA

We met Irena, a former Communist Party Member, at the international church in Moscow and heard her fascinating story. She specialized in Indonesian languages and had been assigned the job of a translator for a delegation of Indonesian Christians visiting Russia on the one thousandth anniversary of Christianity in Russia. After the celebration, the Indonesians invited the Russian Orthodox Church to send a representative to Indonesia for a Christian celebration in their country. The Orthodox Church assigned a priest to represent them, and Irena was to accompany the priest as a translator. Having studied in Indonesia as a student, Irena excitedly prepared to go. However, just two hours before she was to leave for the airport to fly to Indonesia, the priest called and informed Irena that he could not attend. Irena was heartbroken—having looked forward to the trip—and told the priest she would cancel her plans to go. The priest replied that she didn't need to cancel her trip and could represent the Orthodox Church in his place. That Irena was an atheist and a member of the Communist party was not a problem.

The Indonesian Christians befriended Irena during her time there and ultimately led her to the Lord. When she returned to Russia, she attended the international church, where we met her. Irena shared her story with us and then told us that she used to be an atheist but had doubts. We were surprised by the comment, but she said honest atheists don't know with certainty they are right. I invited her to my ladies Bible study, which caused a reaction, as one lady whispered to me one evening that the women thought Irena was with the KGB. Irena, however, had truly come to Jesus and influenced her family for Christ. She later taught Russian at a Christian college in the States, where her son was studying. Returning to Moscow, she became the representative for the Protestant denomination where her son had attended college and she had taught. We found that many Russians—though atheists like Irena—had doubts.

Internal Collapse
and Crime

≋

D<small>AILY LIVING DURING THE INTERNAL COLLAPSE OF THE</small> S<small>OVIET</small> U<small>NION</small> provided perspective. Life was hard, but God provided. Stores ran out of food, banks ran out of money, gasoline was hard to get, and violence increased.

Though the only items on the store shelves were pickles, Russians had ways to get food. Their resourcefulness inspired us as they stocked up food at home, had channels through work, and stored homegrown vegetables in root cellars and on balconies.

When we first arrived in Russia, the only way to get money was to carry it in on your person. Later, American Express opened offices and would cash checks if you had an account and give you dollars. Everyone wanted dollars, as the ruble was so unstable. The exchange rate kept changing, and it was a challenge to find rubles. Once, when I went to the bank to change about fifty dollars, I came home with a grocery sack of small bills in Russian currency. The bank had run out of larger bills. Since it was difficult to find anything to buy, neighbors carrying home a bag often asked each other what they had bought and where they had found it. A neighbor saw me carrying my bag home from the bank and asked what I had purchased. I mumbled something evasive. How could I explain a sack of money? Fifty dollars wasn't much to me, but with the crazy exchange rate, it was a large amount for Russians. Eventually, kiosks to change money, guarded by armed former soldiers, appeared, and changing money became easier. But I always felt a little uneasy using them. A couple of years later, ATM machines appeared where you could get Russian rubles and charge your US bank at a good exchange rate.

Finding gasoline for our little Fiat was a challenge. Lines were long. Sometimes enterprising Russians stood on the side of the road with a can of gas for sale, and we were happy to purchase gas from them. Not only was it easier to get gas, but we were helping local Russians. One day, Peter was playing with his toy cars and lined them all in a row; he told us they were waiting for gas. Somehow, we always found enough gas for the car.

With the fall of the Soviet Union, there was a lack of government control, and different mafias controlled different areas. Sometimes, a business had to pay one mafia to protect them from another mafia. Occasionally, we heard gunfire at night as they fought for power. They might burn down a business that didn't comply or shoot the business's owner. Those who could afford it installed steel doors in their apartments. We did this after someone unsuccessfully tried to break down our wooden door. We felt like we lived inside a vault when our new steel door clanged shut. We also had an alarm on our car. One of the American Campus Crusade staff's children had a knife pulled on him in an elevator. Another missionary friend was beaten almost to death when he tried to rescue a neighbor who had been attacked by local youths. A neighbor who sent his dogs against the youths rescued our friend. Another foreign woman was robbed and murdered in her apartment. Russia felt like the Wild West. Although we lived in government chaos, we didn't feel overwhelmed or terrified. One day at a time, God took care of us and carried us. Even when a country collapses, God doesn't, and he is faithful.

One day, Vance awoke to the sound of our car alarm going off. After the initial panicky feeling, he thought to himself, *At least the car is still there.* He went outside and found the front passenger window broken. He had left a large bag full of photocopied student notes for the training center on the front seat, which was missing. The new (empty) cash box he had purchased was still sitting on the seat, untouched. It appeared the thief grabbed the bag of ministry papers and, hearing the alarm, left before taking the cash box. I wondered if one day, we would hear of some thief who came to Christ through those stolen notes. Other staff had tires or entire cars stolen.

It was a definite inconvenience but not a crisis. Vance couldn't leave the car with a broken window, lest another thief steal the car. Not sure just what to do, he went upstairs to our good friend and neighbor, Slava. As soon as Slava heard what had happened, he called into his office at the Soviet Academy of Sciences and told them he would come in late to work. He then drove Vance to an auto flea market we didn't know even existed. They could find a window, but unfortunately, it didn't have the metal attachment at the bottom of the window needed to attach the mechanism to roll the window up and down. Vance and Slava installed the window in the up position, and we felt safe to use the car again.

A few days later, another Russian friend took Vance to the government auto repair shop to have the missing piece added to the window. They informed Vance that they didn't have the equipment to add the metal attachment at that facility, so insisted that he purchase another window with the piece already attached. After asking what the price would be, Vance found that it would only cost a couple of dollars for a new window with the needed part attached, so he gladly had the new window installed and put the spare window in the trunk.

A couple of weeks later, we were having our regular staff meeting at a staff member's home, and our director arrived an hour late. He apologized for being late and told us his car window had been smashed. Knowing he owned the same kind of car we did, Vance asked which window was broken.

When he said it was the right front door window, Vance replied, "That's no problem; I have a spare window in my trunk." Amazed at this unusual provision, the men then went downstairs and installed the spare window in our director's car.

JULIA

WHILE VANCE STUDIED RUSSIAN IN A CLASSROOM, I HAD A TUTOR COME to our home so I could stay with three-year-old Peter. My tutor, Julia, was also a mother with two school-age boys. She came while her boys were in school, and we had a great time together. She made learning fun—and I enjoyed studying Russian. I loved the language and the culture. Peter, always a quiet, cooperative child, never seemed bored and kept himself occupied during my Russian lessons.

Julia opened my eyes to the family and spiritual lives of Russians. Four times a week, she arrived at our apartment, often with a small wooden toy to illustrate a Russian fairy tale. I paid her for these and for lessons and soon had an impressive toy collection. For the first time, I understood English grammar, as Julia drew diagrams and gave illustrations. Then she explained Russian grammar. Russian words change depending on how they are used in a sentence. For example, a noun used as a preposition has a different ending. I never mastered Russian but learned enough to converse and feel comfortable in daily life.

Julia was twenty-nine. She had become a Christian about a year before and attended Bible studies. She sometimes spoke about God, saying how wonderful it is to think the Lord cares about her and her family and has a plan for them. A personal relationship with God, someone she can talk with, was new to her and to many Russian people.

Julia not only made learning enjoyable but gave me a glimpse into the growth of new believers as the Gospel spread in the new openness of post-Communist Russia.

Mysterious
Threads

≈

Sometimes, God allows us to see in this life the mysterious threads woven by God into the tapestry he is creating. Russian was a mysterious thread. At UCLA in the 1970s, a foreign language was a requirement for graduation. As a young student, I searched the listing for language classes and discovered to my astonishment that every class was already full, except for Russian. So I signed up, wondering how on earth I would ever find any practical use for it. Russia was the Evil Empire, and we were engaged in the Cold War. I would never go there and had never even met a Russian. However, learning the alphabet and how to pronounce the letters was fun. Grammar was another story, and I never got my mind around it very well. Language was not my best subject. I did better in science and math.

Later, on staff with Campus Crusade for Christ, I sat next to my trainer from Houston—Jewell Erickson—at staff training in Colorado, listening to a speaker. He encouraged the audience to consider the language we studied in college. Perhaps God was calling us to serve there. We looked at each other and laughed. Jewell had also studied Russian.

I was in my forties when we moved to Russia, and for this woman who is not great in languages, the switch from Arabic to Russian was only by the grace of God. The Russian alphabet, pronunciation, and basic phrases came right back, even after twenty years, and I had a jump-start on the language. I loved speaking Russian and still do, when I get a chance. Now when one of those mysterious threads pop up that don't seem to fit in with the rest of my life or serve a purpose, it helps to remember the Russian language thread.

Shopping
Adventures

≈

Unpredictable, unexpected, and unusual all described shopping just after the fall of the Soviet Union. When we first arrived, there was little food in the stores. Then we learned of a company in Europe that would truck in food. We bought items from them, such as a freezer, soap, motor oil, and fun food like chocolate chips. After finding they charged eighty dollars for an ironing board, a Russian friend—Nick—bought us a local ironing board for a few dollars. Nick's grandmother—who lived outside of Saint Petersburg—bought it and sent the ironing board via a friend who worked on the train. Then Nick brought it to us on the subway and the bus. Our table for the TV and video came from some staff friends who had just moved by truck from Poland.

Once things settled down politically, food returned to the local stores. Shopping proved to be quite an adventure in our local grocery store. The items were not available on open shelves but organized in different departments of the store, with a counter at each. Only the clerks had access to the items. First, I walked to each station to order what I wanted from that department. There were at least five small departments. At one, I would ask for a kilogram of cheese. I waited while they weighed the cheese. They kept the cheese and gave me a slip of paper with the amount of money I owed. At another station, I would order sugar and flour, which they also weighed and gave me a paper for. I had to stand in line at each station to order and receive a slip of paper. Sometimes, I would take the children and put them in different lines. If they got to the front of the line before I returned, they weren't happy, as they hadn't learned the vocabulary for shopping and couldn't order, so they got in the back of the line again.

After I stood in all the lines and had a handful of papers, I stood in another line for the cashier. At first, I spoke to the cashier—telling her the amounts for each station. But I was still learning the language, and I overheard a lady behind me exclaiming that some people are so slow. So I handed the cashier all my slips of paper, and she added them up. Then I had to return to each station, stand in line, and finally receive the item. I ended up with a bag of groceries, which I deposited in my personal wheeled shopping cart. Most of the year, I pulled the cart home several blocks through the ice and snow. Fast food and restaurants were almost nonexistent in the early 1990s, and getting food took a lot of effort.

Later, as the free market appeared, we paid a start-up Russian company to bring us food. We never knew what would arrive. Once we received twenty-four chicken breasts; about eight pounds of pork; two boxes of quail eggs; two pounds of butter; a big bag of shortbread cookies; about two pounds each of apples, tomatoes, cucumbers, onions, and carrots; and four pounds of onions, all for twenty dollars. I fried all the little quail eggs for breakfast. We never lacked food, though some meals were interesting. Gradually, things improved, although prices increased, and many Russians had difficulty because of the expense.

Vance also shopped at local stores while he was out practicing Russian and came home with interesting things to try, including bottles of cherries and plums, ice cream, cookies with apple jam inside, pomegranate juice, various breads, and different hot cereals.

Russians often stocked up on things they found in the stores and then traded with friends. I traded whole oat cereal for rolled oats with my language tutor. The newspaper was filled with items to trade: a rug for a TV, a car for an apartment, and much more.

As in Egypt, instead of planning menus and looking for ingredients in the store, I purchased what was available and then figured out what to do with it. Even today—being back in America—I still go to the store, buy what is on sale, and then figure out what to do with it. This is so different from my first years of marriage, when I made up recipes for a week of meals and then bought the ingredients. In Russia, I stocked up on items when they were available.

Testimony of Teddy Bears

≈

THE FALL OF THE SOVIET UNION CAPTURED THE ATTENTION OF THE world, including the church. Missionaries, Bible colleges, and humanitarian aid flooded into the vacuum created by seventy years of oppression. Josh McDowell, an apologist with Campus Crusade for Christ, organized a humanitarian effort called Care Lift and brought supplies for children's hospitals, including teddy bears for sick children. The hospitals at the time lacked even basic supplies such as tubing for IVs. Churches and US businesses gave teddy bears and other supplies, and many volunteers came to Russia to help distribute the gifts. So many people gave teddy bears, there were more than all the children in Moscow hospitals. So we invited the missionary children to take two teddy bears each. Our amazed children told us there was a room piled with teddy bears almost reaching to the ceiling.

Still, there was a mountain of leftover teddy bears, so our staff came up with a plan to reach out to the Russian school our missionary kids met in. Our students learned Christian worship songs in Russian. We arranged with the school principal to hold a series of assemblies in the main auditorium so we could have a program for all the students and offer the leftover teddy bears and other items, which included school supplies. Our students sang Russian worship songs on stage, and then Gosia—a Polish staff woman who spoke excellent Russian—gave the

Gospel message. We watched as students raised their hands to receive Christ. After the assemblies, students walked down a hall to receive teddy bears and supplies handed out by our staff. It was like Christmas and contributed to the euphoric feelings of the country shortly after the fall of Communism. At least one of those teddy bears still resides in our family, now worn with age.

UNLIKELY
COMPANIONS

≈

U NDER COMMUNISM, CHRISTIANS USUALLY COULD NOT ATTEND THE universities. When Gorbachev instituted glasnost, Campus Crusade for Christ International sent staff and students to Russia on short-term trips. As a result, some students had already come to Christ before we arrived in Moscow. Those who had received Christ and graduated from the university, and who we felt were qualified, were invited to join CCC staff. They joined the training center to become equipped to reach the students of the former Soviet Union. Most of our trainees were in their twenties and had been Christians less than two years. As they grew stronger in their Christian faith, traditional cultural and religious barriers broke down between them.

Four beautiful Christian women from diverse backgrounds lived and ministered together. Christina came from a Christian home in East Germany. Sarah was from a Jewish background and had come to the Lord through Jews for Jesus in Russia. Sveta had been a Communist youth leader, and Nora was a Muslim from Central Asia. So a Jew, a German, a Communist, and a Muslim all came to Jesus and now lived and ministered together at a university in Moscow. We held meetings at their apartment, and the atmosphere felt like heaven as our diverse group sang praises to God in Russian.

Christina married a godly man in the ministry from her country.

Sarah moved to Israel. Sveta married a pastor, and they serve with their many children in Siberia. Nora married, and they serve today among the Muslims of Central Asia. What a joy to watch God transform lives and break down walls in the most unlikely ways.

ADVENTURES
WITH BETTY

≈

Y OU NEVER KNOW THE ADVENTURES GOD HAS FOR THE DAY OR THE
interesting variety of people you may meet. I couldn't have imagined
the people Betty, a former coworker from Cal State Fullerton who was
visiting Moscow, and I would meet that day.

We began at Moscow State University, the leading university in
Communist Russia, and talked with an athletic coach named Julia, out
on the grass. Betty gave her a Gospel tract. Julia invited our family to
swim at an indoor pool where she taught children. Then we lunched
at a student cafeteria. In my limited Russian, I ordered tomato salad,
mashed potatoes, soup, and tea. I wanted to order meat, but the Russian
word for "meat" sounds like "month," and I got mixed up. We also
ended up with the wrong soup and ate hot milky cereal instead of
cabbage soup. Such is the unexpected life of a language learner.

Next, we met a physics student while lost in a maze of halls. I
asked her, "Where is the Metro?" in Russian. She spoke English and
offered to take us to the Metro, as she was going herself. We found
she and her brother were Christians. On the way to the Metro, we
met an American family from our church. He was a visiting professor
teaching religion at Moscow State.

Needing rest, Betty and I sat in the lobby of a nice hotel to drink
a coke. Next to us was an American woman whose husband was the

anchorman for the ABC Evening News in New York. He was doing a documentary. We talked with her about the Lord; she seemed very interested and possibly already a Christian. She had flown part of the way to Moscow with Billy Graham. Asking us to wait a moment, the woman returned with a bag for us filled with duty-free items such as perfume and makeup, explaining that people had given her a lot of free samples.

Topping off an already abundant day Betty had her hair done at a Russian hotel, and we headed for the Bolshoi Theater with the Russian ballet, where we enjoyed a glorious evening of *Swan Lake*—for only twenty dollars a ticket. You never know the adventures God has in store each day.

Losing Peter

≈

Wᴇɴ Pᴇᴛᴇʀ ᴡᴀꜱ ꜰᴏᴜʀ, ᴀʟʟ ᴛʜᴇ Cᴀᴍᴘᴜꜱ Cʀᴜꜱᴀᴅᴇ ꜱᴛᴀꜰꜰ ɪɴ Rᴜꜱꜱɪᴀ and Eastern Europe met for a large conference in Prague, Czechoslovakia. The fellowship and main sessions encouraged the adults, while the children got to know each other in their own programs. The children learned songs and entertained the adults by coming up on the stage to sing. Peter happened to be standing at the stage's front. He stretched up to sing loudly right in the microphone, resulting in his voice carrying above all the other voices. People around me kept asking who that kid was.

While exploring Prague with another family, we lost Peter in a bus station. Trying to stay calm and think through where he might be, we walked around the station. Vance checked the men's restroom, where he found Peter, sitting on the sink, washing his hands. He had recognized the universal sign for restrooms and walked in by himself. We learned that Peter was smart and logical, but we made it clear he shouldn't go off by himself.

CHOCOLATE AND OTHER MEDICATIONS

≈

My FAMILY TEASES ME WHEN I HAVE A SQUARE OF DARK CHOCOLATE—claiming it is medicinal. But I have good reasons for my actions.

In the early 1990s in Moscow, pharmacies contained various bottles of mysterious solutions, and Russian people used herbal medicines. Antibiotics, Novocain, aspirin, IV tubing, birth control, feminine hygiene products, and most of the medical items considered standard in the United States were in short supply or didn't exist. People just had bronchitis for months. We heard the average woman had six abortions as birth control, though I never confirmed this. Many Russians avoided the dentist, as there was no Novocain. Someone said Americans were identifiable by their excellent teeth. We speculated that most of the money went to the military; this theory seemed to be true the more we learned about Communist Russia.

As Americans, our family had access to a foreign medical facility in downtown Moscow. We used this occasionally, and I went there with a case of strep throat. I am allergic to penicillin, and after three courses of other antibiotics, I was feeling a little strange and wondered if I had a secondary infection. Returning to the foreign medical facility, a doctor from India examined me, said I was all right but suggested I pick up some chocolate on the way home to revive my energy. It worked. I felt a lot better after consuming a bar.

So that is my rationale for keeping a stock of dark chocolate in the cupboard today. A couple of squares helps most ailments, and I suspect it may even be preventative.

SPIRITUAL NEEDS

≈

IN MOSCOW, I MISSED THE GOOD BIBLE TEACHING AND ALL THE FRIENDS from our church in Merced, California. Our church in Russia used a formal liturgy, and I wasn't used to that style of worship. We missed fellowship, even though more missionaries were arriving all the time; we gradually got to know them and our new Russian friends, who were mostly unbelievers or young Christians. Life was full between family, language learning, and just learning how to live. Vance and I were tired, and that also contributed to episodes of my being bedridden with back problems. However, I found comfort in scripture and the Russian forest. I wrote in a letter home:

> I have been taking walks in the birch forest and memorizing scripture to music and praying. That has been the highlight of my day, and the loveliness of tall, slender birch trees with sunlight filtering through and the green undergrowth filled with winding pathways awes me and quiets my spirit. It's easy to praise God in such a place. It's a real gift.

Looking back at my life, I see a pattern that began in college and—though not always present—has continued until the present day. Walking in nature and making up tunes to memorize scripture has had a powerful impact on me; somehow, the rhythm of my steps with the tunes and words and nature have embedded God's word into me so I remember and retain it. Then God's Spirit brings it to mind applying it to different life circumstances. "For the word of God is living and active and sharper than any two-edged sword and piercing as far as the division of soul and spirit, of both joints and marrow, and able to judge the thoughts and intentions of the heart" (Hebrews 4:12). God met my spiritual needs, even in the distant land of Russia.

Our First Moscow Thanksgiving

≈

As our first Thanksgiving in Moscow approached, snow had covered the landscape for a month. We wondered where we would get a turkey. We had always found turkeys in Egypt for Thanksgiving at a local poultry market where they sold live turkeys and chickens. They killed these on the spot and then cleaned and plucked them. But in Moscow, with food hard to find, we didn't know where to find a turkey. It looked like we would need to have one flown in from abroad, which would be very expensive.

Noreen Dambman, the wife of one of our Athletes in Action staff, solved this problem when she arranged for a local hotel restaurant to prepare a Thanksgiving meal for all of us. The restaurant was on the top floor of the tall Central House of Tourism Hotel, just down the street from where we lived. We all brought candles, table decorations, pies, traditional vegetables, and salads. The restaurant did a good job finding turkeys and cooking them, along with other traditional foods. We had a lot to be thankful for during the brief time we had been in Moscow. The coup had resulted in more opportunities, and though there were only about a dozen of us at the time of the coup, many had arrived since then. Over one hundred Campus Crusade for Christ full-time and short-term staff attended the Thanksgiving feast. Some staff provided music. The children sang and did a skit. We hooked up our

TV and video in a back room for cartoons and football games. Most people stayed four to five hours.

Being separated from relatives during holidays brought us closer to our family of fellow missionaries and made traditions even more special. The atmosphere created in the restaurant transported us away from the stress of living in a world of unknowns into a familiar spot of home. Memories of this first Thanksgiving with coworkers in a newly opened country still fill us with warmth.

Becoming
Third Culture

~~

BEFORE MOVING OVERSEAS—IN CROSS-CULTURAL TRAINING—WE learned that after living in another culture for a while, we no longer fit into any culture. I remember thinking I had a choice: to fit in or to have a bigger picture of the world. I decided then I would rather have a bigger picture. It's a little like moving from a small town to a big city and then returning to the small town. It's hard to find someone who understands, unless they have had a similar experience. In our cross-cultural training, we learned that after assimilating some of each culture, we create a "third culture," which can result in no longer fitting into either culture.

In November 1991, I wrote home:

> It's interesting to me that I feel more comfortable now with foreigners than with Americans, unless the Americans have also lived overseas like us. I find it hard to relate to the new staff from America, even those my age. They, in turn, seem amazed at how I am so unafraid of getting out into Russian life.

I experienced reverse culture shock after moving back to America but am now comfortable living here again. It is always a joy to speak Arabic or Russian with an immigrant, and I feel at home with them. I guess a person never stops being third culture.

GOD IS OUR ROCK

≈

I LLNESS PLAGUED US OUR FIRST WINTER IN MOSCOW, YET WE FELT A PEACE and a sense of God's provision. I spent many weeks at home, and while the pain from my herniated disc improved, I caught one virus after another, first a cold, then the flu. Then an automobile wheel sitting in the hall fell on my foot—with the rim bruising it badly. I hobbled for a couple of days and then went with Vera to have an x-ray at a Russian clinic. Gratefully, I didn't break it. However, I noticed their supply of medicine was pitiful. I couldn't find alcohol, Band-Aids, or anything similar. The Russians often used herbal medicine. I wrote home on December 29, 1991:

> Thanks for all the Christmas gifts.... We like the mugs, and I especially like the one about hope. Things here aren't tough, but I would say they're a challenge. We feel God meeting all our needs in abundance, especially compared to Russians. I feel like this country is fluid, not solid. But the Middle East was that way too. It's just a little more fluid here. God is a rock. It's kind of nice to be in a situation where He has to be our rock. It's so easy to depend on something else.

One Day at a Time

≈

Somewhere in my life's journey, I wrote the following poem, which still speaks to me today.

One Day at a Time

One day at a time, Lord,
I give you today.
Live through me, love through me, show me Your way.
Tomorrow's problems, I can't comprehend.
My eyes cannot see what lies 'round the bend.
Tomorrow's too much of a burden to bear.
I'm not meant to deal with such worry and care.
So all my tomorrows I lay at Your feet
and trust that today, all my needs You will meet.

SPORTS

≈

I GREW UP SKIING IN THE CALIFORNIA AND UTAH MOUNTAINS, BUT winter in Moscow surpassed anything I had known. Leaves fall off the trees in late August, and except for pine trees, nothing green appears until May. Seven months of snow is normal. But cold weather didn't stop the athletic Russians, and we found many winter sports to enjoy.

Across the street, they transformed the community tennis court into an ice-skating rink. We had come prepared and brought ice skates from America. One day, Amy, Peter, and I ventured across the street with our ice skates. Sara and Vance were out and visited the rink later in the day. I wrote home on January 11, 1992:

> A man helped us by showing us a building where people went to put their skates on. There were about forty people skating, mostly children. Someone turned on some music, and a skating class of children began. Two ladies tried to explain where I could sign up my children for a class. Another man examined my skates and said they could be sharper. All this was in Russian, so I only understood the general ideas. Peter took off right away on his double-bladed skates. Falling didn't seem to bother him. He was more interested in a friendly dog that had wandered in and the boys playing ice hockey at the end of the rink. Amy skated

slowly and fell on her tailbone. After a while, she'd had enough. Everyone was happy to get home for lunch.

Russians didn't let a little cold weather stop them from enjoying the outdoors. It was 2 degrees Fahrenheit when my friend Vera invited us to go sledding across the street with her and her son. After putting on long underwear (I wore two pairs), pants, snow pants, warm socks and boots, scarves, mittens, and hats, we walked through powdery snow that squeaked when we stepped on it. The children rolled and jumped in mounds of snow; three to four feet deep. I wrote home on January 20, 1992:

> There were about twelve children on the hill. Solid ice was under the snow from the recent thaw. It made a great slick surface, and many kids just slid down on their pants. After an hour of sledding, my toes ached, even inside wool socks and lined boots. Amy's cheeks were pink, and Peter only had one eye showing through his balaclava hat. Van said we looked like we'd come in from the Arctic when we came home. It was good to thaw out. A few more degrees, and it will be too cold to go out. We have a chart about what to wear at different temperatures and when it's too cold to take the children out playing (-20 centigrade). Today was -17C. Vera said it was OK. One hour was enough!

The Russian culture pursues excellence, and we found that—in contrast to America, where kids are involved in many sports and activities—Russian kids pursue one thing to perfection. Sara loved gymnastics, so we put her in a Russian gymnastic program. The coach wanted her to come twenty-one hours a week. She was only seven, and we thought three days a week was plenty. Two other missionary children joined Sara in the Russian program. The coach wrote a program for our girls, focusing on building strength, and had two of his Russian students show what they were to do. This included twenty chin-ups and deep knee bends with another child on their shoulders. These girls were very strong.

Amy took ballet, which she had studied in America and the Philippines. The teacher said she had the body and talent for ballet, and we noticed a lot of improvement. Later, Peter would take gymnastics with Vera's son and the son of missionary friends.

SUNNY FIELDS
(*Солнечные полях*)

≈

IN APRIL 1992, AFTER A VERY INTENSE WEEK OF MEETINGS IN THE
ministry, our family spent a refreshing time in the country with two
other families. I wrote home:

> It [the hotel] was about two hours out of Moscow. It
> was so interesting to see the countryside, it's really
> beautiful, with forests and rolling plains of farmland.
> The country starts right outside of Moscow. Since
> there's no private land, you can explore anywhere.
> We passed many dachas [summer homes] and little
> villages that looked very poor, and several military
> installations, which seemed strange. It was hard to
> imagine we were actually driving down those roads.
> The hotel was in a lovely place, set on a hill with a pine
> forest behind it and a broad plain below with a winding
> river. We walked down to the river across farmland
> and through the quiet forest. The resort hardly lived
> up to its name—Sunny Fields. A cold spell hit, and we
> had lots of rain and snow flurries. We went for walks
> anyway and enjoyed the beauty. The hotel itself was
> quite nice, we had a two-room suite for a total of eight

dollars per night. Everything was traditional Russian, and there was wood paneling on the walls and pretty wooden furniture. Meals were about sixty-five cents per day. We usually ate at 9 a.m.: hot cereal, meat, mashed potatoes, coleslaw, and tea; 2 p.m.: hot cereal, soup (very good), juice, meat, and a starch; 5 p.m.: tea and cookies or bread; and 7 p.m.: meat, mashed potatoes, coleslaw, hot cereal, and tea. I enjoyed the food though it was high in fat and low in vegetables or fruit. I wouldn't want it as a steady diet, but it did taste good. We rented the sauna facility for one dollar per hour. It was three rooms and a bathroom, a hot rock sauna, a very small cool pool, and a room to sit and drink in (we had tea). The kids liked the pool, and it was interesting to see a Russian sauna. We also explored the adjacent young pioneers camp, which was empty now. There were lots of playgrounds, basketball, soccer, and other facilities, and rows of dormitories. It was fascinating and left me with many questions. We hope to go back to Sunny Fields again. We understand it used to be for people in the construction industry but now those people can't afford it. I think they're trying to attract business. It's awesome to think there are many establishments like that trying to figure out what to do now that their former way of life has collapsed.

In May, we returned to Sunny Fields for a staff team retreat for six days, bringing along eight kids and four Russian babysitters. The babysitters took the children horseback riding and for other fun activities. They also taught the older four children Russian. The countryside was lovely. I wrote home:

Spring is finally completely here, and it's incredibly beautiful. All the barrenness is replaced by a burst of green in different shades. Dandelions cover grassy fields, and delicate flowers of purple and white lie among undergrowth in shady forests of pine and birch. Everywhere in the countryside, people are planting, along the highways on any patch of ground—fifty people are planting potatoes. The land here—of course—isn't private, so it's open to anyone. On the roads on weekends, streams of cars with plants in the back or a bed on the roof, head out to their dachas. People here depend on the food from their dachas to help feed them in the winter. Gardening isn't just a hobby. This time it [Sunny Fields] lives up to its name. Our room overlooks a vast panorama of rolling green fields and forests, with little villages and a winding river. It looks like the countryside in northern Europe but more vast and empty. Today, we walked in the forest. It was so pretty, a fir tree forest. The only sounds were the birds, and many wildflowers were blooming. The countryside is incredibly beautiful and even more so for the long winter. Also, it seems less crowded and more pristine than anything I've seen. I was enjoying a cup of tea from the samovar in our suite. It's a great instrument, a big silver (or stainless steel) container for water with a heating element inside and a spigot. A small teapot sits on top and is heated by the steam from the water below. Russians pour a little tea from the pot into their cups and add a lot of hot water from the spigot. They drink tea all day.

We would continue to enjoy the countryside when we joined the Russians in moving to a country home during the summer.

THE SUMMER DACHA

≈

SOMETHING MAGICAL HAPPENS WHEN THE SNOW MELTS IN MOSCOW. AN almost compulsive urge to plant infects the population. I felt it too, as colors—made more brilliant in contrast to a long white winter—burst forth in every direction. It was intoxicating.

Our family joined the Russians in sending the mothers or grandmothers and children to the countryside for the summer. Gosia and I met with Mr. Kuts, an older Russian man who was renting his country dacha for the summer. We made the arrangements and soon found ourselves in a quaint two-story cabin in a gardening community just outside Moscow. This community had rows of cabins—each on about one-half acre and connected by dirt roads. Most had outhouses—including ours. In the outhouse, I found piles of old newspapers and prepared to throw them away when Mr. Kuts found me and objected. I was throwing away the toilet paper. Under the toilet seat was a bucket, which Vance emptied into the compost (this was the source of our lush garden). Next to the outhouse, a wooden room housed our shower. This worked when the water pressure was strong enough in the hose to fill up a tank near the roof. Under the water tank was a place to light a wood fire to heat water. We took showers, occasionally.

Mr. Kuts's family had the dacha for years and developed a lush garden with plum trees, a couple hundred strawberry plants, currant and gooseberry bushes, raspberries, and more. I discovered I loved gardening so much that not having water in the house didn't bother me. Our kitchen sink was in the garden—which looked a little strange standing alone outside, a dish drainer perched on top. It appeared the sink had gotten lost on its way to the house. Close to the sink, a vine-covered arbor sheltered a picnic table, where we had our meals. The house had a bottled gas stove. Sometimes, we got water into the pot on the stove by sticking the hose through the kitchen window.

Mr. Kuts's family had made the dacha cozy. It felt homemade and probably was. Unlike our city apartment—a cookie-cutter copy of so many others, even to the same wallpaper, the dacha was unique. The upstairs was divided in half—with one room facing the back garden and the other room facing the front. The girls took the upstairs. Everything was furnished, including souvenirs from the Arctic Circle, where Mr. Kuts had worked in the mining industry.

Though we missed Vance during the week, as he returned to Moscow, Luda, our English-speaking neighbor, took us on adventures.

I found a letter written to Grandma Nordman and Judy on July 16, 1992, that captures my daily life at the dacha with the children. I wrote:

> The sun has just set (10:30), and I've just put the kids to bed. We've become Russian; everyone sleeps in till 8:30. It's been hot this week, about 90 degrees. Three days we went to a nearby lake. The water was kind of murky but not bad, it was pretty with grassy banks and trees and blue sky with white clouds. Some cows grazed nearby. I really enjoyed the exercise, and the kids had fun. We went with our neighbor, Luda. We've had some more spiritual discussions. I sense she's very open and may already believe somewhat. She is somewhat afraid of offending her Jewish grandmother. Both she and her husband are part Jewish. She said many of the educated people have Jewish blood, but the wealth belongs to the Slavs. I'm afraid my Russian practice has been neglected recently.

Luda and I are busy with the children when we go to the lake, and there's so many interesting things to discuss with her. I feel too limited by Russian. I try to spend mornings helping Amy practice the 3 Rs. I want her to know her addition and subtraction up to 20 by heart. We keep working on printing, spelling and grammar, and reading. I seem to spend the rest of the day cooking or sweeping or picking berries. I decided berries are a lot of fun to eat but very tiring to pick. I'd rather buy them, and I'll be glad when berry season is past. I've tried currants stewed, as jelly, and as preserves, and decided they're not worth the trouble. The best way to eat them is fresh off the bush a few at a time. The white and red currants are OK, but none of us like black currants. Our strawberries are abundant but small [sometimes very small, though sweet]. Two hours of work yields about one and a half pounds of berries and a lot of sneezing. I'm allergic to something in the strawberry patch. We're picking raspberries, but I only get one and a half cups a day, so we bought some to make jam. We made 9 large bottles of strawberry and raspberry jam this week. Making jam is a big process. It's been a good experience, but I don't need to repeat it every year. Next comes the gooseberries, then the plums and apples.

Van's been in Moscow all week, and I miss him. But I think I'd go nuts with us all home all day long in our tiny apartment. Also, sometimes our apartment seems like Grand Central—phone calls, visitors—I need a break! The children have had time here to relax and play for hours and climb trees and run. Gardening is an outlet and helps me relax, but I need to be careful to not let it consume me. I didn't realize how much I like it. People have said I'm really becoming Russian by living in a dacha, but I think I found a part of Russian culture that has been me all along. I see myself in many parts of Russian culture, and it's nice to be in a place where it's a pleasure to do what the people do."

AMY, SARA, AND PETER IN A TREE AT OUR SUMMER DACHA

Mr. Kuts, our dacha landlord, was a veteran of World War II and had an interesting experience during the war, when he briefly wore a US Army uniform. He was warned not to tell his story, or he might end up in Siberia. Finally, when freedom came to Russia, Mr. Kuts was free to tell his story, which was written up in *People* magazine. His story can be found online at the link below.

People Magazine, August 21, 1989
https://people.com/archive/red-army-vet-vladimir-kuts-joins-up-with-his-gi-pals-44-years-after-battling-the-nazis-together-vol-32-no-8/

While Vance worked at the training center in Moscow during the week, the children and I explored the area with Luda. We purchased fresh eggs and goat's milk from people living in our dacha community. We also walked to a small village nearby and met a family who raised animals and made hand-painted lacquered wooden spoons. Their industry and creativity impressed me, as it seemed the family also built their home themselves.

I will never forget the day we visited the village lake and swam in its muddy waters. Along with villagers, we sunned ourselves on grassy banks. Cows grazed peacefully among the people. Then, when the children and I got in the water, I looked around and couldn't see Sara, who was seven. Fearing the worst, I dove under the water. It was shallow but so muddy I couldn't see. Finally, after quite a while searching in the water, I got out to look along the bank and found her. She had gotten out herself—probably not caring to swim in such a muddy place. It gave me quite a scare, and I felt such relief. In another lake in Moscow, we witnessed a young man being pulled out of a lake after drowning. They lay him on the bank and covered him with a cloth. I felt so grateful all my children were safe and the day at the muddy lake ended happily.

The plums on our trees were ripe, and the time had come to can them for the winter. In Russia, they sold everything in standard-sized glass bottles with standard-sized lids. We collected the bottles during the year and then used them for our summer canning. The bottles we used were large glass bottles—like a gallon dill pickle jar. Working together as a family, we picked the ripe plums and washed them (I can't remember if we took out the pits). We slid the garden hose through the kitchen window to fill up the pot on the stove. After the plum-filled bottles had boiled long enough, we tipped the pot and the hot water drained out the window onto the weeds below. The whole process took a long time. I remember preparing piles of plums and having fun working together. I can still taste those delicious bottled plums we enjoyed during the long winter months.

Spiritual Fruit

≈

Picking fruit in the dacha was work but also lots of fun. It was also a joy to plant seeds for spiritual fruit. I wrote home:

> Luda is very excited to practice her English with me; she speaks fairly well and has offered in exchange to teach me Russian. I was able to share the Lord a little. She said that she has some problems and wondered if God could help her. We have gone through law two of the Four Spiritual Laws, with many interruptions from our sons, who play together with some difficulty because of the language barrier. Luda said she is very interested and has recently been thinking about God. She felt it isn't a coincidence that we've met. Everywhere I go, I seem to meet interested people.

In September, back in Moscow, I asked the Lord for a sunny day as a birthday present so we could go back to the dacha and pick up some of our things. I wrote home:

> It was a time of saying goodbye to my love of the dacha in a way, though I'll never forget it. The owner is selling it, so we probably won't be going back. For some reason, that place seemed homier and more special than any we've stayed in. But it was a perfect

day, crisp, cool, and sunny. The flowers were just as lovely. We roamed the garden, tasting mint leaves, sorrel, and berries, and explored the house we'd stayed in. Then we shopped in the nearby town as we had before, and I bought a lot of plums and apples. Then Van and I gave out 4 laws [a Gospel tract] to people all around the train station and bus stop. It was great to see people standing around reading the 4 laws.

I have been passing out 4-laws while I wait for Peter's bus [his school bus back in Moscow]. One man said, "I need this. Give me another." Another said, "We need to do this!" [Pass out tracts.] One young woman said, "I believe. I want one for my father. It's shorter for him to read than the Bible." Almost everyone takes one, and many thank me.

Whether it was just curiosity or true spiritual interest, I don't know, but in September 1992, almost everyone seemed ready to learn more about Jesus.

SIMPLE
PLEASURES

≈

WE HAVE THREE WONDERFUL CHILDREN, WHO WERE A PLEASURE TO raise. The simple things they entertained themselves with amazed me. I remember Peter and his friend Daniel enjoying homemade playdough for at least half an hour when they were about four years old. I found them using plastic knives to cut dough into tiny pieces to make a salad. They spent such a long time doing this that I decided they must be detail people.

We also had gained a large collection of small toy cars and trucks. These vehicles had names and families. Our three children spent many happy hours making up stories and events these personalized cars and trucks took part in, and I would find vehicles in a long line, stretching through the house.

I taught the girls some embroidery and crochet. We also made their jeans into shorts and made the remaining cloth into purses, pillows, and a rough-braided rug. The Lord always seemed to give me an outlet for creativity, and we had fun together.

They made forts with furniture and blankets. Boxes held special excitement. Sometimes a box would arrive from the family in the United States with lots of treats. I wrote home, "The kids made spaceships out of the boxes and have flown to Mars. Sara is speaking into a toilet paper roll to communicate with Amy's ship. Peter's gone out for a spacewalk."

I have found that a stable home environment with love, and reasonable, enforced rules and routines calms children, and they become enjoyable companions. I never looked forward to them leaving home, though I wanted them to grow into happy, independent adults following God's unique path for their lives. Our children are a joy, and I loved watching them grow and find pleasure in the simple things.

Moving

≈

Whe would end up living in three different apartments during our four years in Moscow. Each needed a lot of fixing up, which we paid for. Then the landlords would break their agreement and raise the rent—so it was too expensive, and we had to move. The landlords ended up with a nice, fixed-up apartment.

I wrote home on September 8, 1992:

> We are moved into our new flat, and my back is OK, thanks to the help of many friends and neighbors. God sent the right people at the right time, a big Russian man with a roof rack on his station wagon to move the girls' bunk beds and big pieces of wood and a group of women to unpack the kitchen. The training center began the same day! A week later, the girls began school.
>
> I am slowly unpacking, about 10 boxes to go. We're also still having repair work done: plumbing, building shelves, installing a new sink and stove and water heater, reinstalling our steel (front) door, and reupholstering some furniture. We wallpapered and painted (had it done) several rooms and had the bathroom made from

two rooms to one so our washer and dryer could fit, had it tiled, and a new bathtub installed.

I have a lady helping me in the house, Vallya. She cleans and is a pleasant person. I try to be home to let in the workmen (and women) and generally coordinate it. She (Vallya) brings her small daughter, and she and Peter watch *Sesame Street*. Her daughter is no trouble, she seems pretty quiet.

P.S. Van made about 30 liters of canned plums from our dacha! There are still more plums on the trees, but we haven't had time or energy to pick them. The Russians call what we made compote. They certainly work hard at their dachas and store up for the winter!

Even though changing apartments involved a lot of time, energy, and expense, God sent us help; somehow, everything got done.

HEALTH
PROBLEMS

≈

Ｍy back trouble that began from carrying too many vegetables in Egypt continued to worsen in Russia. I had episodes where I could not stand for up to six weeks at a time. Once I wrote home, "I'm down with my back again—not as bad as when I was with you—I can get in bed and barely walk. But I'm basically useless as far as taking care of Peter or caring for the family. It's hard on Van. ... I think it's a combination of stress, having surfaces unusually low in the kitchen, gaining ten pounds, and possibly our futon." When I was well enough to get to church, we asked for prayer and met an American couple. They were new Christians, and the husband was a back surgeon. After listening to my symptoms, he offered to do surgery on my back at no charge. They even offered to have Peter and I stay in their home in the States while I was recovering. I prayed about this but had no peace. I came across a rather scary letter I wrote home:

> Right now, it seems to be affecting the nerve in my right leg, making it hard to walk. If I lay down most of the day, I can walk around the apartment and down to the playground and lay on a bench a lot of the time. This is the third week of this. The worst thing if I wait to get surgery is the possible loss of being able to

flex my right foot upward. That could be permanent. Another possibility is injuring it to the point of extreme pain that can't be relieved. The doctor said that could happen if I fell on the ice in winter. We signed up for an evacuation insurance for me that would air evacuate to a good doctor in Europe.

Then one of our Russian staff asked to bring his mother to see me. Although she was professionally trained in massage, we were hesitant, as some of our Russian friends had suggested some bizarre treatments. Finally, we agreed, and a small Russian grandmother with a bun on her head came to visit. Olga only spoke Russian and exuded a joyful spirit of praise for God. The first time Olga came, she asked me to lie on the bed and folded a small piece of paper back and forth, lit it on fire, and put it on my back. However, her quick fingers placed a glass jar over the paper, which was only burning on the end away from my skin. The fire went out with the lack of oxygen, forming a vacuum, which pulled the skin up toward the jar. Olga guided the glass around my back, which brought the blood to the surface. I felt no pain, and the whole effect was very relaxing.

On another occasion, Olga looked at me and announced that God did not want me to have surgery; he wanted me to exercise. I felt like God had spoken and given me the direction for my healing. Olga came every day to give me massages and exercises. While I lay on the bed, Olga taught me Russian and told stories of her childhood under Communism. My favorite story took place during World War II. Olga's family was out of food. Her mother prayed, asking God to provide for her family as he cared for the sparrows and to please not make them wait. That day, a man arrived from another village with a sack of potatoes. He said God had told him to bring the potatoes to her home. Olga ministered to me in every way; sometimes I wondered if she was an angel.

When Billy Graham came to Russia, children from across the Soviet Union responded and wrote to him. Olga became "Auntie Olga" and operated a Bible study correspondence course to follow up these children. She had twenty thousand children in her correspondence course. Olga used the money I paid her for my treatments to pay the ladies who helped her respond to the children.

When my back was feeling stronger, I had an MRI performed at a Russian hospital with a German MRI facility. Later, in San Francisco, I took the MRI results to a back doctor. He examined it and informed me it sounded like I had needed back surgery, but he took another MRI, which showed that my body had absorbed the bulging disc and would probably never give me problems again. He said sometimes that happened. I still remember that God wants me to exercise. I continue to do daily back exercises and walk regularly. In my time of need, the Lord sent just what I needed, using a small Russian woman with a big faith.

MANY ARE THE AFFLICTIONS

≈

Many are the afflictions of the righteous, but the LORD delivers him out of them all. (Psalm 34:19)

I WROTE HOME ON OCTOBER 13, 1992:

> It's about twenty degrees Fahrenheit and snowing; winter came overnight. The heat in our building isn't on yet because something is broken so it's hovering at sixty degrees in here. Yesterday the phone broke, so it's not without problems here.
>
> At the same time, a very nice neighbor arranged for a telephone repairman. Vallya came to clean my house and buy me bread. I had a nice talk with a secretary from the office, and Gosia came over with her kids, and we had bean soup with plum pie. Another friend arranged for someone to come today and seal our window casings with cotton and tape in preparation for the winter.

Our building also doesn't have hot water because of the same problem, but we do because of the gas water heater we installed. I just heard a nearby building only has hot water. I feel like we're somewhat experiencing what the Russian people experience, except we have more conveniences and more money. One of our (Russian) friends basically saw a savings account that probably equaled twenty thousand dollars dwindle to a few hundred dollars with the drop in the value of the ruble.

I also sense a spiritual battle going on. Recently, someone broke our car window; fortunately, they only took a bag of (ministry) notes. It was still a lot of inconvenience for Van and the secretaries. At the same time, they are having a good ministry with students, and things are going well. I feel like we're in the thick of the battle, many problems and many blessings. It reminds me of a verse: "Many are the afflictions of the righteous, but the Lord delivers him out of them all" (Psalm 34:19).

Please pray for Sara. She continues to be homesick for Merced and Grandma.... My back goes up and down; it's a challenge to know what I can and can't do. There is much I could do!

BUILDING THE
KINGDOM

≈

Watching God work in what we grew up thinking of as "the Evil Empire" amazed us. In fall 1992, we welcomed young university graduates from around the former Soviet Union to Moscow to be trained for nine months as missionaries to their own people. Vance wrote in a prayer letter:

> Things have really been busy at the training center. Everyone is very excited by the quality of our new trainees. Most of them became Christians through our ministry (at universities) and are only a couple years old in the faith. One couple however have been Christians for many years and are from the indigenous Baptist church. All of them have seen fruit from their witness and are in the process of starting small group Bible studies with seekers or new believers (at universities in Moscow).

Our new trainees ministered at the famous Moscow State University—one of the oldest, largest, and most prestigious universities in Russia. Under Communism, Christians were not allowed to attend the universities. Now we were holding weekly student meetings with about sixty in attendance. A famous American country singer—Ricky Skaggs—had some spare days in his tour and offered his time to our ministry. He performed at our meeting to a packed house and shared his testimony. Moscow's leading country western singing group even came to hear him, and several of them indicated decisions for Christ.

Following the concert, eighty-six students came to a weekend retreat held out of town in a pioneer camp, which was a former Communist youth training camp. I wrote home:

> It seems strange to think that the place for teaching youth Communist ideas is now used for a student Christian conference! We are staying in what looks like motel buildings: two stories with halls and rooms with two beds and a bathroom. It's out in the country, and there are perhaps five buildings widely spaced with other buildings; a cafeteria, a gymnasium, a meeting hall, and a large playground outside. It's basically clean and functional and decorated in styles that look like the 1950s. The children (our children) like the conference because our friends are here with their three children who are the same ages as ours. We are next to each other, and some children are sharing rooms.

Back in Moscow, God was at work in my neighborhood ladies Bible study. I wrote home:

> I've seen a real change in several [ladies] as they realize God is with them, they are forgiven and have eternal life. They are so much more joyful and happy than last year. They are all trying to tell others about the faith that has helped them.

We continued to be amazed watching God transform lives, raise up young people as laborers, and build student ministries in a country where only a short time before, they persecuted and killed Christians.

A STRANGE
BALLOON RIDE

≈

Delight yourself in the Lord; and He will give
you the desires of your heart. (Psalm 37:4)

I HAVE FOUND THIS VERSE TO BE TRUE IN MY LIFE, AS GOD KNOWS MY
heart's desires better than I do, and I allow him to meet those desires
however he wants to. This is often not in the way I expect. One of my
desires was to go up in a balloon. God granted this desire unexpectedly
on a cold, winter afternoon in Moscow.

Many people don't realize that Christianity has a long history in
Russia. Under Communism, Stalin demolished the Cathedral of Christ
the Saviour in 1931—the largest Orthodox church ever built. He intended
to replace it with one of his massive wedding cake-type structures with
buttressed tiers to support a huge statue of Lenin—raising his arm
and standing on a dome. It would be a monument to socialism called
the Palace of the Soviets. However, lack of funds, war, and flooding
from the Moskva River halted the project until Khrushchev built the
largest open-air swimming pool on the site—the Moskva Pool. Russians
believed God was behind all the obstacles. When Communism fell, they
built a church again on the site. About one million Russians donated
money for the church, which they consecrated in August 2000.

One Sunday, as our family was driving home from our international church, a strange sight greeted us as we arrived at the top of an overlook. Below stretched the city of Moscow, gray and chilly. Near the road—at the site of the demolished church—a small crowd gathered around a tethered hot-air balloon with a basket underneath.

We stopped and asked what was happening, and discovered money was being raised to rebuild the demolished church by giving balloon rides. I had wanted to go up in a balloon, so Sara and I got in line for a ride. Volunteers would hold the balloon while people climbed into the basket and then let the balloon rise while still attached to ropes—probably a couple hundred feet in the air. The tether ropes lay on the ground while people climbed into the basket, and as I watched the balloon rise, a woman who unknowingly was standing with her feet on either side of a rope rose with the balloon. She must have been five or six feet in the air before they got her untangled. Next, I saw someone climb halfway into the basket when the men lost their grip on the balloon, and it rose with the person half inside. Fortunately, they got inside in midair. But when our turn came, Sara and I jumped in that basket as fast as we could. We rose to a spectacular view of the city in a bitter cold wind. Gratefully, the chilly ride was brief. I left feeling thankful to be safe, and it satisfied my desire to ride in a balloon.

You can find the story of Cathedral of Christ the Saviour at:

Http://en.m.wikipedia.org/wiki/Cathedral_of_Christ_the_Saviour.

BILLY GRAHAM CRUSADE

≋

I WILL NEVER FORGET ATTENDING THE BILLY GRAHAM CRUSADE IN Moscow in fall 1992. Our student ministry rented buses and took interested students. Our family attended on Sunday—the final day—and barely found a seat on the top row of the huge indoor Olympic stadium, even though we arrived over thirty minutes early. Thousands stood outside in the snow. Inside, they packed even the aisles around us, and I barely made it to a restroom and back with one child—picking our way around all the people.

I remember empty stands as most of the fifty thousand people moved forward when Billy Graham gave the invitation. After so many people had gone forward, we found some of our trainees and other staff in the auditorium not far from us. It was a great time of rejoicing.

I have never seen such a massive response to the Gospel. They broadcast the Crusade across the former Soviet Union. The fields in this northern land were white for harvest.

TRIALS AND JOYS

≈

SOMETIMES, LIFE WAS JUST DIFFICULT AND TAUGHT US PERSEVERANCE. But along with troubles came many joys. One day, Vance wrote home to his mother:

> [5 degrees Fahrenheit] Today was quite a day for our car. I started it okay but then found the left rear brake frozen so the wheel wouldn't turn. Then while trying to free it, I found the electrical system wasn't working so the cooling fan on the radiator (it's electric) wasn't working, and the car overheated. Finally, while trying to free up a frozen door lock to lock the car, the key broke off in the lock.

I also wrote home:

> There seems to be a real spiritual battle here this year. Many of us sense it on many fronts. We have a lot of things coming through the prayer chain. One family had their landlady and her grandmother come over and lock themselves in a bedroom, refusing to come out. She insisted the family leave right away. They had to move in with another family, and many people are storing their things. Two days ago, a lady almost died from the flu. One lady I know who has worked on

our staff in this area for many years said she has never experienced such opposition during her years here.

At the same time, our neighbor—Luda, who had come to the Lord—was helping a new believer—Tanya—grow in her faith. And our children were doing well. Sara had her birthday party, which was a great success. All the children played games and ate pizza and cake in a room the size of a bedroom yet had a lot of fun. It's amazing what you get used to. We even found a bust of the ancient Egyptian queen—Nefertiti—in a local kiosk in Moscow. Sara had one just like it in Egypt, but it fell, and her nose broke. We never imagined we would find a Nefertiti bust in Moscow. Our school kids also enjoyed ice skating lessons across the street at the former tennis courts. And Peter was teaching himself to read by playing computer games. Game instructions came in printed form, and he was so motivated to play, I would find him studying instructions written for adults for long periods of time. One day, I found him on the adult flight simulator. He had taken off and was flying. Our lives were full, with trials to help us grow in faith and joys of spiritual fruit and family life.

RUSSIAN PETS

≈

DURING OUR TIME IN RUSSIA, OUR CHILDREN HAD MANY PETS, EVEN though we lived in a small apartment. I will never forget going to the open market for pets, which resembled a flea market. We found a tortoise atop a wooden post, with her body lying flat on the top of the post—legs dangling in the air. We also found a hamster, which greeted us by biting a finger, and a canary.

All these pets had interesting adventures. We discovered why CC the tortoise had a crack in her shell. She loved to climb. She climbed out of her box, climbed a pile of stuffed animals or anything she found, often falling on her back. But CC's favorite place was napping under the wall heaters.

Our hamster, "Mumpsy," was nocturnal and spent nights running in his wheel. He always tried to escape and finally succeeded. We heard him running under our wooden floors at night for a long time until I expect he went on to some neighboring apartment. My canary was in the kitchen; one day, he got out of his cage and became stuck behind a cabinet. I remember having to remove the wood facing to free him.

Russians also seemed to enjoy pets—especially dogs and sometimes exotic animals. One day in winter, Peter and I found an alligator carcass in the playground. Asking a nearby Russian lady, we found the alligator had probably been a pet in someone's bathtub. We enjoyed our more traditional pets, who enriched our lives.

GUINEA PIGS

≈

Buying pets in Moscow was quite an adventure. I wrote home:

Hi! It's Saturday night, and I'm pooped! We've been out looking for guinea pigs. Yesterday the children and I drove around locally for a couple hours. I did get twenty-two pounds of ground beef, a planter box, toy baskets, and a garbage can, but no guinea pigs at the closest pet store. So today the whole family made the long drive across Moscow to the big pet flea market.

First, it's nearly impossible to park. Then we walked by street vendors selling various auto parts and tools and people holding kittens, puppies, and bird cages. Then, tightly holding all the children, we walked across tram tracks, in between trams, and joined the throng of people entering the flea market. We were jostled and moved along by the mob and managed to dart through tables of tools into more quiet aisles of pigeons and various birds. Moving through the stalls, we at last found the guinea pig, hamster, and mice vendors, along with the cage and exercise wheel vendors. We spent a lot of time trying to find out ages, prices, and sex of various guinea pigs, along with general health and color. Our book on guinea pigs suggested two females. Amy finally settled on a brown and white smooth-haired female, and Sara chose a black and white female with swirls in her fur. But we couldn't find the right cage. Remembering that the book suggested a plastic tub, I recalled a store I'd visited the day before that had plastic baby bathtubs. So, with the guinea pigs in a little box, we made our way through the crowd to the car, buying a coke, crackers, and bananas on the way. Van dropped me off by the plastic store, as we couldn't figure out how to drive there (one-way streets). There was a line to get in, and they only let in a certain number of people at a time. At last I got in, bought the bathtub (around seven dollars), and went back to find where the family had parked. They were by a store selling boots, and I looked for some for Sara, leather wool-lined boots for thirty to forty dollars. But we couldn't find the right size. We finally got home after stopping at a nearby store to look for milk, unsuccessfully. But I bought an interesting looking unknown vegetable from a vendor. It looks like a turnip. He insisted we eat it raw and that it's very healthy.

Well, the guinea pigs liked their bathtub house and ash tray food dishes, flowerpot sleeping house, and an exercise wheel. The girls invited a friend over who also brought her guinea pig (also a girl). Sometimes I wonder why I should be so tired. Then I remember what I've done! Well, the hamster is beginning her nightly run in her wheel. Now we have five pets and five people, unless one of the guinea pigs is pregnant!

The guinea pigs—like little dogs—stretched up on their hind legs—heads peeping over the top of their plastic baby bathtub while squealing with delight when we entered the room. The children often held them—and we had to be careful because they would chew the buttons off the television remote controls. The guinea pigs also had outdoor excursions during warm weather.

OUR VILLAGE HOUSE

≈

SUMMER IN THE DACHA HAD BEEN SO REFRESHING THAT WE RENTED A place in the country for a winter family retreat. Our vacation house was outside of town, in a village of about five to ten thousand people. However, I think it must have been more crowded in the summer because most of the houses looked unequipped for winter—without insulation or heat. Our furnished house was moderately clean and had a bathroom inside (not a standard item) with running water, a two-burner gas stove, and gas heating. It was the size of a studio apartment, though it had a large unheated room upstairs we didn't use. The neighbor across the street let us park our car in his driveway. He also had a well outside he had dug himself.

Most villagers didn't have cars and used buses and the train. There were a handful of stores but no restaurants or motels. We loved to walk the snowy little streets and paths with hundreds of little houses and pine and birch trees. We rarely saw people, as most houses appeared empty, and we enjoyed the quiet. It reminded me of the way life may have been in America about one hundred and fifty years ago, except for a few modern products from the stores like coke and candy bars.

Visiting our neighbor one day, we enjoyed homemade bread rolls stuffed with fried onions and cabbage or with meat; we spent an extended time, talking in Russian.

My biggest surprise occurred while I was in the bathroom. I heard knocking and saw a small door in the bathroom wall. Opening it revealed a woman's face. She explained that she was a neighbor and wondered where the owner of the house was. I told her we were renting the house. She smiled and said goodbye, closing the door on her side of the opening. I never saw her again, but I felt comforted to know we weren't alone in the empty winter countryside.

Meetings in
the Woods

≈

IN JANUARY 1993, OVER TWO HUNDRED STAFF AND OVER SIXTY OF THEIR children—mostly Americans—met for a ten-day conference at the Russian White House's conference center, a snowy complex outside of Moscow. It was the only place we could find large enough to accommodate all of us. Vance had participated in the hunt for a place to meet, which even included a trip to Star City, the Russian space center, but it was not large enough.

Various sized buildings lay scattered through the woods. I wrote home:

> It is lovely outside in its own way. The sun so low on the horizon makes me feel I'm in a different world with a different sort of sun. The firs are dusted with snow, and after a snowfall, it looks like someone dumped a box of powdered sugar over everything. The river is so flat and smooth, all ice. Under the snow the grass is still green, and the trees have small buds, waiting to open.

Older staff from America who had lived overseas told stories of how God had protected and provided for them. One day, we had a day off, and Gosia, my Polish staff friend, and I joined others to cross-country ski through snowy woods. As I struggled with my skis, a young Russian man slid smoothly by, disappearing through the trees. I heard these trails connected towns. One day during the conference, everyone went for outreach. Vance, Amy, Sara, and I went witnessing in a nearby town and had an amazing experience.

The town was called Gorky Ten (they numbered towns, and this happened to be Gorky number Ten). Vance, Amy, Sara, and I knocked on a door, and a very nice family invited us in, without even asking who we were. We knew enough Russian to talk a little and found that they hadn't been able to have children. The wife had asked God for help, and then they had a baby boy. After that, she believed there is a God. We didn't know enough Russian to explain the Gospel to them but had "The Four Spiritual Laws" in Russian. So we asked if they would mind reading it since our Russian wasn't good enough. They read it and then both prayed, inviting Christ into their lives. They seemed to understand what they did. We left them with a Russian Bible and another helpful book in Russian.

I don't know what happened to that family, and we weren't aware of any churches or other believers in their area. We felt that a church could have easily been planted in that town if there was someone available to do it. God sent us to a family already prepared to receive him.

My Husband

≈

CAROL AND VANCE

I MARRIED A SPECIAL MAN, GIFTED IN LEADERSHIP AND ADMINISTRATION, adventurous yet steady, fun, funny, complex, brilliant, caring, responsible; I could go on. I wrote home in February 1993:

Van is somewhat less busy. Sometimes he looks tired to me and like he's aged about four years instead of two since we got here. He does handle pressure and chaos well. I'm grateful for such a solid, dependable husband. He's a great leader too, not afraid to make the hard decisions or go against popular opinion for the sake of doing the right thing, or step out and start going with a project when there are still a lot of loose ends, and we don't know where the resources will come from (a man of faith). He really is gifted in organizing and administrating, especially start-up projects. Since everything is in start-up here, it's a great place for him. Van's pretty involved in helping our girl's school start, in the GCTC, and in the ministry, as he's on the leadership team. I'm proud of him. He works hard but tries to balance it with the family. My illnesses give him more time to be with them (the children), but we spend a fair amount of time together anyway, most evenings and Saturday and Sunday.

God has continued to use my beloved husband to start and develop ministries. After Russia, we worked with the *JESUS* Film Project, a ministry of Campus Crusade for Christ showing the feature length film *JESUS* around the world. At the *JESUS* Film Project, he helped begin short-term mission projects in London, Turkey and Japan, and later led the *JESUS* film Missions Trip department. Then God led him to begin the People's Connection, which grew to a full-time team of nine plus volunteers and sent over five million *JESUS* film DVDs to those reaching immigrants in the States and Canada. It's been a privilege to watch God work. Walking alongside my husband has always been an adventure.

EASTER 1993

≋

SPRING FINALLY ARRIVED IN APRIL, AND I WROTE HOME:

> Yesterday we walked into the forest and picked pussy
> willows by a stream. The forest is still quite slushy
> with snow, but everywhere else, most of the snow has
> melted. It's still quite muddy. Yesterday was warm,
> about fifty degrees Fahrenheit. I have a new definition
> of warm now. Warm is when you can take off your
> down parka for a lined raincoat. It's warm when you
> can uncover your head (no hat or scarf) and wear shoes
> instead of boots. I've worn my boots since October.

In another letter, I wrote:

> Easter is a big holiday in the church here. We
> celebrated Russian Easter by making traditional bread
> called kulich—a sweet bread with raisins, nuts, and
> sometimes candied orange peel. We also made pasha of
> curds, sour cream, and sugar, pressed through a cloth
> to remove liquid, with raisins (a little like cheesecake),
> and we dyed eggs by boiling them with onion skins,
> resulting in a brick color. Orthodox Russians usually
> take their food to church to be blessed, then go to
> church Saturday night after 11 p.m. Sunday morning

they go to the cemetery to put flowers on the graves of relatives and return home for a family meal. We decided just to go to our international church service as we had celebrated Easter last Sunday. We also got some circus tickets, so we had an interesting time watching trained bears, dogs and monkeys, and different acrobats and gymnasts.

Easter in Russia was unforgettable, as we told friends, "Christ is Risen!" and received the response, "He is Risen indeed!" The emphasis on resurrection refreshed us, and we still occasionally make kulich.

God Keeps the
Doors Open

≈

After we returned from a busy summer furlough in America, violence erupted in downtown Moscow. Vance sent a prayer letter explaining the situation:

> Last week I attended a meeting of missionary leaders in Moscow. The meeting was called to discuss the new restrictive law on religion that the parliament had passed. Between the time the meeting was called, and we actually met, the parliament was disbanded and the Russian White House stormed. Speaking at our meeting were a leading Russian sociologist and expert on religion, the president of the Russian Christian Legal Society, and a well-known and respected dissident Orthodox priest who was also a member of the parliament (before it was disbanded), Father Gleb. The information they supplied us with about what was going on over the past days proved to be very enlightening.
>
> Evidently, this bill to restrict mission activity in Russia was part of a larger effort to suppress all religious activism. As you may know, the leadership of the

Orthodox Church was chosen by the Communists. Many people consider them to be KGB agents. At the same time the parliament was secretly working on the bill to suppress Protestant activities, the parliament was also giving more power to the Orthodox leaders (not necessarily the Orthodox Church) so these people could suppress dissent within the Orthodox Church. Some priests have evidently even been removed from their churches.

Father Gleb served on the human rights committee in the former parliament and sought to stop this bill but was unable. He said that President Yeltsin very courageously tried to stop this law from being enacted. (According to Father Gleb, the support from America was very important in encouraging Yeltsin to oppose the bill.) After Yeltsin rejected the bill, he returned it to the Parliament for a rewrite. The parliament then made some changes that may have made it worse rather than better and sent it back to Yeltsin for a second time. Father Gleb, who was one of the only people in the parliament opposing this bill, said that no one doubted that the bill would be passed within a matter of two months. He also stated that it was no accident that Yeltsin vetoed this bill and returned it to parliament just four days before he disbanded the parliament. Father Gleb also shared some very interesting facts about what happened after the parliament's disbanding. While the parliament hard liners were holed up in the Russian White House before their violent attack on the television studios on Sunday, October 2, they only acted on one piece of legislation, this bill to restrict religious freedom. After passing the bill, Rutskoi, the former vice president who they appointed to replace Yeltsin, signed this bill into law. It seems that only the disbanding of the parliament has saved us from this bill actually becoming a reality.

The kings of the earth take their stand
And the rulers take counsel together
Against the LORD and against His
Anointed, saying,
"Let us tear their fetters apart
And cast away their cords from us!"
He who sits in the heavens laughs,
The Lord scoffs at them.
Then He will speak to them in His anger
And terrify them in His fury. (Psalm 2)

Looking back, I realize now that had the doors to foreign missionaries closed at that time, the infant ministries and young Christians would not have had the maturity and strength they do today. In 1993, many of the believers had only known the Lord for a few years, and national leadership was not yet in place. Praise God for His protection.

I wrote home in October 1993:

I do sense God is moving here and is not allowing the doors to close. I sense He has great plans for this place, and we've only begun. After living in Egypt, I'm convinced that if God wants us to stay, we'll be able to. I guess I'm getting used to living in uncertain conditions, though sometimes, I long to find a way to be more stable. But God gives me grace, and I find it's my heart's desire to be where He has us, even if it's unstable.

We do have many blessings in the midst of many struggles. I guess that's the paradox of Christianity, how it's difficult yet sweet.… I am at peace. I sense God doing something here in Russia and that people won't be able to stop it. But we still need to pray. Prayer is so powerful yet intangible, especially when it's linked with faith and a promise from the Bible. I'm coming to believe it's the greatest work we can do. We are all well. Everyone has been so healthy this year, and my back is fine. Most mornings, I climb nine flights of stairs seven times (taking the elevator down each time), do back exercises, read the Bible, and pray and take a shower. Also, I try to go for a walk every day with Peter. If I shop daily for about an hour, we never run out of food.

Our life goes on with school schedules, plus piano two times a week for Amy (in Russian), ice skating lessons two times a week for all the kids, language two times a week for me, and tutoring once a week for Amy. The kids describe their school as fun and interesting. They are all learning more Russian—even Peter (in kindergarten). He likes his teacher—a man who makes paper airplanes, plays the piano, and plays basketball while teaching Russian. Sara's Russian teacher cooks with her students, has tea parties, and goes on walks. It's fun to watch the kids grow.

Van's office stuff is still scattered all over our house. I'm getting used to using the microwave in the hall as a place to put backpacks and mail. The Xerox machine in the girl's room is where we put school papers and books we're reading. Van is ready to have his office, and we don't understand why things keep falling through. So we keep praying and working and taking one day at a time. God provides what we need for now and we trust Him for later.

Even during political instability and unsettled conditions, our lives were full of God's supernatural joy and peace.

CREATIVE
OUTLETS

≈

THROUGHOUT MY LIFE, I'VE FOUND JOY IN DIFFERENT CREATIVE OUTLETS, and Russia was no exception. I loved the creative soul of the Russian people. I wrote home in October 1993:

> I think I'm finally adapting to living here; there's a certain beauty and wildness in these northern climates. I like the intensity of it. In summer it's SO green, and the flowers are SO colorful. In winter the air is SO fresh, the snow is SO white, and the trees SO dark. In autumn the colors are SO dazzling. All this intensity comes out in the culture and the arts. I enjoy all that.
>
> I'm cooking more Russian. Today we had beets with butter, potatoes I boiled, then peeled and sautéed with butter, and fresh dill and big sausage links I boiled then fried in butter. I've been peeling and slicing apples and sprinkling them with sugar and cinnamon for breakfast. I also bought a gunnysack of potatoes and put it on our balcony (about ninety pounds of potatoes). Luda recommended it. Now it's potato and apple season. I do enjoy cooking; it's really become a

hobby. One of my favorite things is poking around the local stores and figuring out how to fix the things I find there.

I do have to add that we had some strange experiences with trying unknown food from local grocery stores. Since most food came in brown paper packages with only writing on the outside and no pictures, sometimes we couldn't figure out what we had bought. Once I mistakenly made flat, runny pancakes out of something that wasn't pancake mix, and another time foolishly tasted a clear yellow liquid that resembled lemonade but tasted like gasoline. I think it was concentrated vinegar, which is toxic unless diluted. But most of the time, I enjoyed the creative challenge of finding and learning to prepare Russian food.

NEIGHBORS

≈

Our neighbors, Vera and Luda, became special friends, and we continued to meet to study the Bible. Today, Vera and her husband Vladimer still pursue their career in avant-garde art and travel to New York and other countries for exhibitions and lectures. Luda—who became Vance's secretary—taught me how to cook Russian dishes. I wrote home in October 1993:

> I sense a step forward in our neighborhood ministry. The two women in my Bible study who are disciple type women are still moving ahead. We decided to meet as a couple with just Vera and her husband Vladimer. We found he has a real spiritual hunger and began to believe in God after meeting daily with an Orthodox priest for a year and a half. Luda and I are trying to have an outreach to our neighbors and have visited several neighbors. She says she has to do all the work because her Russian is better than mine! Anyway, I'm excited about the neighbors. I continue to meet more of them as I climb stairs for exercise.

Luda was learning to share her faith with others, and as Vance's secretary, she mothered our young trainees. Typing the training curriculum, she also learned about the Bible and grew as a Christian. I felt blessed to have Luda and Vera as friends.

AT HOME WITH THE KIDS, JANUARY 1994

≈

Often, I stayed home with the children and Vance traveled. Though we missed him, I enjoyed time with my children, and we had fun together. It was easier for me to care for them alone now they were older and able to help. This is what I wrote home on January 16, 1994:

> Hello from snowy Moscow! It's a white world outside with deep, soft snow. Today the kids and I joined other families on a local sledding hill. Then they played house in a playground, cooking pretend food from ice and snow. We had a game of catch with a snowball (that had to be remade when dropped) before coming home. I got to ride home on a sled while Amy pulled. I thought about all the memories the kids will have of snow. Snow is the usual thing here. It seems unusual not to have it. Van is coming home tonight after a five-day trip. Everyone is excited about his return. He got delayed in customs, and I put the children to bed with a promise Dad will come see them. They were reluctant but went.

Another time, all the kids were sick with coughs, so we stayed home, and Vance went alone to a conference in Saint Petersburg. The train left at 1 a.m., and the temperature outside was between -15 and -26 centigrade. I wrote home on February 13, 1994:

> We've had a nice time at home; it's nice to be with the children. I've cooked some of their favorite foods, popcorn, cookies, hot dogs. Today we're having pizza, Peter's favorite, and making heart cookies for Valentine's Day. I'm teaching Sara how to sew. We're making her a summer jumper that's culottes. She helped cut it out and sewed some seams and helped gather. Today I hope to teach Amy to cut out her dress. Sara seems to like it the most right now.
>
> We've been reading a kid's devotional at night that deals with problems kids face today. Our children face only a small percent of the problems. It's almost like America is another culture. Van and I are amazed when we read the book and realize the problems our kids aren't facing. Everyone from their [missionary] school comes from good wholesome families. Well, it's about time to make cookies.

I remember talking to the wife of one of our leaders with Campus Crusade for Christ who had lived in another country. I asked her how to raise children, and she said to raise them overseas. I agree. The missionary community is unparalleled, though not perfect. We had the privilege to raise our children this way, and I wouldn't trade it or the opportunity to spend time with them when Vance traveled.

THE BELLY
DANCER

≈

V ance and I enjoy regular date nights and one evening tried a
new Russian restaurant. It was a pleasant place, except for the loud
music. We were the only customers when—to our surprise—our
good friends and coworkers arrived, also on a date. We decided to
sit separately so we could spend time as couples. They also had three
children at home.

Since we were the only people in the restaurant, we asked if they
would play a classical music tape we had in our car. Enjoying the
atmosphere and romantic time, we noticed two ladies walk in, and
then the music changed abruptly. Familiar melodies from the Middle
East flowed from the loudspeakers when, to our shock, a woman
emerged dressed as a belly dancer, and as she danced, she sidled up
to our coworker. He averted his eyes, though it was hard to avoid the
woman swaying directly in front of his table within arm's reach. About
that time, they decided it was time to go. I don't think they finished
their dinner. We left soon after.

We found out the woman was auditioning for a job at the restaurant
and didn't know the only people in the restaurant were missionaries.
I doubt she got the job after we all walked out. We had a lot of fun
teasing each other later about the belly dancer.

THE LONG DARK WINTER

≈

Moscow has seven months of snow and mostly dark skies, where the cloud-covered sun never rises more than about 45 degrees above the horizon. The sun rose late in the morning and set by midafternoon. Illness and depression struck the population, and I was no exception. Sara expressed the weather in her letter home: "It is a blisered over her and I meen it is snowing. It will freez your hands off." In February, I was home recovering from a case of strep throat—a complication of the flu. I was weak from two different courses of antibiotics and resting in bed. I wrote home:

> I want to somehow balance my life—so I don't get so exhausted. Often, I'm tempted to just go to America and live, just live, out in the country someplace, and just take care of my house and family and go to church on Sundays and have a routine life, sometimes I crave routine, and forget about trying to learn Russian and reach this country. But then I think about how exciting it will be to see someday the results of all this and how the sacrifice is always repaid abundantly in some way. And, besides, God sent us, which is the bottom line.

> Sometimes I think I'm getting too old for all this, and my body's worn out. Then I get letters from friends my

age in America who have health problems, and they're in America! So, in the end, I'm glad for the chance for us to put our strength and our years into something of eternal significance, though I'd have to say it hasn't been easy recently. Many of our coworkers have felt discouraged, and some have had to move, or had their cars stolen. And winter seems eternal, and sometimes illness does too. So we are being made mature and learning to endure, and I am learning to understand sick people. And Van is learning to take care of the kids, and the kids learn to help more. And I am looking forward to the harvest of righteousness and peace in Hebrews 12:11 after we have been trained by this discipline. And then, the sun comes out in Moscow, the world looks brighter, and all the difficulties are forgotten in the glory of it all. It's like spring after winter. You can't believe it's even the same country.

I've never experienced much depression before. I don't think it's in the nature of a phlegmatic-sanguine like me to feel depressed. But I have felt times of depression here, and so have many of my coworkers. I think we are experiencing a little of what Russians experience. Spring is coming, but it still seems so far away. Winter and cloudy days seem endless. Fruit and vegetables are harder to find. I think I understand more why Russians like tragedy. They're depressed and can identify with it. But though they experience the lows, they also experience the highs: artistic excellence, beauty, the Russian countryside in summer, a paradise, as one man described it. When God promised an abundant—full and overflowing—life, it certainly is true. Our lives are full and overflowing with life, love, experiences, ranges of feeling and depth; I could go on. Van says it's like we've already lived more than enough life for one life.

THE PROMISE

≈

IN SPRING 1994, PRICES IN MOSCOW WERE GOING CRAZY. WE AND OUR coworkers suffered under rising rent and food costs, but not as much as the Russian people. In other republics such as Tashkent, prices were even higher. We heard that some people ate only bread and milk. Our apartment, for which we had been paying seven hundred and fifty dollars per month, was now costing us between twelve hundred and fifteen hundred dollars per month. Our office price was also rising. A new Moscow law made it legal for foreigners to buy property, and a window of opportunity in Saint Petersburg caught our attention.

The big villas owned by wealthy Russians before Communism in downtown Saint Petersburg were now for sale. Under Communism, the government had seized the villas and moved multiple families into each home. A family would have a room, and all the families shared the bathroom and kitchen. These families had lived this way for many years and often had conflicts with so little space for privacy. With the rise of the free market, companies sprung up offering to buy the room in the villa and—in exchange—purchase the family their own apartment. Once the company resettled all the families, they sold the entire villa—sometimes to foreigners. One of our coworkers raised money and bought one of these villas.

Prices in Saint Petersburg were going up 15 percent a month, so Vance and I got on an overnight train and went north to talk with realtors. It was fun to tour the beautiful villas for sale, with their high ceilings. I felt like I'd walked into the *Dr. Zhivago* movie. Vance and I had just been deeded a piece of property from Grandma Nordman, so this idea was totally within reach. We also considered buying a building to house the training center and the trainees.

About this time, I received a promise from the Lord. We had always rented but moving so often in Moscow because the landlords broke the contracts and raised the rent was taking a toll on me. I just wanted to stay in one place and not keep fixing apartments only to leave them. It was exhausting. I talked to the Lord about it, and one day, he gave me a promise. I've learned to hear his voice, and this sure sounded like him:

> I will also appoint a place for My people Israel and will plant them, that they may live in their own place and not be disturbed again, nor will the wicked afflict them any more as formerly, even from the day that I commanded judges to be over My people Israel; and I will give you rest from all your enemies. The LORD also declares to you that the LORD will make a house for you. (2 Samuel 7:10–11)

I knew God spoke this to Israel, but I thought I heard the Lord say it was for me too. So I believed it and felt our home must be in Saint Petersburg. However, when we returned to Moscow with the good news, our director said he didn't want the training to move to Saint Petersburg but to stay in Moscow. It was a mystery, and I thought maybe I hadn't heard correctly from the Lord. But God's ways are not our ways. The Lord would fulfill the promise, but not in the way I expected.

Finding ACE

≈

I THINK IT WAS DURING OUR SECOND YEAR IN RUSSIA THAT AMY STARTED having trouble with the math curriculum our school used. We had to do something, and I can't remember where, but we heard about Accelerated Christian Education (ACE). I believe God led us to this curriculum that worked for Amy.

ACE comes out of Texas, and many Christian schools use their mastery-based workbooks. ACE used their curriculum to spread the Gospel in other countries. One of those countries was Russia.

I rode a bus in the dead of winter around the snowy ring road encircling Moscow. Inside a nondescript block of buildings, I found the little ACE school. Russian children sat at their desks, using the English workbooks, which taught basic subjects and the Christian faith. The staff were so helpful and sold me the math curriculum I needed for Amy.

Amy and I worked on math at home together with her new curriculum, and she joined her classmates in school for the other subjects. When we returned to America, Amy used ACE successfully for all her school subjects all the way through high school. Many missionaries return home because of educational needs for their children. God provided for us through the staff of a little mission school hidden away inside a huge building in dark, snowy Moscow.

EGYPT: SUNSHINE AND REFRESHMENT

≈

IN MARCH 1994, OUR FAMILY TOOK A VACATION AND VISITED EGYPT. THE long winter still gripped Moscow, while Egypt and our friends greeted us with warmth and love. I wrote home:

> We got back from Egypt the day before yesterday and had a wonderful time. It seemed so much like home. At first, we could understand what people said, but when we spoke, it came out in Russian. Then we spoke a mixture of Russian and Arabic. Finally, we began to speak mostly Arabic. Our Arabic is still better than our Russian. We spent the first night at a hotel in Cairo, where we usually stayed before or after we arrived by plane. It has a big garden with grass, a playground, and a swimming pool for adults and kids. It also has a big buffet breakfast with traditional Egyptian food as well as Western food. The kids were like young calves let out of a barn. They just ran everywhere and splashed in the kid's pool. The temperature was probably in the 70s (Fahrenheit). When we left Moscow, it was around 32 degrees. We walked to the plane over slippery ice in our street shoes and wearing several layers of clothes.

We didn't want to carry around boots and coats. The kids said it was great to be able to run without worrying about slipping, and Peter said it was nice to go outside without having to put on a coat.

The next day, we went by train to Alexandria and were met by three of our staff, who took us and our luggage to an apartment next door to our friends—Ray and Gail—who have four children. The apartment is inside a nunnery and on the grounds of the international elementary school. So—it was private and secure for the kids to run around. It was completely furnished with dishes, things to cook with, bedding etc., even a washing machine. It seemed so big: four bedrooms, a living room, dining room, two bathrooms, with sinks and closets in each bedroom. Ray and Gail took great care of us and had arranged two open houses, one for our staff and one for our church. We enjoyed talking to everyone. We also spoke at a staff meeting. Egypt now has fifty national staff. We spoke at church and went to the homes of three of our Egyptian staff and to the homes of two American missionary families. So we were busy, but we enjoyed it all.

We also did things that were special to our family: a morning at the zoo and a trip to Montaza—the beach resort and grounds of the summer palace of the last king of Egypt. And we had a look at the last two houses we had lived in. We did a little shopping and bought cotton shirts and underwear, which Egypt is famous for. We also celebrated Easter. The children had a candy hunt with twelve other children. Finally, we said goodbye to our friends in Alexandria and went by train to Cairo. We rented a taxi for a day and went first to the pyramids. Van and the kids went inside. Then we saw the solar boat (for the first time) and the Sphinx. We got some chicken McNuggets (Egypt has changed!) and went to a Pharaonic Village, where things were made to look like ancient Egypt, complete with people acting out their parts. We saw how they made bricks, papyrus, pottery, statues, wall engravings, and perfume, and how they farmed. We also saw papyrus growing, went in a rich man's house, a poor man's house, a temple, and a replica of King Tut's tomb, with replicas of everything just as they found it. The highlight was dressing up in Egyptian costumes and getting our pictures taken. We had a good trip back on Egypt Air, with a short layover in Budapest. It was about two and a half hours from Cairo to Budapest and three hours from Budapest to Moscow. It sure was good to go back, but we saw that our part of the work there was finished—at least for now.

That was our last trip to Egypt, though Peter and Sara visited when they were college students. We are still in touch with Egyptian friends and will always remember their warm love and encouragement—especially coming from the long dark Russian winter of 1994.

DR. BILL BRIGHT

≈

Brethren, join in following my example, and observe those who walk according to the pattern you have in us. (Philippians 3:17)

ONCE—AT A *JESUS* FILM PROJECT DINNER IN CALIFORNIA—WHEN asked to speak about why I continue in ministry, I quoted a poem my daughter Sara had given me about a little lady following me. I talked about following the model of Dr. Bill Bright, a spiritual father figure, and remembering that others are watching and following me. As I spoke about Dr. Bright, I began to weep at the podium, which astonished me. Until then, I didn't realize the depth of my emotion or the role he played in my walk with Christ.

I first met Dr. Bright in 1974, when I joined the staff of Campus Crusade for Christ. I sat with hundreds of other new staff in the outdoor amphitheater at the beautiful CCC headquarters in the hills of San Bernardino, California. After the meeting, I walked to the front and introduced myself to Dr. Bright, saying I just wanted to shake his hand. God had used the materials he wrote about confessing sin and walking in the power of the Holy Spirit to affect my life in a powerful way.

A few years later, Dr. Bright visited Houston, where many financial supporters of Campus Crusade lived. He always liked to visit the staff wherever he went, and everyone met in the home I lived in with Debbie, another staff woman. I felt so honored and enjoyed the staff family time. Dr. Bright and his wife, Vonette, always made the staff feel like family.

When Vance and I served in Egypt, we visited the Holy Land twice, and on one occasion, Dr. Bright was also visiting. I heard he collected cuff links, and our Egyptian director, Mounir, had a pair made in Egypt with Alexandrite stones. I delivered these to him in Israel when he visited with the staff at a conference. I remember his humor and humility. He loved to talk about Jesus and could relate to the man on the street or the Queen of England (which he did upon receiving the Templeton award and then donated the one million dollars to the ministry).

Russia was the country Dr. Bright prayed especially for, and I heard he had given his retirement money to advance the ministry in Russia. In 1994, Dr. Bright came to the graduation of our national Russian staff from the nine-month training school Vance directed. It was a formal occasion, with a dinner and a ceremony. At the dinner, to my surprise, Dr. Bright came to sit beside me for a while, asking how I was. Again, his fatherly care for the staff amazed me. I believe Campus Crusade for Christ had at least twenty-five thousand staff and volunteers internationally, with perhaps five thousand staff in the States. Yet he continued to seek opportunities to express care for us.

Dr. Bright was humble and fun-loving. He trusted God like a child and believed people everywhere would come to Jesus if they only could understand God's great love for them. He didn't defend himself when criticized and continued to move forward with what he believed God wanted, regardless of obstacles or opposition. And we witnessed miracles and millions coming to Christ. His challenge to "Come help change the world" and his signature on correspondence, "Yours for fulfilling the Great Commission in this generation," still motivate me to follow his example and continue in ministry, proclaiming Jesus until he comes.

Summer Beauty

≋

In May 1994, the kids and I enjoyed the Moscow summer while Vance attended a conference in Finland. I wrote home:

> Well, the weather is beautiful today. Russia can be breathtakingly beautiful or dismally gray. When the colors are there and the sun shines, it's almost too intense to look at. It also reminds me of the High Sierras in the summer. The children have Monday and Tuesday off because of a Russian holiday. Today is Saturday. It's such a beautiful day we went for a walk and explored a different forest about a ten-minute walk away. There are three forest parks within walking distance. They are birch and pine forests with paths through them.
>
> This forest had more hills and was more rustic. There was a man-made lake on the other side with a couple of ducks and a big hill with grass and dandelions. It was fun sitting on the hill with the children making flower chains into wreaths, rings, and bouquets. The wind blowing the pine trees and the big sky and lime green leaves of other trees were all so pretty together. A lot of people were out enjoying the day.

We came out of the forest by a Chinese restaurant I had heard of. It was an outdoor snack place. The food didn't look too good, so we just got drinks. Then we walked back, stopping at a Russian store with big lines, where I bought flour, bread, and eggs. Outside I got some parsley from a vendor. They sell fruits and vegetables in separate stores—usually with lines (about ten minutes wait). But only vendors sell greens (parsley, dill, green onions). I like to freeze them to use in cooking. We came home and ate lunch, a make-it-yourself sandwich lunch with bread, roast beef, cheese, pickles, tomatoes, and pears. I just made candied popcorn with peanuts, and the kids are eating it.

Summer in Moscow in 1994 held many delights.

Refuge in Turmoil

≈

My soul, wait in silence for God only,
For my hope is from Him.
He only is my rock and my salvation,
My stronghold, I shall not be shaken.
On God my salvation and my glory rest;
The rock of my strength, my refuge is in God.
Trust in Him at all times, O people;
Pour out your heart before Him;
God is a refuge for us. Selah. (Psalm 62:5–8)

LIVING WITH UNRESOLVED ISSUES HAS TOUCHED MY LIFE AT DIFFERENT times, and each time, I have grown spiritually, though it is probably my least favorite state of being. I wrote home on October 15, 1994:

It's a beautiful Fall, and the trees are incredible, all sorts of leaves all sorts of colors—from purplish red to bright red orange to whole trees of bright yellow and others of mottled green and yellow. The changing light from sun and clouds illuminates one color then another. The air is brisk and clean. I'm glad to live in Moscow just for the experience of Fall. This morning I walked to church alone to go to choir practice before church. Just looking around at nature helps lift my spirit above the turmoil of here and now to God. Then singing praises all morning carries the mood along. I've been thinking a lot about Psalm 62:5–8. There are some situations here that have been trying our patience for some time. I tried appealing for help, but it didn't seem to help the situation. Through Psalm 62, I sensed God telling me to be quiet and wait on Him. My soul finds rest in God alone. There are many emotions when living with unresolved situations: frustration, anger, etc., which all probably don't glorify God. I got a new sense that no matter what is going on in life, my soul can climb into a fortress which is God, and there find rest and peace. So I can find the proper godly reaction, love, forgiveness, joy, to whatever external circumstance there is. God frees us to live above the circumstances by climbing into Him and pouring out our hearts to Him.

Sometimes I think some of the main reasons we're here is to have the children in this godly school and to develop our character and mature us. Circumstantially we could get discouraged. Our job may end this year. It isn't decided yet and I don't know when it will be. Our landlady's daughter raised our rent to one thousand three hundred and fifty dollars. We said no and agreed to leave in six weeks. We don't know what will happen with us after this year, and we don't know where we will live then, lots of uncertainty. So it's a good chance to learn to be still and wait on God. A lot of it is just beginnings of this ministry. Beginnings are unstable and bumpy. Van and I seem to like beginnings in spite of it, and we feel a little like the pioneers who started to feel crowded when more people came—and they longed to move on. There's something in us that keeps longing for the frontier, to move on to the untouched, unreached. We've just got itchy feet even now in our forties. Sometimes I'm amazed we're both that way. I guess we're just made to be starters not managers. God continues to encourage me from the Bible, other Christians, and in different ways. I know in due time we will reap if we don't grow weary in doing good. Please pray for our persistence.

EXERCISE IN TRUST

≈

MOUNTAIN CLIMBING, ZIP LINING, AND SKYDIVING HELP TEAMS TRUST each other and work together. In Moscow, God allowed an unexpected event to bond our leadership team. We met regularly as a team to coordinate the ministry and occasionally had retreats at hotels. One hotel boasted a Russian spa in the basement. Our team took advantage of this, and we all met downstairs with our bathing suits on, ready to relax in the pools. Slippery tile separated small pools of deep water of varying temperatures. I don't remember safety barriers or railings, just slippery smooth tile about two feet wide, separating lots of square pools.

As our team walked through the pools with our bare feet, suddenly and without warning, all the lights went out. The basement was in total darkness—just like a cave. We all froze, wondering what to do to avoid the maze of treacherous pools we couldn't see. Then someone had an idea: Joining hands, we formed a long chain and slowly shuffled forward. All I remember was holding Greg's hand in front of me and trustingly following. No one panicked, and before long, we safely emerged. God had provided a unique and unexpected lesson in trust for our team.

THE CHOCOLATE CAFE

≈

VANCE AND I HAVE ENJOYED MANY MEMORABLE DATE NIGHTS, AND A highlight was dining at a chocolate cafe in Moscow. Waiting outside amid a growing crowd, we wondered why no one was entering the restaurant. Finally, the doors opened, and they ushered in the whole crowd as a group to an empty restaurant.

After we were all seated, a meal arrived in courses. Everyone received the same food. I remember everything revolved around chicken and chocolate. I wondered if the restaurant had some special access to these two products and came up with a creative idea for a restaurant. An egg atop the soup, a small dark chocolate beverage with a little sugar, and many more dishes I can't remember now, except that chicken or eggs combined somehow with chocolate. They served each course to the group, and every person in the room had to finish before the next course arrived. Being a slow eater, I felt pressed to eat faster so the whole room could proceed with the meal. Finally, after dessert, they emptied the whole room so the next group could begin. The chocolate cafe reminded me of the Soviet era, when they did everything as a group rather than individually. We had another glimpse of a culture different from our own and an unusual dinner.

Uncertainty
and Growth

≈

In October 1994, we were having troubles again with the landlady wanting to raise the rent. Also, our job was uncertain. As the Soviet Union broke into separate parts, our ministry would also divide and no longer be centrally run. Our new leaders held varying ideas of how they wanted staff trained. Uncertainty surrounded us. I wrote home:

> This week has been sort of like body surfing when the wave lands on top of you. The hardest thing is riding out the establishment of this ministry as directions are set and leaders chosen. It's living with ambiguity and uncertainty, and the only comfort I have is God's word and His continuing call. The challenge to me is thought control, deciding to think about and live for today by the power of God. Please pray I will do this.

> In most respects, everything is great. Van is stretched and challenged, the kids seem to be thriving, and I'm OK as long as I don't overload. We are seeing people receive Christ with our Russian staff, and people are growing in the Lord. Growth, difficulties are all there,

and God always provides. I love being on the edge of faith, growth, and it's where we are.

In another letter, I wrote about a student conference held at a camp outside of Moscow. The ministry was exploding with growth.

There are over one thousand college students from all over: Alma Atta, Bishkek, Saint Petersburg, Kiev, Lithuania, Siberia, and more places. There are about sixty to seventy from our campus. It's exciting to watch our GCTC trainees teach the basic seminars about Christianity, to hear Russians teaching other Russians (and Cossacks and Lithuanians etc.). They all understand Russian. Many who came weren't Christians, and at least twenty percent have indicated decisions. Tomorrow we're going to a luncheon for students interested in staff. We hear sixty will attend. I think the Lord is working a lot in people's lives here. This is helping get many ministries off the ground. There are many new teams of Americans around the former USSR, and they're the ones who have brought all these students.

The ministry was expanding and getting ready to divide and grow more. Exciting and uncertain, joyful and painful, we felt blessed to be a part of it all.

WHERE IS HOPE?

≈

MOVING AGAIN, JOB UNCERTAINTY, AND FEELING DISCONNECTED WERE hard for me.

On November 16, 1994, I wrote in my journal:

> Where is hope? It seems to be the question of the hour. Where is my hope? Am I down when circumstances are hard, when I have to move, and my life is all disrupted; when we don't have lots of money to buy everything I want for this house right now or even know how much we should buy in light of our situation? Where is my hope? Is it in a nice life right now; in a secure, happy home; in a secure future; in my emotions—if they are up or down? How am I different from those around me who don't know God, who have no hope, whose life now is hard? My hope is in the promises of God. "For I know the plans that I have for you, declares the Lord, plans for welfare and not for calamity to give you a future and a hope" (Jeremiah 29:11). I can stake my life on God's promises. They are always true.

> Let us not lose heart in doing good, for in due time we will reap if we do not grow weary. (Galatians 6:9)

If we have hoped in Christ in this life only, we are of all men most to be pitied. (1 Corinthians 15:19)

If the dead are not raised, let us eat and drink, for tomorrow we die. (1 Corinthians 15:32b)

Therefore, my beloved brethren, be steadfast, immovable, always abounding in the work of the Lord, knowing that your toil is not in vain in the Lord. (1 Corinthians 15:58)

Therefore we do not lose heart, but though our outer man is decaying, yet our inner man is being renewed day by day. For momentary, light affliction is producing for us an eternal weight of glory far beyond all comparison, while we look not at the things which are seen, but at the things which are not seen; for the things which are seen are temporal, but the things which are not seen are eternal. (2 Corinthians 4:16–18)

And there, in the resurrection, in eternity, in God's promises of these and of reward, is my hope.

RELEASING

≈

OFTEN, I HAVE FOUND THAT GOD HELPS ME RELEASE WHEN THE TIME comes to go. This time, his method was through moving—again. Our landlady raised the rent, and we moved to the edge of Moscow, within walking distance of the children's school. I wrote home on December 6, 1994:

> I have an inner peace about the future. We should know in the next month or so if we'll be here next year or not. Please pray we walk daily in the Spirit, praising God and following His voice. This hasn't been an easy assignment, but it's been good for our spiritual growth and good for the kids. It has been like climbing a steep mountain, which was an illustration God gave me when we came here.
>
> Personally, I feel like the things I set out to do in the fall—church choir, Russian study, meeting with Van's secretaries, staff meeting in our home—have all been tossed up in the air because we moved. I'm too far away to get to church very early for choir practice, Russian is on hold as all my efforts are directed to moving, the office is hard for me to get to as we have one car, plus I don't usually drive in winter, and we're too far for

the staff to meet in our house. But I have a peace this move is God's will. I just feel sort of disconnected and haven't really got connected to where we are now. It seems to take a long time to get connected in Russia, and I sometimes wonder if I'm disconnected because it's easier to be moved if you're already pulled up.

We were indeed being disconnected, and God graciously helped us through it by moving apartments.

CHRISTMAS AGAIN

≈

Like the Russians, we celebrated and invited family and friends for special occasions, even though there wasn't much room in our home. It was like living in a large trailer. But like the Russians, we used what we had and enjoyed each other and the holidays.

On December 26, 1994, I wrote home:

> There's a nice Russian custom of either dropping by or calling on a birthday or special day. On Christmas day, we received two phone calls and a quick visit from Russian friends. It made the day special. We had one long table for dinner with ten people. Two little boys sat at a coffee table. The people on one side of the table sat on furniture (not chairs but part of the built-in closets), and our entire room was filled. Nobody could get out except the people on the end and the two little boys. But I think my favorite way to celebrate Christmas is at a long table filled with people. And it's fun to have lots and lots of food.

Christmas in Moscow was a happy time for our family, with the snow outside and friends and family squished together inside, feasting and opening gifts. Our enjoyment was just as great as more prosperous, roomy Christmastimes, and I will always remember the long table with people filling the room.

THE RED OCTOBER CHOCOLATE FACTORY

≈

ONE OF MY FUN MOSCOW MEMORIES IS THE TIME WE HAD A SCHOOL field trip to the Red October Chocolate Factory. Getting downtown was an adventure, as twenty-one children and eight adults took the bus then three different subways and finally a ten-minute walk to the candy factory. Our trip took about an hour, and we could smell chocolate as we approached the large building on an island in the Moscow River. In those days, there were few restaurants or places to buy food, and no one brought lunch.

Inside, we were all assembled for the tour and given white coats and hats. Then we listened to a guide explain how to make chocolate and told we could eat all the candy we wanted. I think tours were a new idea at the factory as a source of revenue. Entering the factory, we walked right down into the machine area where workers helped with candy making and wrapping. Workers scooped up the candy on conveyer belts, giving it to us until our pockets were full. The adults spent all their energy making sure no child put a hand into a machine. Finally, we went to a museum and looked at fancy candy boxes and the pictures of the two Germans who started the factory, later taken over by the state under Communism.

The grand finale was a tea party just for us. Cups of black tea and big bowls of various candies adorned a long beautifully laid table. They told us to eat all we wanted. It was fun, and I still smile thinking about our unusual tour to the Red October Chocolate Factory.

SCHOOL TOUR OF THE RED OCTOBER CHOCOLATE FACTORY

LESSONS FROM PAUL AND BARNABAS

≈

SOMETIMES, CHRISTIANS SEPARATE BECAUSE OF DIFFERENCES IN OPINION of how to accomplish a task. This is not because of sin or wrong theology. The Bible gives an example of this.

> After some days Paul said to Barnabas, "Let us return and visit the brethren in every city in which we proclaimed the word of the Lord, and see how they are." Barnabas wanted to take John, called Mark, along with them also. But Paul kept insisting that they should not take him along who had deserted them in Pamphylia and had not gone with them to the work. And there occurred such a sharp disagreement that they separated from one another, and Barnabas took Mark with him and sailed away to Cyprus. But Paul chose Silas and left, being committed by the brethren to the grace of the Lord. (Acts 15:36–40)

Eventually, Mark evidently returned from his work with Barnabas and became associated with Peter (1 Peter 5:13) and wrote the Gospel of Mark. At the end of Paul's life, Paul requested Mark to be with him. So Paul and Barnabas separated because of a disagreement in how to do something (take Mark or not), and both continued in a successful ministry.

I have experienced this in ministry more than once, and it is usually painful. In the former USSR, when our leaders decided that each country have its own leadership, the person chosen to lead Russia was one of our close friends. We had supported this decision, believing him to be the man for the job. However, our friend who was now the new Russian director and Vance had a disagreement about the best method to train our staff. This was significant because our friend wanted Vance to oversee training the Russian ministry. After more discussion, they both agreed that if they had such a disagreement, it would be best if we weren't on the leadership team for the country. As a result, we began looking for ministry opportunities outside Russia.

I also learned from this that it is important to be behind the vision of your leader. This also applies to a church setting. If we can't follow a leader wholeheartedly, even if it is a difference in opinion about the method used, it is better to go somewhere where we can. It is better for us and better for the ministry. Having two strong leaders not in agreement isn't an effective or pleasant way to operate. What is encouraging about the situation with Paul and Barnabas is that after they separated, the ministry continued to grow and even expanded more while they each pursued their own vision.

We continue to have a good relationship today with our former coworker from Russia, and we have each gone on to other ministries. But I faced letting some of my dreams for our time in Russia die and had to step into an unknown future. I was learning again that the ministry belongs to God—not to me—and sometimes, I need to let it go.

WHAT'S NEXT?

≈

O<small>N JANUARY 24, 1995, I WROTE IN MY JOURNAL:</small>

Dear Lord, I feel the relief of yielding over the GCTC [staff training center], of realizing and accepting our job with it ends this summer. And, I sense it is right, Your will, though I do not understand totally, or think it is the best way to do it, but perhaps now, with the people here, it is the best way. I can only trust Your sovereignty. It is clear to me this is Your will.

You also seem to be leading us out of Russia. This seems increasingly clear, though we haven't made the final decision. I see everything saying, "Go," and nothing saying, "Stay." If we are deceived, please show us. But both Van and I sense this. But then, when I think out of Russia, what is it into? All I sense is, first, America. It's scary, Lord. Imagine, scary to go to America! But it's foreign somewhat because it's changed, and we've changed these fourteen years. Then there's all the upheaval, adjustment, cost, and resettling involved with a move from here to the U.S. and homeschooling— which I've longed four years for—but now that it's upon me, I feel inadequate and wonder if I can do it. So I'm scared, Lord, and it seems as hard and scary to me to move back to America as it sounded to move to Russia. At least I think so. Perhaps I'm premature in assuming this is what we're going to do, but I feel so certain in my being that this is right and will be so. How long we will stay in the U.S. or what our job will be, I can't see yet. I only sense, and I feel I can say with certainty, that You are leading this way, and we must follow. Dear Shepherd, please protect us from the evil one and direct us.

MORE STRUGGLES
AND VICTORIES

≈

As we prepared to return to America for furlough, the spiritual battle, as usual, was clear. At the same time, God was at work transforming lives. I wrote home on April 5, 1995:

> Today we got a prayer request; the Seventh Day Adventist medical clinic was asked to pay protection money by the mafia! They asked us to pray for wisdom. Maybe you could pray for them too. There is a neat story I should tell you. Our family went to a student conference last weekend. There was a student there from Armenia. She said when she was five, she only knew the word, God. Then as a girl, they had that terrible earthquake. Her sister was killed and others around her. She began to think about life and death and began to pray to God, though she didn't know who he was and had no Bible. In Moscow, as a university student, she began studying with the Jehovah Witnesses. But she noticed they didn't study the Bible. Then she met one of our trainees, from East Germany, and has become a Christian this year. She gave her testimony at the conference. This week she

was planning to show the *JESUS* video in Armenian to her brother, who is still suffering emotionally from the earthquake. There are some wonderful Russian Christians here, lights in the darkness, and they are shining. I'm glad to have been here. Leaving is a sort of grieving, but it is absolutely clear we should leave; it just seems to be the Lord's plan, though we don't know yet what we're stepping into. But there is peace.

PACKING

≈

MOVING OUT OF RUSSIA PROVED TO BE MORE DIFFICULT THAN MOVING in. A new law was made charging a retroactive tax on all foreign pets brought into Russia. A Siamese cat was taxed over $1,000 and a gerbil $4.50. There was also a charge to take these pets out of Russia. Fortunately, all our pets were purchased in Russia, and we left them behind with friends.

There were complex rules involving items taken out of Russia. Every book had to have about five items recorded including the title, author, publisher, and a couple of other things. We had at least two hundred books, and Amy and Sara were given the job of compiling this list. There was a government office we needed to work with that was only open briefly. I think it was half a day a week. Since the fall of the Soviet Union, new businesses had sprung up, and one was devoted to help foreigners leave Russia. We hired them to work through the bureaucracy for us. I don't know how we could have done it without them.

We also had a "garage" sale at our home for our friends. Some things were so hard to get that people who knew we were leaving called us up to ask if they could buy an item. We must have had five people asking to purchase our waffle iron.

When we finally finished packing, we mainly had books, videos, gifts and souvenirs, our clothes, and a few other items, such as our wooden end tables from Pakistan. Leaving Moscow was much more complicated than arriving.

BRAZIL? TRINIDAD?

~

I T HELPED TO HAVE TWO JOB OFFERS AS WE PREPARED TO LEAVE MOSCOW. Saying goodbye was hard, and we felt the warmth of coworkers inviting us to join them in two different ministries. I wrote home:

> We got a phone call from Hank Hornstein, a long-time friend, saying he is now going to lead the ministry in Brazil, and would we go to Sao Paulo with him and his wife and set up a ministry and GCTC with executives? Our kids said, "We want to stay in one place: America." They are sad about leaving Russia and their friends but going to America is also nice. But going to Brazil and learning Portuguese? Anyway, we are too worn out right now to go anywhere new, and we need time to recover. But we didn't say no; it's just not the right time to decide anything. It was nice to be asked, though.

In another letter, I wrote:

> We recently have had another job offer, in the Caribbean; we aren't making any decisions now and plan to come home for furlough. This job sounds more interesting. It's in Trinidad, helping to start an English-speaking training center. There is a national ready to be trained to take it over. The time commitment is two to

three years. After Moscow, a sunny spot seems mighty appealing. A nearby island is supposedly the scene of Treasure Island. Please pray we'll know at the right time. Right now, we're just gathering information, and we still need some R&R.

Though our path would take another direction, these new possibilities helped us look to the future God had for us and made it easier to say goodbye.

GRANDMA NORDMAN PROVIDES A HOME

≈

G RANDMA NORDMAN WAS LIKE A SECOND MOTHER TO ME. I COULD TELL her anything, and she was not shocked or emotional (at least not outwardly). She always opened her home to us on furlough and put up with all our boxes and luggage and people coming in and out. She even bore with grace her grandchildren writing on her walls with crayons (that only happened once). Whatever she had, she shared with us. But her small home was getting more crowded as the children grew. Knowing we would have a long furlough, I hoped to rent a house in her neighborhood. Little did I know the extent of her generosity.

We flew from Moscow to Colorado to attend staff training for Campus Crusade. Traveling from there to Las Vegas, where we exchanged rental cars and spent the night, we experienced reverse culture shock when we saw the first person with a pierced tongue. Finally, we arrived in Merced, California, and Vance said he needed to stop at a house to pick up something. This was odd behavior, and it completely surprised me when we pulled up to a beautiful home in the country, and Grandma Nordman opened the door, exclaiming, "Welcome home." She had purchased a home on a half-acre with more rooms so we could all stay with her.

Grandma Nordman's new home was all young children could hope for. There was an apple tree and almond trees in the expansive front lawn. The back yard held our swing set, and behind it was a barn and a field. Her home was toward the end of a cul-de-sac. Neighbors had goats, cows, and other animals, and a family with three homeschooled boys Peter's age lived one street away. It was the perfect place to rest and get used to America. We would live happily with Grandma Nordman for over six months and begin homeschooling the children before moving to our new assignment.

FURLOUGH DAYS

≈

Life with Grandma Nordman was wonderful. We visited supporting churches and friends and joined a homeschool group. The homeschooling family with three boys were in the same homeschool group. It motivated the boys to finish school so they could all play together. Our home was a magnet for local boys. A gardener at heart, I was having fun with Grandma's fruit trees. We picked apples, plums, figs, and nectarines in abundance. I also loved walking with my new friend—Vicki—the mom of the homeschooling family with three boys. It was a delight to talk together as we walked past orchards and fields.

During this time, Vance took a trip to Trinidad to check out the possibility of our moving there. After returning, he had doubts that moving to Trinidad was the best thing for the ministry or for our family. We still had more to do on furlough, but beyond that, the future was unclear. God would soon reveal the next step and provide for our needs in a most amazing way.

THE JESUS
FILM PROJECT

≋

Wᴴɪʟᴇ ᴠɪꜱɪᴛɪɴɢ ᴘᴇᴏᴘʟᴇ ɪɴ Sᴏᴜᴛʜᴇʀɴ Cᴀʟɪꜰᴏʀɴɪᴀ, Vᴀɴᴄᴇ ᴀɴᴅ I stopped by the *JESUS* Film Project office in San Clemente to visit friends. We had many friends working with the *JESUS* Film Project and had talked about working there someday, when we were older, as we felt it was a strategic ministry. On this visit, our friend Mike asked us to stop by his office before leaving. To our surprise, he invited us to come help him with the Macedonia Project, a project to send short-term teams to unreached areas of the world. Mike said they would base us in San Clemente, and Vance could help with Central Asia.

Vance and I had considered moving to Central Asia after Russia— but the Lord seemed to say no. This area of the globe combined the Middle East with the Soviet world. The doors were open there, and the need was great. We met with Mike and his wife, Cathy, a couple of weeks later at a restaurant closer to Merced to talk more. Mike then asked us to help with strategy and training, something Vance was interested in. A couple of weeks later Vance and I took a weekend away in the mountains to pray and make a pro/con list. One thing we liked was that San Clemente was a one-day drive from both Vance's family in Merced and my parents—now in Phoenix. As we evaluated the opportunity, everything pointed to joining the *JESUS* Film Project, so we said yes to Mike. What followed confirmed our decision, as we watched God miraculously provide our needs for this new assignment.

God Provides
a House

≈

Moving to a Southern California beach city with a family of five was expensive. We had little money and no home, furniture, or car. Vance had inherited some money from his grandfather, but as there were five grandchildren and most of his estate was going to Vance's mother, we assumed it wasn't a lot. It pleasantly surprised us to discover it was enough for a down payment on a home. I made a list of what I wanted in a home and began to pray. I just asked for everything I wanted: five bedrooms, a fireplace, trees, and a place for a garden.

Vance exclaimed, "You want five bedrooms in Orange County? Do you know how expensive that is?"

A couple at the *JESUS* Film Project had recently purchased a home, and they advised us to talk with the husband. He told us he had looked at over one hundred homes in the area on paper and visited over forty in person. The best deal was a home in his neighborhood. As he described the property, Vance thought, *That sounds like Carol's list.* Fortunately for us, Orange County was in the middle of a housing crisis in the early 1990s, and home prices were at their lowest in many years. We took a trip to San Clemente to look at houses.

My parents joined us, and we all stayed in a motel. They watched our kids while Vance and I met with the realtor, Nancy, a Christian woman who had helped other staff at the *JESUS* Film Project find homes. When we asked about the five-bedroom home, she replied it was the first place she planned to show us. Coming from overseas, every home looked wonderful. We didn't mind the dead tree in the front yard, the garbage in the backyard, the broken kitchen cabinets, or the white carpet and that the fireplaces and paneling were painted white. The owner had painted everything white to sell the home, which hadn't been repaired for many years. What I noticed was so much space, trees, a place for a garden, and *two* fireplaces. The house was about one mile from the ocean and on a hill, so we could see the ocean over the rooftops. The back of the house looked out on open land owned by a military base, and the slope of the hill separated the neighbors from us. We didn't even feel like we were in a city. I knew this was the answer to my prayer. Every other home we looked at couldn't compare and was more expensive. We said yes to Nancy and signed papers.

Back in Merced, my sister-in-law Sheri gave us some furniture they had in storage. We already had purchased beds for the children and ourselves to sleep in when we stayed with Van's mother in Merced. So in spring of 1996, we moved to a spacious home in a lovely Southern California beach town.

GOD PROVIDES
A CAR

$\approx$

WE NEEDED TO PURCHASE A CAR, AND THE LORD PROVIDED MONEY FOR this from an insurance policy Vance found out he was the beneficiary of from his father. It seemed that a few months before Van's father died, an insurance agent had shown him how he could convert his policy to one that would result in a larger payment. As a result, the policy's benefit was enough for us to purchase outright the much-needed car. A Christian man in Southern California named Sid, who had helped other *JESUS* Film Project staff, purchased a car for us at the Riverside auto auction. When we contacted him, he asked us what type of car we wanted, and we told him we would like a minivan. He then asked what make and model. Having lived overseas for so many years, we had no idea. We visited car dealers in Merced and made a list of all the minivans we liked. We chose the Ford Aerostar, as it seemed appropriate. Sid told us he would look, but the Aerostar had only been in production a couple of years, so he doubted he could find one. Sometime later, Sid called, saying he had found a good deal on a Mercury Villager minivan; did we want it? We looked at our list of cars we liked, and it was on it, so we said yes. Sid said the tax would be less if he had the car shipped to Merced, so instead of us flying down to pick up the car, we wired him the money, and he had the car shipped to us.

The car arrived in front of Grandma's house on a big truck full of cars. It was dark outside when a minivan rolled off the truck and was parked in the driveway. The whole family went outside to sit in it. We couldn't drive it yet until all the paperwork was filled out. We all sat there a long time looking at all the buttons and gadgets and wondering what color the car was. It looked blue by flashlight—which it turned out to be. The kids said it was like being on an airplane. They had grown up in simple Fiats overseas. The next morning, after having a good look at the car, we realized it was the nicest minivan we had looked at and was our favorite. We would have that minivan for about fifteen years.

So in just three months, we had a five-bedroom home with an ocean view, enough furniture to get by, and a minivan. God had provided what we needed to live in Orange County and work at the *JESUS* Film Project. A year later, the housing prices doubled. I remembered the promise I believed God had given me to provide a home of our own. We felt we were right in the center of God's will.

REVERSE
CULTURE SHOCK
... AGAIN

≈

I HAD EXPERIENCED REVERSE CULTURE SHOCK BEFORE ON FURLOUGH. Moving back to the States was an adjustment. At first, our kids all slept in the same bedroom of our five-bedroom home. Everything was too big after living in our tiny Russian apartment, which fit in the space occupied by our new living room, dining room, and kitchen. I marveled at all the big houses with so few people in them. As most people were away from home each day, working or at school, neighborhoods looked so empty.

One day, when Vance and I were shopping, I began loading bags of sugar into the cart, and Vance gently reminded me, "The sugar will still be here tomorrow." It took a long time to give up my large bin of extra food I kept under the stairs in our new home. At church, the youth group planned a food fight, and they assigned Amy to bring peanut butter. She couldn't bring herself to take part, and I understood. In Egypt, the only peanut butter available was made in a small factory in Cairo. We had to ask friends to purchase it for us and then pick it up on our next trip to Cairo. Before that, I roasted peanuts and then ground them in a food processor. Peanut butter wasn't easy to come by in Moscow, either, so how could we throw it? Sometimes, Americans seemed so frivolous.

Then there was the church. I attended a ladies Bible study and wondered what language they were speaking. Slang had changed since I'd left, and I sat and listened to the conversation, trying to figure out the new words. I was used to the missionary community and unconsciously equated them with the Christian community. Almost no one in our missionary community was divorced or had discipline problems with their children. I guess those who did, left the mission field to get help. I found myself angry at American Christians. What was wrong with them? Why didn't their walk match their talk? I felt like shaking people. Christians should confess and turn from their sins and let God be in control. I was just blessed to live around people who did this in the missionary community. I often tell people that the best place to raise kids is on the mission field. It is such an amazing group of people to live around.

Then there was driving. I didn't drive much in Russia because of all the snow. Public transportation was accessible and cheap. In America, I found freeway driving terrifying. I prayed for help and asked God to clear the way ahead of me. Even driving to a neighboring city was stressful, and I felt more comfortable with side streets in our little town. Finally, I had to drive the kids to Colorado for our staff conference and meet Vance, who had flown ahead of us to attend another event. Driving so far finally helped me overcome my fear of freeway driving.

I found that while I was experiencing reverse culture shock, the kids were just experiencing culture shock. America was the foreign country. They weren't moving back home but to a new country. They were born overseas. Once when I asked Peter where home was, he replied that it was in the airport. The weather was all wrong. In the summer, the hills were brown instead of green. In the winter, they were green instead of white. Then there was the ocean. In Egypt, we didn't usually swim in the polluted Mediterranean as we became physically sick. We usually didn't wear bathing suits and expose ourselves. It took a while for the girls to get used to wearing a bathing suit and swimming in the ocean. But finally, we all took up bogey boarding and had great family times, catching waves while the colors from the setting sun danced on the moving water.

I reminded myself that overseas, it took three years to feel at home in a new country. Each year was easier than the last. The same thing happened in America. I grew more comfortable but then alarmed as my awareness of the rest of the world faded. I felt that all the wealth and comfort around me was normal. I know it is not, and our job would provide opportunities for our family to minister again overseas and keep the vision alive. Today, I feel so happy and at home in our city, it is hard to remember the adjustments I had in 1996.

ADVENTURES IN HOMESCHOOLING

≋

As Vance traveled to Central Asia with the *JESUS* Film Project, I began ten years of homeschooling. Many people dread the teenage years in raising children, but these years were my favorite. We made the upstairs bedroom into a schoolroom with a large finished piece of wood for the desks. Vertical wooden dividers separated the surface into desks, and I had a metal desk at the end. With a view of the ocean and the hills, we called ourselves Ocean View Academy.

Each day, we began with forty-five minutes of cleaning the house. I bought a book called "Speed Cleaning" and did what it said. We each had an apron and a caddy of cleaning supplies. I laminated cleaning instructions for each area and taped them inside cupboard doors. I was learning right along with the kids, and together, we kept our house in order. Then we had devotions beginning with music. Peter and I played guitar; Amy learned the drums, trumpet, and keyboard; and Sara had her flute, which she had learned to play in Russia. I enjoyed beginning the day singing praises to God.

Through the years, I used several different curriculums. Amy continued with Accelerated Christian Education workbooks, which worked so well for her. Peter and Sara used different curriculums at different times, including Abeka, Calvert, a literature-based curriculum, an internet Christian school, classes for high school offered through a Christian college, and classes at the local community college. Vance said we should really call homeschooling alternative education. As the children became teenagers, I felt my job was to research and provide tools that fit each child. They were responsible to study and learn. I helped them when they got stuck or helped them find help. We were also part of two different homeschool groups, which provided testing, field trips, resources, and help for parents. Many kids from our church were also in the homeschool group, and our children were part of a community of teens and families who shared our values. We faced no problems with substance abuse or sex or many of the issues facing teens today. Homeschooling provided flexibility to visit Grandma in Merced and to take family mission trips. We also started and hosted a teen public speaking club in our home, which turned out to be one of the greatest adventures of all. I learned right along with my kids; it was challenging and fun.

BACK TO TURKEY

≈

M Y GOOD FRIEND SUSANNA TOLD ME SHE WAS PRAYING OUR WHOLE family would come to Turkey. I wondered how that could ever happen. A little while later, it surprised me to hear that the *JESUS* Film Project wanted to send short-term teams to Turkey. Vance was asked to help pioneer the outreach in Turkey, so we made plans for the summer. Amy was fifteen, Sara thirteen, and Peter ten years old.

Landing in Istanbul—a bustling modern city on the Bosporus— the kids and I toured while Vance went to a meeting. We visited an ancient church—Aya Sophia—and the Blue Mosque opposite it. An underground cistern made by reusing discarded marble columns supplied water for the ancient city. One column caught us by surprise. It had a marble base with Medusa's snake-covered head standing upside down in the water. The huge covered bazaar and many Turkish carpet shops fascinated us. Vance and I celebrated our anniversary with the kids having lunch overlooking the Bosporus at the Topkapi Palace. Touring those magnificent buildings, where the sultans lived with their harems, was fascinating. As a family, we visited a museum and an amusement park, enjoying a Turkish meal while reclining on cushions. Finally, we boarded a boat for the trip down the Bosporus into the Aegean Sea and south to the city of Izmir. The weather was perfect and the views breathtaking as we glided by buildings and mosques into the open sea. Soon we would be in our own rented home in Kusadasi on the Aegean Sea.

OUR FAMILY IN A TURKISH CARPET SHOP
(SHOPKEEPER'S FACE BLOCKED FOR PRIVACY)

As we stepped off the boat in Izmir, Susanna greeted us. She had found a furnished beach house we could rent in the city of Kusadasi. We rode in a small van to a Turkish vacation community on a beach of the Aegean Sea. Outside our rented home, plants surrounded the building and attached patio. Inside was a large room containing the kitchen, dining area, and living room, which opened to the patio containing a second table and chairs. The kitchen included a stovetop and refrigerator. A spiral staircase led upstairs to three small bedrooms and a bathroom on the second floor. One large bedroom made up the third floor. Balconies off the bedrooms had clotheslines, where we dried our clothes. Sara's job for the summer—for which we paid her—was to wash our clothes in the bathtub.

Vance and Peter fit right into the neighborhood, as physically, they looked like Turks. Turkish boys Peter's age walked to the local grocery store in the mornings to get fresh bread for the family. Peter joined them—walking about a block to the small store. We settled in, rented a car, and explored the area.

No one ended up joining us in Turkey for the outreach, so we had to do all the cassette distribution ourselves as a family. Very few

Turks owned video machines at the time, so we purchased a thousand audiocassettes of the *JESUS* audio drama based on the film, which we stored in our home and carried in our car. It was legal to give out the cassettes because they had a stamp from the Turkish censor board on them. This was such a miracle. Back in 1980, when Vance and I first came, there were only about a hundred known Turkish believers among forty million people. Now there were at least fifteen small churches, and the government had approved the *JESUS* film. I could feel the difference in the spiritual climate. The dark, oppressive spiritual atmosphere was lifting. Soon we would plant more seeds of light meeting people and offering a *JESUS* cassette.

Using our rented house as a home base, we planned trips down the coast of the Aegean, east across the coast of the Mediterranean, then north to the center of Turkey, and finally back to the Aegean and north up the coast back to Istanbul. We included visiting the sites of the seven churches of Revelation in our trips, and Vance taught our family the book of Acts as we retraced the steps of Paul. Everywhere we went, we met people and offered a *JESUS* cassette, giving away nearly one thousand cassettes over the summer. We bought gasoline for the car a liter at a time so we could give away more cassettes to the attendants. We stopped at little stores, buying one bag of potato chips at a time to give more opportunities to give cassettes. Our kids enjoyed lots of snacks, purchased one bag at a time. We made up a song to the tune of "Old MacDonald Had a Farm": "The Nordman family went to Turkey, eee eye, eee eye, oh. And on their trip, they bought some gas, eee eye, eee eye, oh. A liter here and a liter there ..." Then we added things: With a chip chip here and a chip chip there, or with an ice cream here and an ice cream there. Everywhere we went, people were happy to receive the audiocassettes. In one jewelry store, after giving a cassette to a clerk, several clerks wanted copies, saying they were very interested in this.

Once, we stopped by a group of ladies having lunch seated on the ground in the countryside, resting from their labors in the fields. I got out of the car with a handful of cassettes and handed them out, and we drove off. Without a doubt the most foolish thing I did was to lean out the car window as we were passing a truck with colorfully dressed ladies from the field in the back. I held out a cassette, and a lady reached out and took it. She could have so easily fallen from the moving truck. Once, while driving by a field, a man ran toward us, waving his arms. We stopped and gave him a cassette. I still do not understand why he waved at us, as our car looked like any other car. I wonder what the end of the story is with that cassette. We had a wonderful time as tourists, spreading seeds of light as we went.

At the southwestern tip of Turkey, where the Aegean and Mediterranean meet, lies the resort city of Bodrum. High on a hill stands an ancient Crusader castle, overlooking a sparkling bay and many yachts below. We toured that castle and sat at a long rustic table in a large stone hall with high ceilings. We sipped beverages and listened to beautiful music while gazing through openings in the ancient stone down to the blue harbor below. We gave out audiocassettes all over that tourist area, and after spending the night, we drove east to the mountains the next day. But something was wrong with the car. High on a small mountain road, the car just quit working. The kids and I got out and helped watch for cars while Vance got our car going downhill and popped the clutch to start the car. Then we all got in the car and headed up the hill again. At the same spot, the car again stopped working. We repeated this procedure several times, with the same results. Finally, we gave up and went back to Bodrum to get the car checked out. We spent another night there, giving out more cassettes. We gave one to a man who said he dreamed about Jesus. We gave out another to a young woman who said she was meeting with someone to study the Bible. We sensed the hand of God leading us back to Bodrum. The next day, they fixed the car, which had a weak fuel pump. We drove back up the mountain and this time continued east along the Mediterranean.

The tree-covered mountains along the southern coast of the Mediterranean are lovely, steeply meeting the sea and forming many coves with turquoise water. I envisioned pirate ships in those coves as we twisted and turned along the narrow road. We stopped to buy figs and olive oil soap at roadside stands, giving cassettes each time. The kids began to groan, feeling sick with all the twisty driving. Suddenly, the road ahead opened, and a huge stone fortress loomed into view at the water's edge. We stopped and bought tickets to go inside the walls, gazing at the turtles swimming in the surrounding moat.

Almost no one was inside the huge area—bigger than a football field. Ancient stone turrets, rooms, and walkways surrounded a large sandy open area. There were no railings or restrictions of any kind, and I couldn't bear to watch as Sara and Peter scrambled up the winding stone steps about eighteen inches wide on the outside of a tower, with no railings. When they were about three stories above me, I could see them waving happily from the top. Amy and I found another way to get there, slowly picking our way over the broken stones. We stood at the top, looking out to sea, and clambered through dimly lit stone rooms with sandy floors. No one was there, and it looked like they had left the fortress untouched since the Crusaders had been there. All the twisty roads and sick feeling faded in the excitement of that discovery, and I felt God had given us a surprise treat.

Arranged marriages were common in the Middle East, and I often marveled at the process. An Egyptian man working in another country came back to Egypt looking for a wife. He heard about an available girl, and the families met together with the girl and the young man. They got engaged; he went back to his job in another country and came back later to marry. I don't think they really spent time together until they were married. Perhaps culture has changed now that the world is smaller, and the internet connects us all. But in the late 1990s, out in the ruins in the countryside of Turkey, things had changed little. We stopped the car to climb around some old ruins, where a young man about seventeen years old was selling books. Amy noticed him watching her and thought it was safer to get back in the car. The young man came up to Vance and ten-year-old Peter, saying that he would like to marry our daughter.

Vance thought he was referring to thirteen-year-old Sara and said, "She's too young."

He replied that he was interested in the other one. Peter's jaw dropped open. This teenager wanted to marry his sister? The young man couldn't understand what the problem was. He was older than Amy and could provide for her. Why wouldn't we leave our daughter with him out in the ruins in Turkey? He was very polite and didn't give us any problems as we drove away with our daughter, grateful to have her safe with us. Though all people have many similarities, I was reminded again just how different our cultures are.

I can't remember the city, but I can still see in my mind the Turkish tourists strolling the streets along the coast of the Mediterranean. We observed a cultural shift since the last time we had visited in 1980. Now, alongside covered ladies, women strolled in tight clothes and high fashion. Many people seemed to give up religion altogether and become secular. But the religious and secular still existed side by side. The culture appeared to be polarizing, and along with secularism came a loss of family values and innocence. This was disturbing.

That evening, our family noticed a magnificent ruin of what looked like an old palace perched on a small island about half a mile off the coast. The weather was beautiful and the water warm. We rented a paddle boat and, bicycling the foot pedals, headed for the island. Vance swam alongside while the rest of the family navigated through small boats. As the sun set, lights appeared on the ruin, and we marveled at its beauty. We didn't get out to explore the island, as it was late, and we turned the boat around toward the shore. But all the little lights on the land looked the same. Where had we come from? We just headed for shore and fortunately found the place we had rented the boat from. I will always remember our night adventure and the contrast of ancient and modern, religious and secular, as change came to Turkey.

Stopping to eat at a McDonald's on the coast of the Mediterranean, we gave away several audiocassettes. After eating, we drove on to visit the ruins of Perga, where the apostle Paul had traveled. We noticed a police car motioning us to pull over and assumed we had been going too fast. The officer asked if we were foreigners and then had Vance get out of the car. When asked what was in the pouch he was carrying on his belt, Van pulled out an audiocassette. They then directed him to get into the police car, while a second policeman got in our car with me and the kids. As we were being driven away, I asked the officer where we were going. He replied that we were going to the *Jandarma* (the police station). By God's grace, we remained calm.

At the police station, they escorted the kids and me into an office, while Vance talked with the police outside by our car. They opened the trunk and transferred piles of audiocassettes to the desk in the office where we were. I told the kids to let Dad handle things. Amy thought it was a great adventure, Sara was indignant that they should hold us, and Peter just watched quietly. Outside, the police asked Vance why he had the cassettes. He replied that he worked for Inspirational Films, and this was the audio of our movie we were giving people.

When asked why he had so many, he replied, "Because people like them."

The policeman laughed. Vance showed them the receipt that we always carried with us, showing we had purchased the cassettes in Turkey. Since the cassettes had been manufactured in Turkey, they all had a sticker from the censor board indicating they were approved.

Vance asked, "Did I do something wrong?"

They didn't reply but needed to check things out. This would take a while.

Vance joined us in the office, behind him was a cabinet with handcuffs hanging in it. The weather was hot. The police were very nice and brought us a fan and water to drink. Peter had a deck of cards in his leather pouch, and we passed the time playing bridge. Vance had taught the family how to play during the pleasant evenings we spent at our beach home on the outdoor patio. With no TV, we enjoyed having tea and playing bridge. After two or three hours, the policeman returned, having checked out our story. We were free to go. When we asked if we could take our cassettes, he replied that we could and requested a cassette for himself. As we drove away, the police waved goodbye. The police must have talked a long time about the American family with all the cassettes. Hopefully, we will meet some of them in heaven.

It was after 6 p.m. by the time the police allowed us to go, so we missed visiting Perga on that trip. After our ordeal with the police and sitting in a hot office all afternoon, Vance said we would stay in a nice hotel that evening along the Mediterranean. It was dark by the time we saw a large hotel ahead of us by the sea. After we checked in and went to our rooms, Vance called the front desk to see if the pool was open. He didn't know the word for "pool" in Turkish and tried words for it in other languages. When he tried the word *"basseen"* (the Russian word for "pool"), the man began speaking to Vance in Russian. It seemed we had checked into a hotel used mainly by Russian tourists. So Vance spoke with them in Russian and found that the pool was closed that evening, but we could swim in the ocean if we wanted. Vance and I went for a night swim in warm, buoyant water, and the girls watched *Jaws* on TV (as if we hadn't already had enough excitement at the police station). In the morning, I went to the pool and did water exercises with the Russian tourists, feeling right at home. After an eventful experience, we were grateful for such a happy ending.

A special treat was the home of Saint Nicholas in Antalya. You can see it on YouTube by searching for Turkey: Home of Saint Nicholas. Walking through the ancient church and learning about his story gave us a new understanding of the origin of Santa Claus.

At the center of Turkey lies Cappadocia—a historical region in central Anatolia. I have never seen a similar landscape with rocky spires of dusky orange and cream, jutting into the blue sky. The spires are dotted with black holes, which are homes carved into the volcanic rock. Below the surface lie anthills of homes, where tens of thousands of people once lived. Long tunnels connected the underground cities. Today, tourists can visit several levels of an underground city complete with wells, air shafts, churches, and even an underground stable.

Our visit began with checking into a motel—actually, an ancient cave home that had been converted to a motel room. The motel owner also ran a Turkish carpet shop, and the stone floors were softened with colorful carpets. We even had a bathroom and electricity, which contrasted with ancient carvings on the ceiling and nooks carved into the walls where pigeons once roosted. The temperature in our comfortable dwelling was a consistent cool. Outside, the summer sun and vegetation greeted us as we explored the area and took a tour of an ancient Christian training center. Paintings of Biblical stories covered the ceilings of cave churches, and we sat at a long table carved from stone where our forefathers once ate. When marauding enemies invaded, the Christians moved into the underground cities, blocking the entrances with large stones. The long tunnels carved through the rock were narrow and dark. I could hardly imagine living like that for months at a time, with thousands of others. On the surface, there was no trace of all the life underneath. If only the stones could speak and tell the stories of all those believers who had gone before us and lived in that strange stone world of Cappadocia.

The thermal springs in ancient Hierapolis have been used for centuries in healing. The apostle Paul founded a church there, and tradition says they crucified the apostle Philip there. Later, the town grew to one hundred thousand inhabitants and became wealthy. During the Byzantine period, the city remained an important center for Christianity.

When Vance and I first visited the thermal springs in 1980, there was only one other person swimming in the bubbly, warm waters. In the late 1990s, returning with our family, the place swarmed with Russian tourists. We joined them, swimming below the surface of the pool to view ancient stone columns and then emerging into the warm air to rest on broken stones scattered throughout the pool. Our children had goggles to help see underwater, and the Russian children asked to borrow them. Understanding some Russian, our children loaned the goggles to others. Our kids blended right in, as they looked like the Russians. In contrast to our previous trip nearly twenty years earlier, when Vance and I swam in silence under the stars with blooming oleanders perfuming the air, this was a noisy, happy crowd. We heard that shortly after our visit, the pool was closed because of so many tourists. Later, we learned that only two places in the world contain this unusual landscape. Our family visited the second in Yellowstone National Park, and it reminded us of our swim in the healing waters of Hierapolis.

The summer was ending, and we headed north to our departure point in Istanbul. On the way, we stopped at the ruins of the ancient city of Troy, which archeologists continue to uncover. There was a modern wooden horse that served as a play structure for children. It amazed us how small the city is and how much archeology is still being done. I think it was on this trip that Sara got an ear infection. We gave her an antibiotic but not as soon as I'd hoped. We felt bad, as she suffered with pain until the antibiotic took effect; gratefully, she recovered. We finally flew out of Istanbul and had a layover in Germany. Everyone was excited to spend a day in Germany. Unfortunately, everyone got sick except for me. I went back and forth to a store, bringing food, while the rest of the family lay in bed, watching TV in German. We were grateful that the next day, the trip to America was uneventful.

London Bridges

≈

WHEN OUR CHILDREN WERE IN THEIR EARLY TEENS, WE WENT AS A family to London to help begin a project to give New Testaments and *JESUS* videos to wealthy Arabian Gulf Arabs vacationing in the British capital. A small group of others joined us from different countries in the adventure. Three other teens from our church came with our family: Charlie, Quentin, and Jennifer. Our ministry rented a large house in the suburbs of London for Vance and I and the six teens. It was a lot of fun. The boys had a room, the girls had a room, and Vance and I had a room. Downstairs, we shared the living area, the garden room, and the kitchen. Each morning, we had breakfast together, and then everyone helped make our lunches. Each day, we walked through the neighborhood to the bus stop, taking a bus to the commuter train, which traveled into central London. We met the other members of our team at a church where we had devotions, training, and tea. After the training, we packed Arabic New Testaments and *JESUS* videos into plastic bags to distribute. The bags were big because of the videos, and we could only carry about eleven videos at a time in our backpacks.

In the afternoons, we traveled to the Hyde Park area of London, where many Arabs liked to visit. We stood on the street and offered our packets to Arabs who passed by. Some took them, though most did not. Afterward, we sometimes found New Testaments people had left on a ledge. Though they didn't want them, they respected them and didn't throw them away. We had some interesting discussions, and I remember Jennifer having a conversation while surrounded by a group of covered Saudi women. We all grew bolder.

Some highlights of the summer were celebrating the Fourth of July (finding hot dogs and buns in England was a challenge), listening to the boys making jokes about the fat pigeons, and somehow not getting on the bus and walking all the way home in the rain together, soaking wet yet having fun. We also toured the British Museum with a guide, who explained how many of the artifacts testified to the truth of the Bible. The London project continued year after year, and we went several more summers, though not all of us every time. More teens from our church also went to London on the project. One year, our family visited the English countryside after the project, staying at a bed-and-breakfast on a working farm. We also visited our ministry in France, staying in the home of some of our staff and touring Paris.

As the years progressed, we learned how to be more effective in distributing materials and shifted from videocassettes to CDs and then to DVDs. Gradually, the project grew in the number of participants and the number of DVDs handed out, until we distributed over twenty thousand DVDs and New Testaments each summer. After 9/11, we saw a marked increase in interest. Arabs wanted New Testaments, and we had trouble keeping enough in stock. Over the years, interest in Jesus has continued to grow among the Arabs, as violence in the Middle East has increased. In the beginning, most Arabs who would talk to us just wanted to argue, but over time, more asked sincere questions. Some Arabs prayed to receive Christ with our team members on the streets of London. Once I gave a packet to a young man who wanted to talk more about Jesus. Arab Christians who joined our project were available to help, and soon, one of them came over to help me, taking the young man aside to answer his questions in Arabic. After a while, I looked over and saw the young man praying. Whenever we found interested Arabs, we introduced them to one of our Arab team members, and they led many to faith in Jesus right on the streets of London. I don't know how many tens of thousands of packets have now been distributed. I remember with fondness the fun times we had with six teenagers, living in the suburbs of London, and the joy of telling others about Jesus.

AMY AND SARA DISTRIBUTING JESUS VIDEOS AND NEW
TESTAMENTS ON A RAINY DAY IN LONDON

JAPAN

≈

THE MINISTRY IN JAPAN WAS REQUESTING SHORT-TERM MISSIONARIES. Our short-term mission team discussed who would lead the trip. Our pastor's two sons, who were part Japanese, had visited Japan with their college and became connected with a Japanese church in the suburbs of Tokyo. Everything fell into place, and we led a team to Japan and worked with the Japanese church. The girls were away at school, and Peter accompanied us, along with our pastor's son and a handful of others. We planned to go just before Christmas and offer a CD with a portion of the *JESUS* film, internet links, and black gospel music on it. Japanese love black gospel music. A woman in our church sewed red Santa hats, and we bought green aprons and scarves to complete the outfits we wore on the streets.

Japan was outside the box for me. I knew almost nothing about Asia. But it was a lot of fun, and since I love fish, the diet was interesting too. Everything seemed to have buttons and remotes, including the toilet, which had a heated seat. The vending machines served both hot and cold drinks, and the noodle restaurant was fantastic. Nothing in the beautiful mall or shops fit me, so shopping held little temptation. Size twelve was too big for the petite Japanese women.

We enjoyed the Japanese church that hosted us, and I will never forget the baptism service for both a college student and an older woman who had attended a foreign Christian school as a girl. She had married a non-Christian, but after he passed away, she decided she believed in Jesus and his promise of heaven. I thought of those missionaries so long ago and the fruit from their work so many years later.

Tokyo was decorated for Christmas even more than American cities, and Christmas carols in English played over loudspeakers. However, most Japanese didn't seem to know what Christmas was all about. To them, it was a romantic holiday, and they ate Kentucky Fried Chicken and cake with strawberries. They knew about Santa Claus but not about the story of Jesus. We offered the *JESUS* CDs while bowing and saying, "Merry Christmas." We were not the only ones on the street offering things. There were many Japanese passing out Kleenex packages with advertising. We accumulated many Kleenex packages. We bowed so often that it became a habit, and once, after returning to America, Peter bowed to a waiter in a restaurant.

One of the brave, or perhaps foolish, things I did was visit my college friend Karen, who is married and on our Japanese staff. She is American Japanese, and her husband a native of Japan. I had an English translation of the transportation system, and I referred to it while transferring trains. We had no cell phones then, and nobody seemed to speak English. I thought later that I could have gotten lost, and I was alone. I just knew that the symbols marking our train stop looked like a coke and french fries: 立川. But I successfully made it to Karen's house, and we had a nice visit. She lived in a traditional Japanese home, and it was fun to see her in this new setting. Our pastor's two sons married the two daughters of the Japanese pastor, and they have children of their own and serve as missionaries in Japan. It was a privilege to help bring the Gospel to Japan (and a lot of fun too).

BRUNO

≈

AMY HAD WANTED A DOG FOR A LONG TIME. WE TOLD HER THAT SOMEDAY, when we lived in a house, she could have a dog. Finally, that time came in San Clemente, and the family went to the Adoption Day at PetSmart. There he was—the golden Labrador she wanted. Bruno was half Labrador and half Shar-Pei. He had the size of a Labrador and the muscle and strength of a Shar-Pei. He grew much larger than his former family had expected, and they could not keep him without a yard. Bruno was a magnificent animal—weighing about ninety pounds, with rippling muscles as he ran. Perhaps because he lost his first family, Bruno never liked to be left behind when we traveled and especially hated to be left enclosed. At first, he ran out the door when he could get a chance, and we had to run after him when he went into the drive-thru at Carl's Junior down the street from our home; luckily, no cars hit him.

We took Bruno along whenever we could, and he often made the seven-hour car trip with us to Grandma Nordman's house. Bruno had a spot on the floor by the kid's door in our minivan, where he could stand to look out the window or lie down. Bruno slobbered a lot, and slime covered the window, door, and upholstery near him. We carried a beach towel for protection. At Grandma's house, he again dashed out the front door, visiting the neighbors and barking at their dogs, causing a general commotion. Vance went after him and gave him a spanking. After that, Bruno listened to Vance. Sometimes, he would listen to the rest of us.

Bruno had a complex personality. He had the happy, friendly nature of the Labrador and the love of fighting true of the Shar-Pei. He especially loved to fight with other male fighting dogs and didn't mind getting bloody. We learned to stay far away from those dogs. At the same time, he was fearful of children outside the family and especially of noises. The clothes drier was a monster in the basement. I would do laundry and look up to see Bruno watching from the top of the stairs with a worried look. We live near a military base and had to give Bruno sedatives when they had artillery practice. He shook, slobbered, and tried to get under furniture.

Pain didn't seem to affect Bruno much. We put up a metal shock fence around the vegetable garden. Bruno didn't care if he got shocked and walked right through the fence. He chewed through so many things, we wondered that he had any teeth left. When he chased a skunk, his nose to the skunk's rear end and raised tail, Bruno hardly responded to the spray full in his face. It wasn't the first time we had to wash him with a concoction to remove the skunk smell.

Our family traveled a lot, and we couldn't always take Bruno. This was a problem. People came to feed and care for him. If left in the house, he ate the wall and the wood blinds. If left in the yard, he chewed through the fence and escaped. When tied up in the yard, he pulled out the railroad ties holding up our tiered landscaping and chewed the post helping support the second story of the house. Finally, we bought a professional kennel with a six-foot chain-link fence and a door with a padlock. We returned to find him escaped again, a metal bolt holding the hinge was broken and his blood everywhere. Once, Bruno was lost for a couple of weeks after one of our trips. We had about given up hope when we received a phone call. A woman found him and was feeding him cat food. She called the phone number on his tag, and we retrieved Bruno. He was so thin and happy to be home, he never wandered far away again.

Bruno lived until he was fourteen, surviving several strokes which impaired half his body. I think at the end of his life, he couldn't see or hear much. With hearing loss, he finally found peace from the bombing at the military base behind us. Bruno was our family dog. He was loveable, exasperating, and quite a character.

SAN CLEMENTE PETS

≈

Our family acquired many pets. Peter had a cat and a cockatiel and later fish. Sara had rabbits and turtles, everyone shared guinea pigs, and Amy also had a parakeet and several hamsters.

We had several cats before we got Thimble. I wanted a cat that lived both indoors and outdoors. I thought our local pet shelter was extreme when I learned I had to sign a paper promising the cat would only live indoors. They told me it was too dangerous outside for cats. So we drove to a neighboring city and purchased a kitten from a pet store. This cute kitty became ill, and Peter carefully nursed it. However, we finally returned the kitten to the store and got another cat from another place. We left this kitten with friends once when we traveled, and we heard that an owl had carried it off. We tried again and ended up with a nice male cat we named Koshka, which is the Russian word for "cat." Koshka had a relaxed temperament and loved to wander the neighborhood. One day, he came home without his collar, and my neighbor returned it, saying she left her window open so Koshka could come in and play with her cat. He left his collar behind. But one day, Koshka didn't come home. Finally, we went back to the local animal shelter and signed the paper that stated our cat would live indoors. We took home a female calico about a year-old named Thimble.

Someone had adopted Thimble before and returned her to the

animal shelter. She was very quiet and shy, hardly ever meowing and afraid of some men. She and Bruno kept a respectful distance. Thimble lived with us about fourteen years, finally learning to trust us. She and my mother had a special relationship; Mother talked to her, and she would meow back. Thimble died of old age while sleeping in a favorite sunny spot on the carpet. She was patient, intelligent, and easy to live with.

Harley the cockatiel came to us from friends at the *JESUS* Film office. One of our coworkers wanted a Harley-Davidson motorcycle but instead bought a cockatiel and named him Harley. Harley could be very noisy and made such a commotion at home that our friend's wife covered his cage with a cloth to quiet him. When we got Harley, he hissed whenever we tried to cover his cage for the night, so we left him uncovered in our dining room. Often, there were evening activities with our teenagers, and Harley liked to join in, making lots of noise. We let him fly outside his cage in the house sometimes. Once when we were having a chicken dinner, he swooped down and flew off with a piece of chicken. We also discovered he was chewing on the wood blinds behind his cage. One day, Harley fell off his perch and broke his neck. I wonder if he just didn't get enough sleep.

Floppy was Sara's lop-eared bunny, a dwarf with ears that hung down. He was cute in his rabbit hutch in our backyard. But he looked lonely, and when our neighbors found a lost bunny in their yard, we took it as a companion for Floppy. The new bunny was small like Floppy, with ears that stood up. However, the new bunny grew into a very large rabbit, and we discovered baby rabbits one day. Floppy would stand guard, protecting his very large female. They had many babies which were so cute, many with one ear up and one down. We gave them all to a pet shop, except for a black male Amy named Licorice.

We also had many guinea pigs, as they also had babies. One friendly male was the head of the tribe. He loved being washed in the sink and then dried with a hair drier; stretching out on his back to feel the warm air on his belly.

Sara's two turtles were small when she brought them home from college, and they lived happily in an aquarium in the dining room. But they kept growing until they were the size of salad plates. They could stand on their toes and flip themselves out of the aquarium and walk off. Learning they would grow to the size of dinner plates, we took them to a local reptile shop, where they joined other turtles who were hibernating in the mud. I'm sure they were much happier in their large turtle-friendly environment.

Now all our pets are gone, and as Vance and I often travel, we feel this is for the best. I enjoy the wild birds outside, and we provide them with a birdbath and fountain. I guess I will always like to have God's creatures nearby.

Young Speakers
for Christ

≈

I COULDN'T BELIEVE WHAT I WAS SEEING. WERE THESE POISED, ARTICULATE speakers really teenagers? Where did they learn this? Our family was visiting a speaker's club run by a homeschooling friend. We wanted to sign all our kids up right away. Unfortunately, the club was full. Disappointed, we returned home and then had an idea. Why couldn't we start our own club? Vance's parents had been in Toastmasters— an adult public speaking club—and Vance had been in student government in college. We gathered information from our friend's club and from Toastmasters, and launched into the unknown, calling our club "Young Speakers for Christ."

We invited homeschooling kids we knew and immediately had a group of eleven. Many were boys in middle school, and some evenings ended up in giggling. But we seemed to meet a social need for homeschooling teens. We met every other Friday evening in our large living room and invited family members of the club to observe. Gradually, the group took on a life of its own and started to grow. When we numbered over twenty students, we divided into two clubs, one run by another family. Then our club grew again to over twenty students. It was like having a giant party every other week, and all our family worked together to make it happen.

At first, Vance ran everything, Peter moved furniture and set up chairs, and the girls helped with getting the house ready. We also had refreshments afterward, and people stayed for a long time, talking and having fun. Then we elected student officers, who ran the club with Vance's help. We felt this developed leadership. All the students learned to speak publicly, and we hoped they would combine their faith in Christ with their new skills to speak with clarity and boldness about the Lord. We had wonderful young people who loved God and lived moral lives.

One of my favorite stories is about Ben. He first came as a young teenager who had some trouble speaking. But Ben wasn't shy, and he loved to speak in public. The other students encouraged him, and he just kept on speaking and improving. Later, Vance and I attended a high school graduation. The main speaker was Ben. As I listened to his excellent and moving speech, I began to cry. He had done it. Ben didn't give up, and he was fantastic. Later, when he was a college student, I heard him preach in church. It was powerful. Ben is now a husband, a father, and a lawyer.

Young Speakers for Christ continued about five years and is one of those things I look back on in wonder. It just seemed to happen, and I believe God was in it.

DEBATE CLUB

≈

I HAD ENTERED ANOTHER WORLD. WITH A NEW VOCABULARY AND new ways of thinking, I embarked on a steep learning curve and joined other moms and their teens in the adventure of debating. My former pastor's wife—Kathy—has always been a role model for me. The homeschooling mother of eight children, Kathy also helped administrate our homeschool group and led the debate club.

The nationwide homeschool debate organization had grown large, with chapters on the local and state levels. Moms and teens met regularly to watch videos and study debate manuals. Then the teens grouped into partners and researched the topic assigned for the year. During the years our children Sara and Peter debated, we studied income tax reform, immigration, and agriculture. The teens followed the rules of debate, preparing speeches, and gathering evidence to support their case and refute other cases. The parents learned to judge, and younger siblings timed the speeches.

I had never been interested in politics or debate, but this became more fun than being involved in sports. I loved going to the regional debates and became friends with the other moms there, as we spent a day together judging debates and celebrating the hard work our kids did. And the kids were amazing—dressed like businessmen and women in their suits. We listened to speeches that could have come from the mouths of lawyers or public officials. We learned so much about each subject, listening to all the creative ideas and interesting facts gathered through months of research.

Sara and her partner, Jennifer—our pastor's daughter—made a powerful team and won debates on the local and state levels. It was fun to watch them as they learned to be kind and respectful along with giving a strong argument delivered with passion. Sara's logical mind combined with Jennifer's passionate delivery worked together to win many debates. I joined our pastor and his wife and another family to travel with the teens to the national debate tournament held in Tennessee. Though Sara and Jennifer didn't win on the national level, being there inspired us.

Thousands gathered for the national debate. Large families of homeschoolers came to support their teens and help with judging and timing speeches. Here were a multitude of teens—most of whom loved God and appeared to be responsible and respectful. It gave me hope, and I wished more people could see what I saw. This was something positive happening in our country I didn't see on the news. The Home School Legal Defense Association, founded by Michael Farris, sponsored the debate. In 2000, Michael Farris founded Patrick Henry College near Washington, DC, which we visited. They were training young people to enter the government. Both the kids and I grew and learned from our amazing experience with homeschool debate.

REFLECTIONS ON
RAISING TEENAGERS

≈

I DON'T KNOW HOW MANY TIMES I HAVE HEARD SOMEONE BEMOAN THE trials of raising teenagers or dread the coming rebellious teen years. But I found raising teenagers to be the most fun years. I wondered why. I think it began when we lived in Egypt.

I learned so many things from the Egyptians. In the 1980s, they were a traditional culture, with strong extended families. Most people never moved and had such large extended families they didn't have much time for other relationships. Their social lives centered on family events with cousins and aunts and uncles. It was a little like the movie, *My Big Fat Greek Wedding*. I thought being a teenager and being rebellious were synonymous. But I realized I was wrong. I didn't see teenage rebellion in Egypt. Though they had problems too, family ties were strong. I learned a lot about the family in Egypt.

Returning to America, I wanted to keep this family connection. I had learned about discipleship from our ministry and decided that my children should be my disciples. Jesus didn't leave his disciples behind to go have a ministry. They lived together and took part in ministry together. They were connected. So it made little sense to me to leave my kids to pursue ministry. I always thought we ministered as a family. We were involved in this together, and I wanted to take our children along.

But so many things in our culture work against being connected as a family. In Russia, I think we had the best school I've ever seen with small classrooms, great kids, and godly teachers. I believe it's what God had for us. But I missed the kids. They were gone all day and had activities and homework after school. I felt like I hardly saw them. How do you disciple your kids and pass on your values if you're not with them? I believe God leads parents to different forms of education. Every child is different, and every educational situation is different. But these were the thoughts going through my mind.

When we returned to America, we found that churches we visited had separate programs for teens, and most adults seemed to have little or no idea about what went on in them. Wasn't there some place we could be involved in church as a family? I felt like the culture and even many churches didn't promote family connectedness but separated us. I knew there must be a better way and began to search. It meant being countercultural—being different. I found what I was looking for in the homeschool community and in a little church with many homeschool families. This church was like a big extended family, with people of all ages working together. The teens and older adults served side by side on the worship team and teaching Sunday school. Everybody knew each other, and we saw each other during the week at our Speaker's Club and homeschool events.

The vast majority of homeschooled children I know became responsible adults who are still a pleasure to know. Many maintain relationships with each other even now that they are establishing families of their own. I am grateful we found a way to stay connected as a family, and I believe God led us that way. It is possible to enjoy the teen years.

FLORIDA?

≋

WHEN WE CAME TO WORK WITH THE *JESUS* FILM IN 1996, THE OFFICE was in two locations: San Clemente, California, and Orlando, Florida. The department we worked with was in San Clemente. This seemed good for our family, as Vance's family was about an eight-hour drive north, and my parents were an eight-hour drive east. They had moved to Arizona while we were overseas. So we were right in the middle of our extended families. Our director assured us we would not be moving to the main headquarters for our ministry in Florida. Years later, though, he stepped down, and a new director took his place.

Vance was directing the *JESUS* Film Mission Trips team, and we were on a team retreat in the local mountains when we all sat at a table and heard the announcement about our office moving to Florida. All the team sat silently, absorbing the unwelcome news. We decided not to talk about it then and quietly left the retreat.

As Vance and I prayed, we seemed to hear the Lord say, "Get on the road to go to Florida." When we talked to our family, they were all fine with us moving. Sara and Peter were away in college, and Amy planned to move with us. I didn't feel like I could move farther from my parents, as I am an only child, and they were old. My parents said they would move to Florida too. Red flags began to come up. Going to Florida felt like we were walking up a steep hill that just got steeper.

One day, when we were driving, we came to a signal. We stopped as the light changed to yellow but the cars beside us continued through the light. Inside me, I heard the words that this is what would happen to us. Everyone would go but we would stay. Then my father learned he had cancer and said he wouldn't be going anywhere. Then my mother said she was fine in Arizona, except for the time of year when it was humid, when she couldn't breathe (she had a lung condition).

That was the last straw. She couldn't live in humid Florida, and I couldn't be so far away from them. Also, though we liked our team, we were more passionate about the Middle East than short-term missions. We knew we shouldn't move to Florida. Looking back, I think it would have been hard on the team if we had said from the beginning that the director wasn't moving. The team didn't want to move. A younger man from our Mission Trips team moved to Florida and took Vance's job as director. He has built that ministry until it is large today. Our leaders said not going to Florida meant leaving the *JESUS* film, which left us with the question, what would we do next?

Reaching
the Nations
among Us

≈

I F WE WEREN'T MOVING TO FLORIDA, AND WE HAD TO LEAVE THE *JESUS* film, what would we do? We considered what we were passionate about. In our lunchroom at the office, I could usually find Vance talking about Islam and reaching Muslims. People would come and go, and he would continue the conversation. This was his passion. We didn't really want to leave Campus Crusade for Christ but decided we would, if God directed us. We checked into ministries within our organization where we could reach Muslims and not have to move. There were at least five. One was working with international students. We attended their conference and were excited at first, but it gradually faded and just didn't seem right.

Another ministry involved working with faculty on university campuses and taking them on trips to the Middle East. A couple from the faculty ministry came to talk with us. The wife asked us who we were and what we did. I had to think about that one. Who were we, anyway, and what types of things had we done? Well, we began the training center in Egypt and began the training center in Russia. We were on the first teams to begin summer projects in Turkey, London, and Japan. We began Young Speakers for Christ. What do we do? Why, we begin ministries. It all fit. Vance and I had once taken a test that said we were both designers and developers but not managers. So it made sense we should begin something again.

Then, one November day, Vance woke up with an idea. We should give the *JESUS* film to every Muslim home in America. This thought continued to grow. Then an e-mail from Phil, a major donor to the *JESUS* film, was forwarded to us, saying he wanted to give the *JESUS* film to every Muslim home in America. The e-mail was forwarded several times until it came to us. When we contacted Phil, his reply was, "Supernatural!" We talked with Paul Eshleman, founder and original director of the *JESUS* Film Project, and he liked the idea. He said to write a proposal. Paul carried the proposal to our headquarters, and it went up to the vice president of our organization. They told us to go ahead, that we didn't have to move, and they even loaned us a hundred thousand dollars to start!

That summer at our staff training, we saw our old friend, Don Dearing. Don was unsure what he would be doing the coming year and asked about what we were doing. After we shared our vision with him, he asked if he could work with us. He lived in Florida at the time and worked at our headquarters. Don said he would help with developing our materials. Later, after returning home, we met Ev and Alise Davis at a meeting discussing reaching Muslims in Southern California. Ev had directed the prayer ministry, and they had also worked with the *JESUS* Video Project. Ev and Alise offered to handle prayer and follow-up and join our team. Our old friends, Jim and Juanita Wyatt, were returning from overseas and joined our team, helping with the database and promotions.

We felt like we had jumped on a moving train. The *JESUS* film was mainly an overseas operation. Yet there were immigrant and refugee ministries in the United States who wanted to use the film. We had learned from our German ministry how to put sixteen audio tracts on one DVD. We found a local manufacturer and replicated a hundred thousand copies of a sixteen-language DVD in Muslim languages. Replicating in this quantity helped cut costs dramatically. We focused on partnering with other organizations and churches to see the DVDs distributed. Russ, a semiretired businessman, became our distributor and handled sales and shipping out of his home. We later learned that the owner of the replication company was a Muslim himself, but he was so excited by the DVD he put a display in his office and offered free DVDs to his customers. Phil later found us a Christian DVD manufacturer who had even better prices.

After creating our DVD with sixteen Muslim languages, we began receiving requests from churches and ministries for DVDs with other language combinations. Don worked with our studio in Florida, while Steiner—a graphic artist with the *JESUS* film—developed artwork for the DVD sleeves with other language combinations: Indian, Chinese, international students, and more. We replicated up to one hundred thousand at a time. Jim and Juanita later felt the Lord leading them to the military ministry. We knew we would miss them. Jim always kept us laughing. Shortly after losing Jim and Juanita, the Lord sent Ray and Gail—our coworkers from Egypt, who had recently returned to America. Ray's experience with computers, overseeing websites, and working with strategy was a great asset. Gail was able to help with the database and social media. Volunteers also joined us: Dick, Connie, Nancy, Ruth, and Hannah. Our team met by videoconference every other week and in person once or twice a year. Ev and Alise handled our follow-up from seekers who contacted us by phone or email on the back of the DVDs.

We even received requests from other countries, including our ministry in Canada, who bought hundreds of thousands of DVDs. We eventually shipped over five million DVDs to customers and partners in the United States and Canada. It had been truly a supernatural experience. And because we didn't move, my mother lived the last year and a half of her life in our home, and we stayed involved in the lives of our children. God's paths—though mysterious at times—ultimately are always best.

PAINTING
BEAUTY

≈

WHEN OUR LEADERS ANNOUNCED THE NEWS OF MOVING TO FLORIDA, many California staff were sad, thinking of all those we would leave behind. A pastor came to talk to us, using the following as his text:

> Finally, brethren, whatever is true, whatever is honorable, whatever is right, whatever is pure, whatever is lovely, whatever is of good repute, if there is any excellence and if anything worthy of praise, dwell on these things. (Philippians 4:8)

The pastor encouraged us to be alone awhile and think about what he said. I took a walk and found a trail along the ridge of a hill overlooking the ocean. As I gazed on the beauty, I believe the Lord spoke to my heart: "Go ahead and paint. Paint what is lovely." I realized that much of painting is learning to see. Noticing lights and shadows, shapes and colors, requires focus and concentration. Looking at a tree for several hours imprints that image on the mind. So painting lovely things imprints loveliness on the mind. I bought a paintbrush (everything must begin somewhere). Next, I took a class that fit into my life and budget. It was a watercolor class offered through our city. My teacher, Betty, is one of those bubbly, joyful souls who delights in encouraging her students to aim high. I took the next step and signed up for another class in town, a pastel class taught by an excellent teacher. I felt like someone poured hot sauce on my brain. New discoveries exploded. Light changes color. Just paint shapes, and on and on. I still wanted more and signed up for a plein air class, setting up my easel outside and painting from life. Oil painting intrigued me with its textures and infinite variations of rich color mixes. At last, I found my greatest love in painting God's beautiful creation out of doors. Hearing the ocean, feeling the wind, smelling the salt air, all contributed to the imprint of loveliness on my mind. Gradually, the sadness of loss receded, and lovely images took root inside me. I never tire of learning to see the beauty that surrounds us, if we only look.

Vance encouraged me and helped me develop a website: www.carolnordman.com. My friend Lisa printed artist cards and a brochure with my paintings and testimony. In the brochure and on the website, I shared how to trust Christ. I set up my easel outdoors and hung the brochures on the back of the easel so people passing by could take them. I talked with many people who came by to watch me paint. I was having so much fun. I met other artists and shared my faith with some of them, as God opened doors. I attended a study for Christian artists led by a local art professor.

Doors kept opening before me. During an art workshop, I sat with two ladies eating lunch. They talked about those born-again people who were unkind and judgmental. Then they looked at me and asked what I believed. I think God helped me as I replied that I followed Jesus. They looked thoughtful, and one woman said she liked Jesus. It is fun to blow apart stereotypes. Many people have never met a true follower of Christ.

We are the light of the world, and darkness exists in many places. Artists have a powerful voice, and we need to bring the light of Christ into dark places and disciple creative people to use their gifts to expand the kingdom. Often, when people won't take a *JESUS* film, they will take an art card with my website on it, containing the plan of salvation and links to grow closer to God. I continue to paint and now to write. God always has new adventures.

APPENDIX

MY FATHER

≈

My father, Robert Francis McMahon, was born in 1920. He had an older brother, Bill, and later a younger brother, Jack. When my father was young, his parents divorced, and he lived with the extended McMahon family until his mother could take care of the boys on her own. It was hard for my father to be separated from his mother, Mildred. Mildred found a job with the railroad and later married Mr. Edwards, who formally adopted the boys, changing their names to Edwards. They lived in Hollywood and later in Venice, California. The three brothers enjoyed riding the train and hiking in the mountains, often living off the fish they caught as they hiked and camped. My father continued to have a love of hiking the rest of his life.

My parents met in school and attended Venice High School. My mother's name was Alice Ede, and students were lined up alphabetically. Bob Edwards and Alice Ede stood next to each other. As they both were redheads with brown eyes, people sometimes thought they were related. When they were twenty years old, they eloped to Yuma, Arizona, when their parents couldn't agree on a wedding location. My father got a job as a postman, and life seemed good until a doctor told them they couldn't have children. Then World War II began. My father was in the Navy and moved around the United States for a while. My mother followed, trying to find housing and jobs so they could be together as much as possible. She was working for the shipyard, I think in San Francisco, when my father shipped out. The ship was in international waters when the war ended. The GI Bill helped pay for his education, and my father was the only one in his family to go to college. He went to the University of California, Berkeley and studied electrical engineering. He got a master's degree and a good job, eventually moving up into an executive position. He worked on automobile accident research, ozone layer research, and more. Later in his life, he even worked on the Hubble Space Telescope. He specialized in quality control. Eventually, he received a PhD in biomedical engineering from the University of California, Los Angeles, receiving a government grant to study the regrowth of nerves.

When my parents were thirty-two, unexpectedly, I was born. My parents then lived near my mother's parents in Glendale, California. Imagine their joy, as they had wanted children for so long, and the situation seemed hopeless. They gave me most everything I wanted. I knew my parents loved me, and I had a happy childhood.

My father was intellectually a genius. He was a gentle, quiet man who loved the outdoors. Slender and athletic with thick dark red hair and brown eyes, he stood six feet tall. His hair turned brown in midlife, and he lost most of it. He liked to talk and referred to his Irish roots to explain it. He especially liked to explain things and teach me. We toured many factories and took long car trips to explore other states and Canada. I always felt my father was there for me when I needed him. He loved to talk about his research, but the vocabulary was beyond me. Once I remember asking him to talk to me as if I was five years old. Later, he said that advice helped him when talking to other people.

Our family went to church, usually a Presbyterian church, but not regularly. We attended the service but didn't get involved with the people. Our family of three usually read books in the evening together, occasionally talking. It seemed like every weekend, we drove somewhere to hike or to swim in the ocean.

My father often changed his mind. In fact, none of the three of us enjoyed making decisions. When I was older, we put a box on the table and voted on decisions. I remember often setting out on the weekend to go somewhere, perhaps the mountains. Partway to the mountains, my father might say, "I see a cloud over the mountain. Let's go to the desert," or, "Let's go to the beach." Eventually, my mother packed the car with what we would need for several destinations. We didn't progress from point A to point B according to a plan. Rather, we flowed. This helped me later in life when we lived in other countries where things rarely went as planned.

Poverty as a child living with a single working mother meant my father worked from a young age. He didn't want to be poor again, and having money was a goal he set. When he moved up into the executive office of a company, we had a lot of money and lived in Encino, California. This was close to Hollywood; Clark Gable's home was nearby. Many neighbors had maids. We moved six times when I was growing up, eventually living in a five-bedroom, three-bathroom home in Northridge, California, where I attended junior and senior high school. It was then that my father decided money wasn't the answer. Rather, love was the answer. He graduated from UCLA with his PhD just before I entered UCLA as a freshman. He sold the house, moved into a furnished one-bedroom apartment, and only owned what fit into two small cars. He chose not to work, and he lived with my mother, the woman he loved.

I think my parents came close to going on welfare, and I received a state scholarship for college because we didn't have much money. Later, my mother went to work for the county, and because of her job, they had retirement later. My father had a temporary job; perhaps that's how they had money to buy a home outright in the retirement city of Sun City West, Arizona, where they lived happily retired for about twenty years.

My father developed his own religion based on his research and felt religion evolved. He said that Vance and I were on the right track, but we needed to evolve and join his religion. He didn't believe in the deity of Christ and felt things could be explained from the natural world. He read the Bible constantly and read the materials from our mission organization, interpreting them to fit his viewpoint. Though we didn't agree about spiritual issues, we always knew we loved each other. I don't remember any anger or harsh words. These were uncharacteristic of my gentle father.

As my father grew older, he became convinced that he would not die; he believed scientists would discover a way to reverse aging. Perhaps this was connected to his research about nerve regrowth. In his mid-eighties, my father learned he had bladder cancer. It had spread, and operating wouldn't help. I asked many people to pray, perhaps hundreds. It concerned me he would die not knowing the Lord.

One day in the hospital, my father cried out, "I've sinned! I've sinned!"

I said, "Daddy, just ask Jesus for forgiveness."

He then cried, "Lord, we need forgiveness!"

I asked him, "Daddy, what do you think will happen to you when you die?"

He replied, "If I believe in Christ, I get a new body."

I asked, "Do you believe in Christ?"

He replied, "Yes."

Because he had previously denied the deity of Christ, I asked, "Do you believe Jesus is God?"

He replied, "He is indistinguishable."

I asked, "Is that yes or no?"

He said, "Yes, of course." Then he added, "I want God's plan, not mine because mine isn't working so well."

My father asked God for another year of life. He went on dialysis and lived another year. During that year, he constantly watched Christian television, read a book by Randy Alcorn about heaven, and truly was a changed person. He said, "I know that Jesus is with me. I've known that for some time. I'm looking forward to being with Jesus. He seems like a nice person."

I was able to be with my parents in their home in Arizona during the last two weeks of my father's life. Hospice helped us, and whenever his care became too difficult, God always sent the help we needed. At the end, they gave us a lovely hospice room with two recliners for my mother and me. This room had a CD player with a CD playing hymns. When my father could no longer talk, I held his hand and looked into his eyes. There was peace and trust. This brilliant scientist was trusting

God like a child. Even the chaplain remarked about the atmosphere of peace in the room. Privately, he told me he had been a preacher before he became a chaplain. He said as a chaplain, he was supposed to confirm the faith the patient already had and not tell them about his own faith. He said that people die the way they live. I told him about my father, who had so recently changed to trust in Christ.

My mother and I found a wonderful lunch restaurant that served homey comfort food. One day, while we were at lunch, my father left this earth to be with Jesus. It was so obvious that he was gone when I looked at his body. We had his body cremated and took his ashes to the veteran's cemetery in Riverside, California. My cousin Mike and his wife Deonne came to the cemetery, along with Vance and our children, where uniformed men shot guns for the salute. Later, my mother said that watching my father die took away her fear of death.

I thank God for giving me a loving father, and I look forward to seeing him again.

My Mother

≈

My mother, Alice Lucille Ede, was born in 1920 to Alan and Margaret Ede. She had a brother, Don—seven years older. Her father was an engineer and designed Marina Del Ray in Los Angeles County, California. He had a good job that carried them through the Depression. I expect my mother went to church. As a child, she remembers singing "Jesus Loves Me" on public transportation.

My mother was a classy lady. She was beautiful, athletic, and smart, and had a dry sense of humor. She was quiet and gracious. I never remember her raising her voice, losing her temper, or saying anything unkind about anyone. I think she could have easily lived in a royal family. Yet she wasn't proud and was polite to everyone. My mother didn't know how to cook or clean house when she married and learned both over the years. She was an editor in high school, and I think she could have been an artist. She liked to sketch people, and at one time, when I was a girl, she painted in oils. She also sewed and did upholstery.

My mother studied English at the University of California and loved literature and all things related to words. She often helped me in this area when I was in high school. Like my father, she grew up hiking in the hills of Southern California and continued hiking into retirement. She also played tennis. She secretly hoped to drive a giant earth-moving machine and to experience the peaceful life of being a cow in a meadow. Like me, she didn't especially enjoy going downhill when skiing. She told the story of a ski lesson when she fell, and the instructor had to coax her to get back up and try again. She finally gave up skiing, though we went for many years when I was growing up.

My mother was such a nice person. She went to church occasionally, usually to the Presbyterian church with my father. In midlife, she was baptized and joined the Crystal Cathedral, which was near their home. When I asked Mother how she knew she would go to heaven, she replied it was because Jesus forgave her sins. She had all the right answers, yet she didn't seem to grow stronger in her faith. I thought it must be because my father didn't have a personal faith.

She moved in with us for a year and a half after Daddy died, before she passed away at age eighty-nine. Not long after she moved in, she told me one day, "I believed in God, but Jesus was fuzzy. So I just asked him to come into my life. He is so real to me now." I asked Mother what the difference was between her previous experience with God and now. She replied, "It's a personal relationship now." She had recently made that decision. We lived with my mother for about another year.

During that year, we attended Bible studies and experienced a new closeness. We also took painting and drawing classes together. She had always wanted to live near her grandchildren, be a part of wedding preparations, and have a cat. She got to do all these things the last year of her life and was active until two weeks before she died. All our children came home to stay for the summer, and we planned Sara's wedding. Mother watched Sara try on wedding dresses, went to a bridal shower, and attended the wedding and reception. She died about two weeks later.

Mother had heart failure and was on hospice. Sara came back from her honeymoon with Joshua and prepared to move to Minnesota, where Joshua would be a recruiter for the Marines. We had my birthday dinner, and then Peter returned to college, and Vance and Amy left with Sara and Joshua to help drive their possessions to Minnesota. They said goodbye Monday morning. It was just Mother and I in the house, and I was hoping I could meet her needs. That evening, her heart began to beat erratically. The hospice nurse instructed me over the phone to give her morphine every hour and to ask someone to spend the night to help. My girlfriend, Lisa, had just offered to spend the night if I needed help, so I called her. Lisa and I sang and read the Bible to Mother as she lay with her eyes closed, as if asleep. In the morning, Lisa went home, and another friend, Norma, and her daughter Vanessa came to help. I made a bed on the floor beside my mother and got some sleep. As the day went on and hospice continued to instruct us, I knew Mother was slipping away. I told her it was okay to go, and that she didn't need to be concerned about anything. I said goodbye for now, knowing she would soon be with Jesus and my father.

Our German neighbor, Brunhilde, came to sit with Mother and me. I noticed a wrinkle on Mother's forehead and went to the refrigerator to get some medicine. When I returned, Brunhilde said Mother had stopped breathing. I knew she was gone. As if on cue, people began to arrive. Another neighbor—a fireman—disconnected the oxygen. Our pastor and his wife, Bruce and Kathy just happened to come by. Within minutes, without knowing Mother had just left, the house was filled with people. We notified hospice and the funeral home. At their suggestion, I waited in my room as they took Mother's body. After that, I was almost never alone until Vance returned. I truly felt carried. Norma spent the first night. Peter came from college and spent the day. I got a phone call from Vance, reminding me to give hospice the extra oxygen tank, just when they were coming for the tanks. I had such peace, and the sorrow I felt was overtaken by the joy of knowing where Mother is. I have a picture in my mind of my parents now in heaven. They look young and happy—two attractive redheads radiant with love. I can't wait to see them again.

MOTHER'S CANCER STORY

≈

WHEN MY MOTHER WAS EIGHTY-ONE, THEY DIAGNOSED HER WITH STAGE one breast cancer in both breasts. Two years before, at seventy-nine, she had open heart surgery and recovered. My mother's doctor recommended a double mastectomy. My parents weren't comfortable with this and came to our home to talk it over with us.

My mother had a book listing the best doctors in America. My parents said these were the doctors the doctors themselves went to, and they didn't cost more—they were just good doctors. We had used this book before to find a good doctor for my mother-in-law, who broke her arm and then had two unsuccessful surgeries before using a doctor from the book, who finally gave her a successful surgery resulting in healing the bone.

My mother found a doctor about an hour away in the city of Santa Monica. It was election day, and we had just voted for the new California governor. We all felt the seriousness of Mother's situation, and the atmosphere in our car was sober. Finally, we found the medical building in Santa Monica and went into the doctor's office. He wasn't the doctor she expected, and we waited in the hall by the elevator to return to our car. We noticed two men who had been waiting near the elevator since we arrived. We wondered what they were there for. One was on his cell phone, and the other looked like he might be his bodyguard. The bodyguard-looking man was wearing a brass bear pin, like the bear on the California flag. My father asked him about his pin and if he was with the University of California. He gave a vague answer to change the subject. As we were waiting for the elevator to go downstairs, suddenly an unmarked door opened, and out walked Arnold Schwarzenegger—the movie star and candidate for California governor. The elevator opened, and we all entered. As the elevator descended, my father introduced himself to Arnold Schwarzenegger, who responded politely. My father mentioned that he had also lived in Venice, California, and they chatted briefly. We were all in a daze as we got into our car. Amazement replaced the sober atmosphere. Did that really happen? It helped lighten the atmosphere.

As we drove home, we passed the University of California Irvine Medical Center, and my mother said there was another doctor in her book—Dr. Butler—who worked at that hospital. We got off the freeway and had lunch and then drove to the medical center. As we exited the elevator, I noticed an announcement that Dr. Butler was having a seminar for the public on breast cancer, and it would begin in about fifteen minutes. We found the room and discovered a large table with chairs and refreshments for the handful of people who came to talk with Dr. Butler. We spent a couple of hours asking questions. As we left, Dr. Butler said he could treat Mother.

We really liked Dr. Butler, and he recommended two lumpectomies, which was much less severe than the mastectomies. When my mother went in for surgery, it was October 31, Halloween. I waited with my father until we could see her. They had injected blue dye into Mother to check for more cancer and found none. The doctor came to tell us the operation was a success, and she was in recovery but that we should wait, as she looked blue. After a while, they told us to come in, but that she now looked green. It was quite a shock to see Mother, still groggy from the medication, with skin the color of the Wicked Witch of the West in the movie *The Wizard of Oz*, white hair, and red bloodshot eyes. She fit right into Halloween.

Mother had almost no pain and quickly recovered at home. I felt

God had carried us through the whole process and given us some fun moments to lighten the atmosphere. I sensed his hand and am grateful to have had my mother for another eight years. The cancer never returned, and she could care for my dad at the end of his life and then spend over a year in our home. I thank God for His provision.

Would You Like to Know God Personally?

The following four principles will help you discover how to know God personally and experience the abundant life He promised.

1 *God **loves** you and created you to know Him personally.*

God's Love
"God so loved the world that He gave His one and only Son, that whoever believes in Him shall not perish but have eternal life" (John 3:16, NIV).

God's Plan
"Now this is eternal life: that they may know you, the only true God, and Jesus Christ, whom you have sent" (John 17:3, NIV).

What prevents us from knowing God personally?

2 *Man is **sinful** and **separated** from God, so we cannot know Him personally or experience His love.*

Man Is Sinful

"All have sinned and fall short of the glory of God" (Romans 3:23).

Man was created to have fellowship with God; but, because of his own stubborn self-will, he chose to go his own independent way and fellowship with God was broken. This self-will, characterized by an attitude of active rebellion or passive indifference, is an evidence of what the Bible calls sin.

Man Is Separated

"The wages of sin is death" [spiritual separation from God] (Romans 6:23).

This diagram illustrates that God is holy and man is sinful. A great gulf separates the two. The arrows illustrate that man is continually trying to reach God and the abundant life through his own efforts, such as a good life, philosophy, or religion —but he inevitably fails.

The third principle explains the only way to bridge this gulf...

3 *Jesus Christ is God's **only** provision for man's sin. Through Him alone we can know God personally and experience God's love.*

He Died In Our Place

"God demonstrates His own love toward us, in that while we were yet sinners, Christ died for us" (Romans 5:8).

He Rose from the Dead

"Christ died for our sins...He was buried...He was raised on the third day according to the Scriptures...He appeared to Peter, then to the twelve. After that He appeared to more than five hundred..." (1 Corinthians 15:3–6).

He Is the Only Way to God
"Jesus said to him, 'I am the way, and the truth, and the life; no one comes to the Father, but through Me'" (John 14:6).

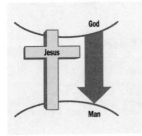

This diagram illustrates that God has bridged the gulf that separates us from Him by sending His Son, Jesus Christ, to die on the cross in our place to pay the penalty for our sins.

It is not enough just to know these truths...

4 *We must individually **receive** Jesus Christ as Savior and Lord; then we can know God personally and experience His love.*

We Must Receive Christ
"As many as received Him, to them He gave the right to become children of God, even to those who believe in His name" (John 1:12).

We Receive Christ Through Faith
"By grace you have been saved through faith; and that not of yourselves, it is the gift of God; not as a result of works that no one should boast" (Ephesians 2:8,9).

When We Receive Christ, We Experience a New Birth
(Read John 3:1–8.)

We Receive Christ by Personal Invitation
[Christ speaking] "Behold, I stand at the door and knock; if any one hears My voice and opens the door, I will come in to him" (Revelation 3:20).

Receiving Christ involves turning to God from self (repentance) and trusting Christ to come into our lives to forgive us of our sins and to make us what He wants us to be. Just to agree intellectually that Jesus Christ is the Son of God and that He died on the cross for our sins is not enough. Nor is it enough to have an emotional experience. We receive Jesus Christ by faith, as an act of the will.

These two circles represent two kinds of lives:

Self-Directed Life
S – Self is on the throne
† – Christ is outside the life
● – Interests are directed by self, often
   resulting in discord and frustration

Christ-Directed Life
† – Christ is in the life and on the throne
S – Self is yielding to Christ
● – Interests are directed by Christ,
   resulting in harmony with God's plan

Which circle best represents your life?
Which circle would you like to have represent your life?

The following explains how you can receive Christ:

You Can Receive Christ Right Now by Faith Through Prayer
(Prayer is talking with God)
God knows your heart and is not so concerned with your words as He is with the attitude of your heart. The following is a suggested prayer:

> *Lord Jesus, I want to know You personally. Thank You for dying on the cross for my sins. I open the door of my life and receive You as my Savior and Lord. Thank You for forgiving me of my sins and giving me eternal life. Take control of the throne of my life. Make me the kind of person You want me to be.*

Does this prayer express the desire of your heart?

If it does, I invite you to pray this prayer right now, and Christ will come into your life, as He promised.

How to Know That Christ Is in Your Life
Did you receive Christ into your life? According to His promise in Revelation 3:20, where is Christ right now in relation to

you? Christ said that He would come into your life and be your friend so you can know Him personally. Would He mislead you? On what authority do you know that God has answered your prayer? (The trustworthiness of God Himself and His Word.)

The Bible Promises Eternal Life to All Who Receive Christ
"God has given us eternal life, and this life is in His Son. He who has the Son has the life; he who does not have the Son of God does not have the life. These things I have written to you who believe in the name of the Son of God, in order that you may know that you have eternal life" (1 John 5:11–13).

Thank God often that Christ is in your life and that He will never leave you (Hebrews 13:5). You can know on the basis of His promise that Christ lives in you and that you have eternal life from the very moment you invite Him in. He will not deceive you.

An important reminder…

Do Not Depend on Feelings
The promise of God's Word, the Bible—not our feelings—is our authority. The Christian lives by faith (trust) in the trustworthiness of God Himself and His Word. This train diagram illustrates the relationship among fact (God and His Word), faith (our trust in God and His Word), and feeling (the result of our faith and obedience). (Read John 14:21.)

The train will run with or without the caboose. However, it would be useless to attempt to pull the train by the caboose. In the same way, as Christians we do not depend on feelings or emotions, but we place our faith (trust) in the trustworthiness of God and the promises of His Word.

Now That You Have Entered Into a Personal Relationship with Christ

The moment you received Christ by faith, as an act of the will, many things happened, including the following:

1. Christ came into your life (Revelation 3:20; Colossians 1:27).
2. Your sins were forgiven (Colossians 1:14).
3. You became a child of God (John 1:12).
4. You received eternal life (John 5:24).
5. You began the great adventure for which God created you (John 10:10).

Can you think of anything more wonderful that could happen to you than entering into a personal relationship with Jesus Christ? Would you like to thank God in prayer right now for what He has done for you? By thanking God, you demonstrate your faith.

To enjoy your new relationship with God...

Suggestions for Christian Growth

Spiritual growth results from trusting Jesus Christ. "The righteous man shall live by faith" (Galatians 3:11). A life of faith will enable you to trust God increasingly with every detail of your life, and to practice the following:

G *Go* to God in prayer daily (John 15:7).

R *Read* God's Word daily (Acts 17:11); begin with the Gospel of John.

O *Obey* God moment by moment (John 14:21).

W *Witness* for Christ by your life and words (Matthew 4:19; John 15:8).

T *Trust* God for every detail of your life (1 Peter 5:7).

H *Holy Spirit*—allow Him to control and empower your daily life and witness (Galatians 5:16,17; Acts 1:8).

CAROL NORDMAN

The Spirit-filled Life

Every day can be an exciting adventure for the Christian who knows the reality of being filled with the Holy Spirit and who lives constantly, moment by moment, under His gracious direction.

The Bible tells us that there are three kinds of people:

1. **Natural Man:** One who has not received Christ.

Self-Directed Life

S – Self is on the throne

✝ – Christ is outside the life

● – Interests are directed by self, often resulting in discord and frustration

"A natural man does not accept the things of the Spirit of God; for they are foolishness to him, and he cannot understand them, because they are spiritually appraised" (1 Corinthians 2:14, NASB).

Christ-Directed Life

S – Christ is in the life and on the throne

✝ – Self is yielding to Christ

● – Interests are directed by Christ, resulting in harmony with God's plan

2. **Spiritual Man:** One who is directed and empowered by the Holy Spirit.

"He who is spiritual appraises all things" (1 Corinthians 2:15, NASB).

3. **Carnal Man**: One who has received Christ, but who lives in defeat because he trusts in his own efforts to live the Christian life.

Self-Directed Life

S – Self is on the throne

✝ – Christ dethroned and not allowed to direct the life

● – Interests are directed by self, often resulting in discord and frustration

"I, brethren, could not speak to you as to spiritual people but as to carnal, as to babes in Christ. I fed you with milk and not with solid food; for until now you were not able to receive it, and even now you are still not able; for you are still carnal. For when there are envy, strife, and divisions among you, are you not carnal and behaving like mere men?" (1 Corinthians 3:1–3).

The following are four principles for living the Spirit-filled life:

1 God has provided for us an abundant and fruitful Christian life.

"Jesus said, 'I have come that they may have life, and that they may have it more abundantly'" (John 10:10, NKJ).

"The fruit of the Spirit is love, joy, peace, patience, kindness, goodness, faithfulness, gentleness, self-control; against such things there is no law" (Galatians 5:22,23).

Read John 15:5 and Acts 1:8.

The following are some personal traits of the spiritual man that result from trusting God:

- Love
- Joy
- Peace
- Patience
- Kindness
- Faithfulness
- Goodness

- Life is Christ-centered
- Empowered by Holy Spirit
- Introduces others to Christ
- Has effective prayer life
- Understands God's Word
- Trusts God
- Obeys God

The degree to which these traits are manifested in the life depends on the extent to which the Christian trusts the Lord with every detail of his life, and on his maturity in Christ. One who is only beginning to understand the ministry of the Holy Spirit should not be discouraged if he is not as fruitful as more mature Christians who have known and experienced this truth for a longer period.

Why is it that most Christians are not experiencing the abundant life?

2 Carnal Christians cannot experience the abundant and fruitful Christian life.

The carnal man trusts in his own efforts to live the Christian life:

- He is either uninformed about, or has forgotten, God's love, forgiveness, and power (Romans 5:8–10; Hebrews 10:1–25; 1 John 1; 2:1–3; 2 Peter 1:9).
- He has an up-and-down spiritual experience.
- He wants to do what is right, but cannot.
- He fails to draw on the power of the Holy Spirit to live the Christian life (1 Corinthians 3:1–3; Romans 7:15–24; 8:7; Galatians 5:16–18).

Some or all of the following traits may characterize the carnal man—the Christian who does not fully trust God:

- Legalistic attitude
- Impure thoughts
- Jealousy
- Guilt
- Worry
- Discouragement
- Critical spirit
- Frustration

- Aimlessness
- Fear
- Ignorance of his spiritual heritage
- Unbelief
- Disobedience
- Loss of love for God and for others
- Poor prayer life
- No desire for Bible study

(The individual who professes to be a Christian but who continues to practice sin should realize that he may not be a Christian at all, according to 1 John 2:3; 3:6–9; and Ephesians 5:5.)

The third truth gives us the only solution to this problem...

3 Jesus promised the abundant and fruitful life as the result of being filled (directed and empowered) by the Holy Spirit.

The Spirit-filled life is the Christ-directed life by which Christ lives His life in and through us in the power of the Holy Spirit (John 15).

■ One becomes a Christian through the ministry of the Holy Spirit (John 3:1–8.) From the moment of spiritual birth, the Christian is indwelt by the Holy Spirit at all times (John 1:12; Colossians 2:9,10; John 14:16,17).

All Christians are indwelt by the Holy Spirit, but not all Christians are filled (directed, controlled, and empowered) by the Holy Spirit on an ongoing basis.

■ The Holy Spirit is the source of the overflowing life (John 7:37–39).

■ In His last command before His ascension, Christ promised the power of the Holy Spirit to enable us to be witnesses for Him (Acts 1:1–9).

How, then, can one be filled with the Holy Spirit?

4 We are filled (directed and empowered) by the Holy Spirit by faith; then we can experience the abundant and fruitful life that Christ promised to each Christian.

You can appropriate the filling of the Holy Spirit right now if you:

■ Sincerely desire to be directed and empowered by the Holy Spirit (Matthew 5:6; John 7:37–39).

■ Confess your sins. By faith, thank God that He has forgiven all of your sins—past, present, and future—because Christ died for you (Colossians 2:13–15).

■ Present every area of your life to God (Romans 12:1,2).

■ By faith claim the fullness of the Holy Spirit, according to:

His command: Be filled with the Spirit. "Do not get drunk on wine, which leads to debauchery. Instead, be filled with the Spirit" (Ephesians 5:18).

His promise: He will always answer when we pray according to His will. "This is the confidence we have in approaching God: that if we ask anything according to his will, he hears us. And if we know that He hears us—whatever we ask—we know that we have what we asked of Him" (1 John 5:14,15).

How to Pray in Faith to be Filled With the Holy Spirit

We are filled with the Holy Spirit by faith alone. However, true prayer is one way of expressing your faith. The following is a suggested prayer:

Dear Father, I need You. I acknowledge that I have been directing my own life and that, as a result, I have sinned against You. I thank You that You have forgiven my sins through Christ's death on the cross for me. I now invite Christ to again take His place on the throne of my life. Fill me with the Holy Spirit as You commanded me to be filled, and as You promised in Your Word that You would do if I asked in faith. I pray this in the name of Jesus. As an expression of my faith, I now thank You for directing my life and for filling me with the Holy Spirit.

Does this prayer express the desire of your heart? If so, bow in prayer and trust God to fill you with the Holy Spirit right now.